The Seafood Cookbook

The Seafood Cookbook

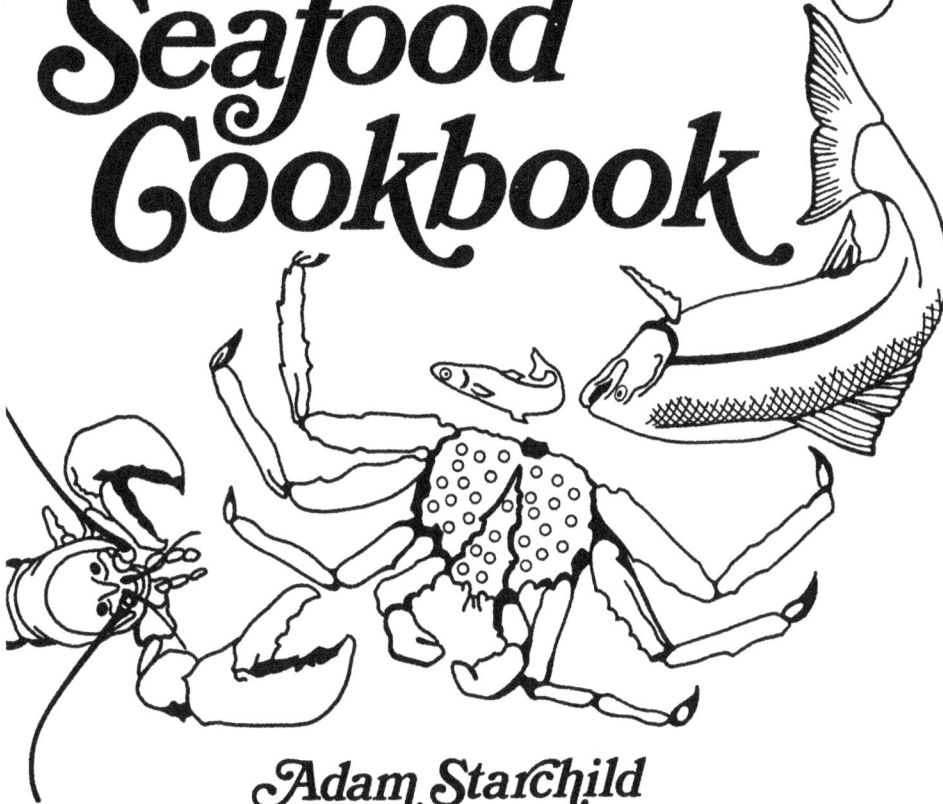

Adam Starchild

The Seafood Cookbook

by
Adam Starchild

ISBN 1-58963-016-5

Creative Cookbooks an imprint of Fredonia Books

Fredonia Books
Amsterdam, The Netherlands
http://www.FredoniaBooks.com

Contents

Introduction

The many moods of seafood offer mankind an ocean of low-calorie variety with a world of interesting flavor. Combined with a bit of imagination and a dash of color, this diverse, complete protein, aquatic bounty adds to our pleasures at table, whether on the beach or in a formal dining setting.

Because seafood can be ruined by overcooking or careless handling, it challenges the cook, but the pleasure the palate derives from its delicate flavors and textures is the reward for culinary care. Recipes herein are simple enough for the beginner but still satisfying to the more experienced; modern shortcuts are included, as well as tried and true standards. Substitution of varieties of seafood allows the use of what is available at any time, and of the cook's originality. Many dishes can make use of cooked fish left over from a previous meal, and most recipes can be multiplied to serve groups.

The many moods of seafoods are good any day of the week for any meal of the day.

Choosing Fish

When buying a whole or drawn fish at a market, observe the following points to ensure freshness:

Eyes: Bright, clear, full and bulging.
Gills: Reddish pink, free from slime.
Scales: Adhering tightly to the skin, bright colored with characteristic sheen of the fish.
Flesh: Firm and elastic, springing back when pressed, not separating from the bone. A cut surface should have a waterlike shine.
Odor: Fresh, free from objectionable odors.

Frozen fish can be used interchangeably with fresh fish. Purchase only firmly frozen, undamaged packages of fish from a freezer kept at or below zero degrees. Thaw before cooking, then use as fresh fish.

Storing Seafood

Whole fish spoil more rapidly than dressed ones, and the warmer any fish is, the faster it deteriorates. That is why sport-caught fish should be dressed and iced or otherwise kept cold until taken home for proper refrigeration. Wrap dressed raw fish, freshly caught or store-bought, in moisture-vapor-proof paper or heavy waxed paper, or put it in a tightly covered container so that the fish will not dry out. Then store it in the coldest part of the refrigerator (other than the freezer). Do not hold raw fish for more than a day or two .

Cook fish that cannot be refrigerated and use at once. If it must be kept without cooking or refrigeration, it can be preserved for two or three days by this method: Cut the fish into fillets (see Index). Cover all surfaces with as much salt as will cling to them, using about one cup of fine salt for each five pounds of fish. Pack fillets in a deep container for four to six hours, then remove them from the container and rinse off any excess salt. Wipe the fillets dry and keep them in a cool place.

All raw seafood can be cooked, then chilled and stored in the refrigerator or freezer. If stored in the refrigerator, put cooked seafood in a covered container. If stored in the freezer, wrap it in moisture-vapor-proof paper. Do not hold cooked seafood in the refrigerator longer than three or four days. Do not hold it in the freezer longer than three months.

Place frozen seafood in your freezer immediately after purchase unless the fish is to be thawed for cooking. Whether in your freezer or the store's, a temperature of zero degrees or lower is needed to preserve the quality of frozen seafood. Above zero degrees, chemical changes make the fish lose color, flavor, texture, and nutritive value. Even at this temperature storage time should be limited. It is a good practice to date the packages as they are put in the freezer. Do not hold raw seafood in the freezer longer than six months.

Canned seafood should be stored in a cool, dry place; it should not be stored longer than a year.

Getting Fish Ready to Cook

Most fish sold in the market are already cleaned and dressed. However, if you catch a fish, you will need some basic cleaning and dressing instructions. Follow these steps:

1. Scales are removed most easily from a wet fish, so soak the fish in cold water for a few minutes. Lay the fish on a table and hold it firmly with one hand. Holding a blunt knife or spoon with its edge almost vertical, scrape off the scales, working from the tail toward the head.

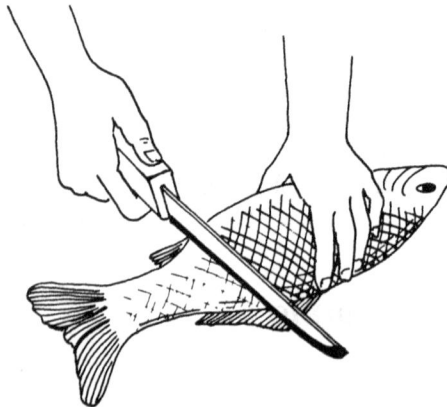

2. Slit the belly from the neck to the vent, slit it crosswise from gill to gill, and remove the viscera. Clean the cavity in cold running water. To remove the head make a crosswise cut above the collarbone down to the backbone, and break the backbone against the edge of the worktable. The head should snap off. Slice off the tail.

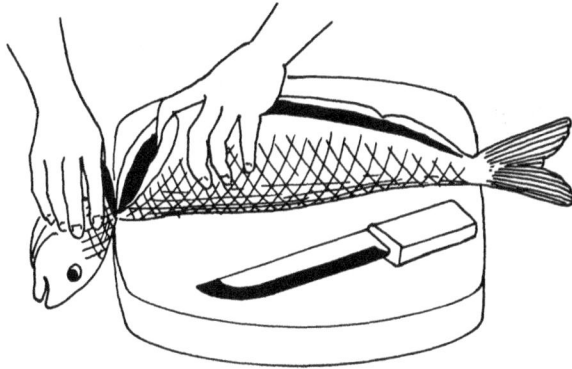

3. Never remove fins with a knife or shears. Instead, cut into the flesh at both sides of the fin along its entire length. Grasp the fin firmly with pliers and give a sudden pull forward toward the head. This removes the "nuisance bones." Rinse the cavity in cold running water. The fish is now dressed and may be sliced crosswise into steaks, or filleted.

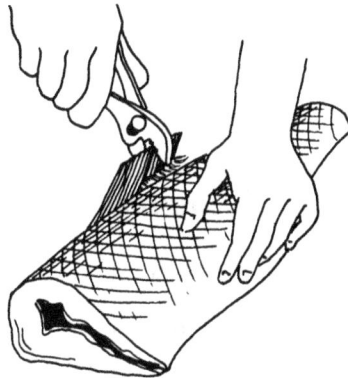

4. Fish need not be dressed to be filleted, but remove the scales if you are not removing the skin. Using a very sharp knife, cut through the flesh along the back ridge from the tail to just behind the head. With the fish on its side, slice the flesh crosswise just above the collarbone until the knife gets down to the backbone. With the knife's edge working at a flat angle toward the tail, cut the flesh from the backbone and rib bones. Lift off the entire side of the fish in one piece. Turn the fish over and fillet the other side.

5. To remove the skin, place the fillet, skin side down, tail end toward you, on a flat board. At the tail end, make a cut to begin separating the flesh from the skin. Press the knife between the skin and flesh with the blade edge angled slightly upward and toward the head end. Pull the skin toward you and work the knife forward, keeping the blade as close to the skin as possible. The skin is not generally removed except when fish pieces are to be breaded or used in chowders.

After working with fish, remove the fishy odor from your hands and utensils by washing them in strong salt water, then in hot, soapy water. Ginger lightly sprinkled on fish removes much of the odor and improves the taste. Try it on strong-flavored fish.

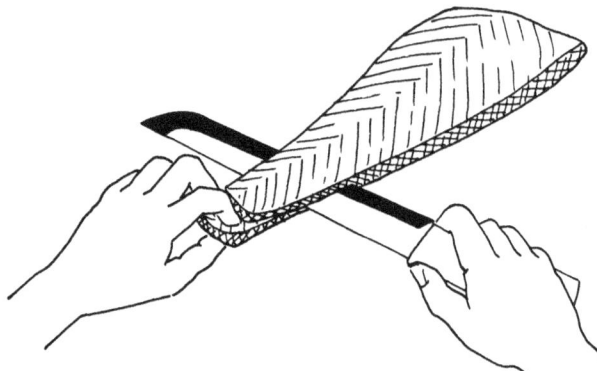

Thawing

If you prethaw frozen seafood, you are less apt to overcook it than if you cook it while frozen. Schedule thawing carefully so you can cook the seafood as soon as it thaws, and never hold thawed seafood longer than a day before cooking.

If the frozen seafood is wrapped only in parchment paper or cellophane, enclose it in a second wrapping of moisture-vapor-proof paper. The additional wrapping will help prevent deterioration as the fish thaws. Place the package in the refrigerator and allow twenty-four hours thawing time for each pound of frozen fish. If quicker thawing is necessary, place the unopened package under cold running water, allowing one to two hours thawing time for each pound of fish. Never thaw fish at room temperature or in warm water, and never refreeze it. After thawing, cook as fresh fish.

Frozen fillets and steaks may be cooked without thawing but will need additional cooking time. However, steaks or fillets that you plan to bread or stuff must be thawed in advance or the breading will not adhere to the fish, nor will the fish and stuffing cook evenly. Fish portions and sticks should not be thawed before cooking.

Cooking Fish

We cook fish to develop its flavor, to soften the small amount of connective tissue present, and to make the protein easier to digest. Cooking fish at too high a temperature or for too long a time toughens it, dries it out, and destroys its fine flavor.

How can you tell when fish is cooked? During the cooking process the watery juices of raw fish become milk colored, giving the flesh an opaque, whitish tint. This color change is unmistakable. When the flesh takes on this tint to the center of the thickest part, the fish is completely cooked. If it cooks even a minute longer, it begins to dry out. When the fish is thoroughly cooked, the flesh will readily come away from any bones and will separate easily into flakes. Because most cooked fish tends to fall apart, handle it gently.

Poaching fish: Poaching is a method of cooking in a simmering liquid. Wrap the fish in clean cheesecloth or muslin (a dish towel will do) and place it in a wire basket. Do not lay fillets or steaks on top of each other. Simmer very gently in enough water to cover the fish. For each four cups of water add one-half teaspoon salt and one tablespoon vinegar or lemon juice. Spices, herbs, milk, or wine may also be added to the water. Simmer five to ten minutes or until fish flakes easily. Drain and serve with a sauce.

Cooking fish for salads: Place a piece of fish on a greased piece of aluminum foil and season it with salt and pepper. Wrap the foil around the fish, making a double fold on the top and sides and pinching the foil to make it watertight. Place the package in boiling water. Cover the container and when the water returns to boiling, time the cooking period. Allow about ten minutes for each one-inch thickness of fish if fresh; if frozen and unthawed, allow twenty minutes. Chill the fish before flaking it for salads.

Steaming fish: Wrap fish as you do when poaching. Place it on a rack above boiling water; do not put the fish in the water. Cover the pan tightly and steam for twelve to fifteen minutes per pound or until fish flakes. Sprinkle seasoning over the fish after removing it from the steamer. Use about one-half teaspoon salt and one-eighth teaspoon pepper per pound of fish.

Steaming in the oven: Wrap fish as you do when cooking it for salads. Instead of placing the packet in water, place it on a shallow pan and bake at 450 degrees. Allow fifteen minutes cooking time for each one-inch thickness if fish is fresh, or twenty-five minutes per inch thickness if fish is frozen and unthawed.

Baking fish: This is the most common method of preparing fish. Fish may be baked with or without stuffing. Dry a dressed fish and sprinkle it lightly inside and out with salt and pepper, allowing about one-half teaspoon salt and one-eighth teaspoon pepper per pound of fish. Rub the fish with oil or butter, or lay strips of bacon over it. Place it in a greased pan and bake it uncovered at 400 degrees for ten minutes per pound of unstuffed fish or fifteen to twenty minutes per pound of stuffed fish. The fish should be nicely browned and loose under the skin when done.

Broiling fish: Brush fish with butter or lay pieces of bacon over it and place it two to six inches from the source of heat. A broiler set at 375 to 400 degrees gives the proper heat. Broil until the fish is well browned. Fish steaks are usually turned once during broiling; add salt and pepper after the fish is turned, or when the cooking is half done. Fillets or steaks require five to eight minutes broiling on each side; the length of time depends on the thickness of the steak or fillet. Split fish need not be turned; broil six to eight minutes. Broil whole fish over an inch thick about ten minutes on each side. Season with salt on the inside and brush lightly with salt, pepper, and butter on the outside before broiling.

Charcoal broiling: Charcoal broiling is a dry-heat method of cooking over hot coals and in recent years has become a popular form of recreation. Fish, because they cook so quickly, are a natural for this cooking method, but use thicker cuts of fish, as they tend to dry out less than thin ones. Dressed fish, fillets, and steaks are all suitable for charcoal broiling. If frozen, thaw the fish in advance. Because fish flake easily as their cooking nears completion, try to use a well-greased, long-handled, hinged wire grill to hold them. To make sure that the fish will be juicy and flavorful, baste it before and while cooking with a sauce that contains some oil or butter. Broil the fish about four inches above moderately hot coals for ten to twenty minutes, depending on its thickness.

Frying fish: Frying is cooking food in fat. When frying, choose a fat that can be heated to a high temperature without smoking. A smoking fat has begun to decompose and gives food an unpleasant flavor. Because they can reach higher temperatures without smoking, vegetable oils are preferable to animal fats.

The temperature of the oil is extremely important. Too high a heat browns the outside of the fish before the center is cooked. Too low a heat gives a pale, oil-soaked product. The most satisfactory frying temperature for fish is 350 degrees. After frying, drain fish immediately on absorbent paper to remove excess oil. Keep the fish in a warm oven until all pieces are cooked.

Frozen fish used for frying must be thawed in advance. Separate the pieces and cut them to uniform size.

Frying methods are:

1. *Deep fat frying* is cooking in a deep layer of fat or oil. It is a quick cooking method and an excellent way to prepare seafood. For it you need a heavy, deep saucepan or French fryer with straight sides, a fry basket to fit the fryer, a deep fat frying thermometer, or an electric fryer with automatic temperature control. Use enough oil to float the fish, but do not fill the fryer more than half full. Allow room for the fish and for the bubbling of the oil.

You may dip the raw fish in a liquid and coat it with a breading, or dip the fish in batter. Wipe the fish dry before dipping so that the batter will adhere to it. The coating keeps the fish moist during the frying and gives it a delicious crispness.

Place only one layer of fish at a time in the fry basket and allow enough room so that the pieces do not touch each other. This prevents the temperature of the oil from dropping suddenly and ensures thorough cooking and even browning. When the oil has heated to the proper temperature, lower the basket into the fryer slowly to prevent the oil from bubbling over the sides of the cooker. If the oil is the right temperature when the fish is added, a crust forms almost immediately, holding in the juices and preventing the oil from soaking into the batter and fish. Fry until the coating is golden brown and the fish flakes easily, usually three to five minutes. Drain on absorbent paper.

2. *Pan frying* is cooking in a small amount of oil or fat in a frying pan. When well controlled, it is an excellent way of cooking dressed fish, fillets, and steaks. But of all the ways of cooking fish, pan frying is probably the most frequently used and most frequently abused.

The general procedure is to dip the fish in a liquid and then to coat it with a breading. Heat about one-eighth inch of oil in the bottom of a heavy frying pan. For a pan with temperature control, the right heat is 350 degrees. Place one layer of breaded fish in the hot oil, taking care not to overload the pan and thus cool the oil. Fry the fish until brown on one side, then turn and brown the other side. Cooking time will vary with the thickness of the fish. In general, allow eight to ten minutes.

3. *Oven frying* is not really frying. It is a hot-oven method that produces a taste similar

to that of pan frying.

For oven frying, cut the fish into serving-size portions, dip in salted milk, and coat with toasted, fine, dry crumbs. Place it on a shallow, well-greased baking pan. Pour a little melted butter or oil over the fish, and bake at 500 degrees. The fish does not require turning, basting, or careful watching, and the cooking time is short, usually ten to fifteen minutes. The crumb coating and the high temperature prevent the escape of flavorful juices and give an attractive brown crust.

Microwave Cooking

Seafood is ideal for microwave cooking; it cooks almost as soon as it heats. Most recipes for oven-baked fish can be adapted for microwave cooking by following the manufacturer's recommendations for methods and utensils; the wrong utensil can ruin both food and oven. A "rule of thumb" for baking time is: use one fourth of the shortest time given in the regular recipe; the dish can be returned to the oven for another minute if necessary. Reduce liquid amounts, for there is no evaporation — or browning.

Brining and Smoking Fish

Smoking has been used for centuries as a means of preserving fish. Carp, suckers, buffalo, catfish, salmon, trout, and chub can all be smoked successfully. The safety and quality of the finished product depends on your skill, experience, and knowledge of smoking.

Before you can smoke fish, you must have a smoker. To make one from a fifty-gallon metal oil or alcohol drum, cut the top from the drum with a chisel or a cutting torch. Reduce the diameter of the removed top by about three inches. Suspend this top from three brackets thirteen inches from the top of the drum; it is now a heat baffle. Next, cut a ten- by eight-inch section from the side of the drum near the bottom for a fire-pit door. Make a door of light-weight sheet metal to cover this opening, and attach it to the barrel with a single hinge. Make a tray that fits into the barrel out of one-quarter- or one-half-inch wire mesh. Suspend this tray, which will hold the smoking fish, six inches from the top of the barrel with metal straps. Get a metal or wooden cover for the top of the barrel. This is used to control the draft and to hold the smoke inside the barrel.

To make a wooden barrel smoker, knock the ends out of a large wooden barrel. Nail wooden strips on two sides inside the barrel, a few inches below the top. The ends of the smoke sticks rest on these strips. Place a loosely fitting cover on top. Suspend some type of iron or wooden rods, or a rack of coarse wire mesh at the top of the barrel. Space them far enough apart so the fish do not touch when hung. The barrel will not catch fire if ventilation is controlled and the fire is smothered to form smoke rather than flames. Keep the door and top closed during smoking, allowing just enough air to enter to keep fire smoldering.

Make hooks from fourteen-inch lengths of eight- or ten-gauge steel wire or from coat hanger wire. To do this, bend a loop large enough to slide over a smoke rod in the center of each length of wire; next bend the ends of the wire to the sides and then up toward the loop. The fish hang from these hooked ends, and the hooks hang from the smoke rods. Place a wire-mesh tray on the lowest set of wooden strips before hanging the fish. It will catch any fish that fall off the rods during smoking.

At the spot where you will smoke the fish in the wooden smoker, dig a hole about two feet deep, with a diameter slightly smaller than that of the barrel. This is where you build your fire. Set the barrel directly over the hole. Dig a gradual slope, like a ramp, from ground level to the bottom of the hole. This allows air to reach the fire, and enables you to feed the fire without moving the barrel full of fish. Once you have a smoker, you can prepare the fish.

Use freshly-caught dressed whole or filleted fish. Larger whole fish can be cut into steaks or split lengthwise to, but not through, the back skin so they will lie flat. Wash the fish thoroughly. Use either of the following methods to brine the fish before smoking. One gallon of brine is enough for four pounds of fish.

1. As the fish are dressed, place them in a glass or heavy plastic container in a brine consisting of one and one-half cups of salt to one gallon cold water. Keep the fish in brine for at least twelve hours at forty degrees.

2. For a short brine method, use a brine of four cups salt to one gallon cold water. Brine for fifteen minutes.

Remove fish from the brine, drain and rinse the fish. Place fish skin side down on wire mesh screen or suspend from hooks or wooden dowels. If the fish lies flat, it smokes more evenly. Insert the short-stemmed meat thermometer in the thickest portion of the flesh of the largest fish. It may be necessary to tie the thermometer so it will not slip out of place during smoking.

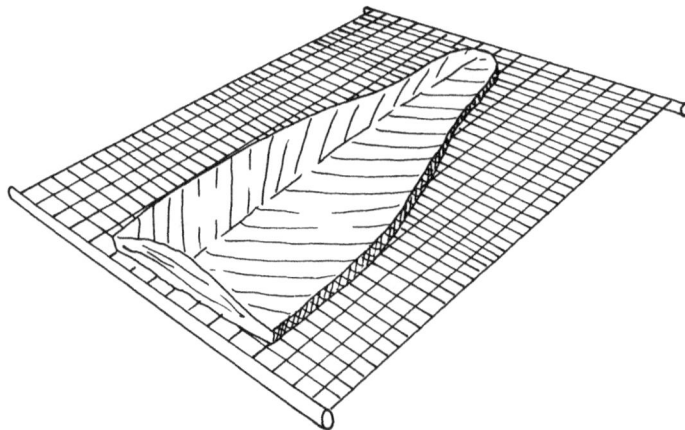

Now build a fire in the bottom of the metal smoker or in the hole dug for the wooden smoker. Start with wood and build up a good bed of coals. (An alternate heat source is charcoal briquettes, burned to a light gray color.) Then add a few wood chips. Keep the fire smoldering, without flames, by adding wet wood chips every thirty minutes, or as needed. Oak, hickory, maple, alder, beech, apple, white birch, or ash wood chips or sawdust produce good smoke. Too much smoke emphasizes the smoke flavor. Do not use pitchy woods such as pine. (If you use a hot plate as your heat source, put wood chips in an iron skillet and the skillet on the hot plate. Keep the chips smoldering until fish smoking is completed.)

When coals are glowing, place the wooden smoker over its hole. Place the fish in either smoker when the air temperature inside reaches 100 degrees. Make sure no piece of fish touches another and that all fish are about the same size and get the same amount of heat. Cover the smoker, keep coals smoldering, and check thermometers occasionally. When the air is 225 degrees and the fish is 180 degrees, maintain these temperatures for a full thirty minutes. This is essential in order to cook the fish and to inhibit bacterial action. Total smoking time is about four hours. As soon as smoking is completed, wrap the fish in waxed paper and place in the refrigerator. Store the fish at temperatures not over 40 to 45 degrees and use within a month.

Pickling Fish

Home pickling is a delicious way to preserve a surplus catch if a few rules are followed. Fish used in a vinegar-spice cure must be fresh and of the best quality. The flavor, texture, color, and keeping quality are affected by the ingredients. Always use distilled white vinegar (not cider vinegar) of no less than five percent acidity; use a fine, noniodized, pickling salt (not table salt); and use regular drinking water in amounts no greater than the amounts of vinegar in the recipe (see Index).

Special Care of Shellfish

You do not often carry home a live fish, but all crabs, clams, or oysters that you prepare in the shell *must* be alive when you cook them. You must therefore know how to keep them alive until they go into the pot. You must also know how to choose them, how to clean them, and how to get them out of their shells.

Clams: There are many types of clams. Littleneck, butter, and razor clams, and geoducks are choice. The cockles, eastern soft-shells (mud clams), and horse clams have fine flavors, but the meat is tough unless ground, chopped, or pounded, and is usually used in chowder.

When you purchase clams in the shell, their shells should be tightly closed. Gaping shells that do not close when handled indicate that the clams are dead and no longer usable.

Butter or littleneck clams are usually steamed. First, scrub the clams under running water. Then, place them in a bucket of clean water, add one-half cup salt, and let them stand for a few hours while they clean themselves of sand. Next, place them in one inch boiling water in a steamer or large kettle. Cover tightly and steam for ten minutes, or until the shells partially open. Detach the top shells, if desired, and serve the clams hot with side dishes of melted butter and cups of strained clam liquor.

Razor clams are very special. If you have an opportunity to dig some, clean them as soon as possible after taking them from the ocean beach. When removing clams from their shells, wear a heavy glove on the hand that holds the clams to protect it from your knife. To remove the clam from the shell, run a knife blade along the inner surface of the shell, and cut the adductor muscles on both sides. To clean, snip off the dark tip of the neck, insert a knife or scissors into the neck, and cut open the body from the tip of the neck to the base of the foot. Remove the gills and the dark part of the clam, which is the digestive tract. Slit the digger foot so it will lie flat, and pick out the small line of intestine that runs through the foot. Rinse away any sand, and the clam is ready to cook.

Geoduck aficionados prize this clam for its long, delectable neck, and although virtually all of the clam is edible, the neck is generally the only part eaten. After removing the geoduck from its shell, cut the neck from the body and quickly blanch it in boiling water; then remove the loosened skin. After skinning it, rinse the neck in cold water and either grind it up for cakes or chowder or thinly slice it. Fry the steaks quickly in butter; overcooking toughens geoduck.

In the store you will find fresh or frozen shucked clams and canned clams. Shucked fresh clams are refrigerated in glass or waxed containers. Choose clams that look plump and have a creamy color. The liquor should be clear and there should be no shell particles. When properly handled, packaged clams will remain fresh for a week or ten days.

Crabs: Almost all of the many delicious ways to prepare crabs begin with cooked crab meat. King crabs, because of their size — five to six feet from the tip of one leg to the tip of the opposite leg, weighing six to twenty pounds — are butchered and marketed mostly as leg meat. Dungeness and tanner crabs may be purchased alive as well as cooked in the shell, or as cooked or frozen meat or canned.

If you catch your own crabs or purchase them live, you must start by cooking them live. Any dead ones should be discarded. To cook properly, place the live crabs in a large pot of already boiling water to which you have added salt and your favorite seafood seasonings such as basil, vinegar, or red pepper. Commercially prepared seafood seasoning mixtures or "crab boils" may also be used. Cover the pot, let the water return to a boil, and cook the crabs for about twenty minutes.

You can safely keep crabs alive for as long as twenty-four hours if you store them in a refrigerator or other cool place. Do not store live crabs in water, as they will quickly use up the oxygen and die. Remember: Throw away any dead crabs before you boil your catch.

If you wish to keep crab meat for future use, only cooked crab meat should be frozen. Never freeze whole crabs, either cooked or uncooked. And under no circumstances should a cooked crab come into contact with any container or surface that has held uncooked crabs. Uncooked crabs may be contaminated with bacteria that could make your boiled crab spoil.

Sitting down before a pot of freshly boiled crabs, you may wonder how anyone could ever find anything edible in that spiny mass of points and legs. There is. By following a few simple steps and using a crab knife properly, you can quickly become adept at picking crabs. An experienced crab picker, like some of the employees at crab processing plants, can pick out from four to seven pounds of crab meat in an hour.

If your first efforts fall a bit short of this, do not give up. With patience your skill may increase to the point at which you can pick the crabs faster than you can eat the meat.

The secret of successful crab picking lies in the use of the crab knife. While special knives are available, any small, heavy knife can be used.

1. Begin by removing the claws. Pull them away from the body and save any meat attached to the end of the arm.

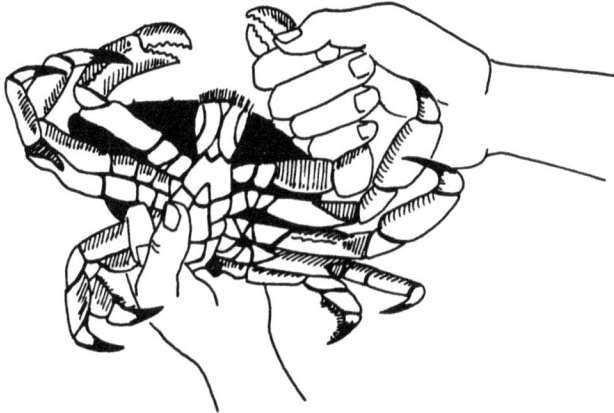

2. Holding the crab knife near the end of the handle, crack the claws with it and remove the meat. If the meat does not come out easily, pry it out of the shell with the knife.

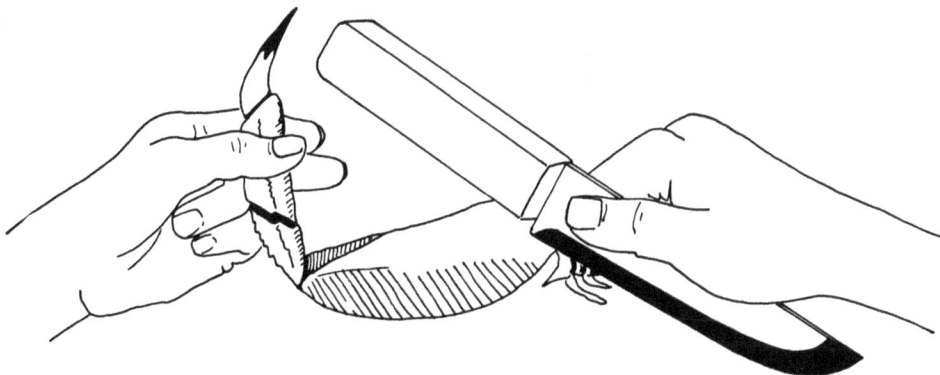

3. Remove the shell that covers the back of the crab by grasping it near one of the spines and pulling up. There is no meat in this shell, so discard it. Using the knife, scrape away the yellowish material, called the fat, lying in the middle of the crab. Some people relish the fat, but most find it rather strong tasting. Cut away the gills, which are the gray

feathery structures found on either side of the crab's back and discard them. *They should not be eaten.*

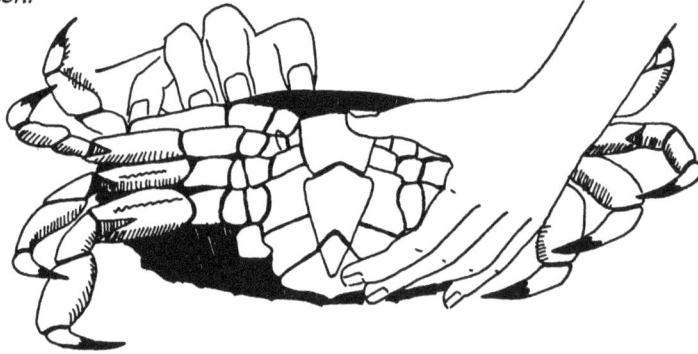

4. Cut away the walking legs. Remove any bits of meat clinging to the cut ends; then crack the legs and remove the meat.

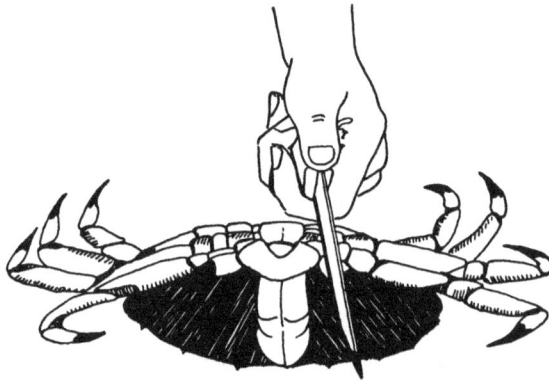

5. Cut the body cavity down the middle, then cut each half into several parts. With the point of the knife, remove the lump meat from the rear portion of the body. Now remove the meat from the remaining sections of the shell by prying upward with the knife.

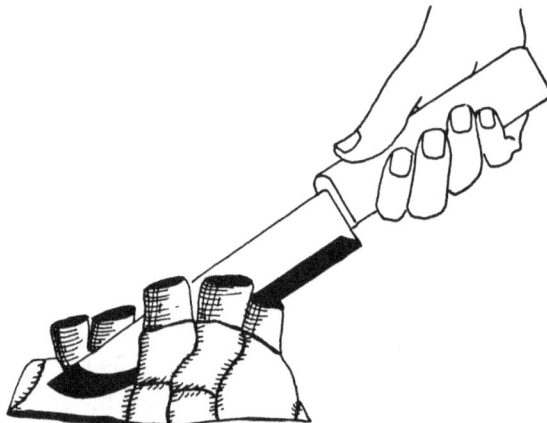

Oysters: If purchased in the shell, these must be alive, too. As with clams, their shells should be tightly closed or should close when handled. Scrub the shells under cold running water with a brush. When clean, insert a strong blunt knife or an oyster knife between the shells of each oyster near the hinge, and with a twisting motion, pry the shells apart. It is wise to protect your hand with a heavy glove, in case the knife slips. When the oyster is open, insert the knife between the shells and cut the muscle that holds the two shells together. Also sever the muscle holding the oyster to the shell. Try to retain as much of the oyster liquor as possible. If you are not serving the oysters on the half shell, drain them and strain the liquor through cheesecloth to remove any particles of shell and sand. Store the shucked oysters and liquor in a covered container in the refrigerator, where they will keep up to ten days.

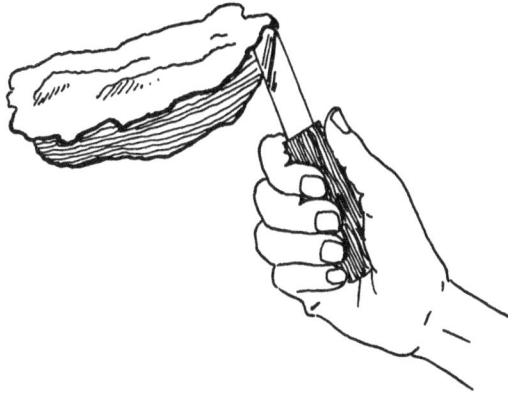

Oysters in the shell may be opened by steaming, but with some loss of flavor. Put the scrubbed and rinsed oysters in a kettle with a very small amount of water — no more than one-half cup for twenty-four medium-sized oysters. Steam them five to ten minutes, or until the shells open. Lift them from the pan carefully so you do not spill the liquor from the shells. When precooked this way, oysters should be used in cooked dishes within two days.

Avoid overcooking oysters. They are toughened by high heat or prolonged cooking. Use moderate heat and cook them just until they plump up or the edges curl.

Use the same criteria for buying fresh shucked oysters as you do for buying clams (see Index).

Scallops: The entire scallop is edible but only the tender white muscle is generally used. Because scallops must be shucked as soon as they are caught, they are not available in the shell unless you take them from the sea yourself. If you do, shuck them by inserting a knife and cutting the muscle free from both shells of each scallop. Rinse them and wipe with a damp cloth.

Before cooking frozen scallops, thaw them until they can be separated from one another.

Shrimp: Shrimp are sold in their shells either raw or cooked, without their shells as fresh or frozen cooked meat, or canned. All cooked shrimp are pink and vary in size from one to three inches in length. The larger varieties are called prawns. Fresh or frozen raw Alaska shrimp are also pink and are sold by the pound with the head and thorax removed. One pound of shrimp in the shell yields one-quarter pound peeled shrimp.

Many recipes use cooked shrimp as the principal ingredient. Here are two ways to cook raw shrimp for use in such recipes: (1) Put one pound of raw shrimp and one-fourth cup salt in one quart of boiling water. When the water boils again, lower the heat and simmer until the shrimp turn pink, about five minutes for small shrimp or eight minutes for large ones. After you drain and cool them, peel off the shells and lift out the dark sand veins.

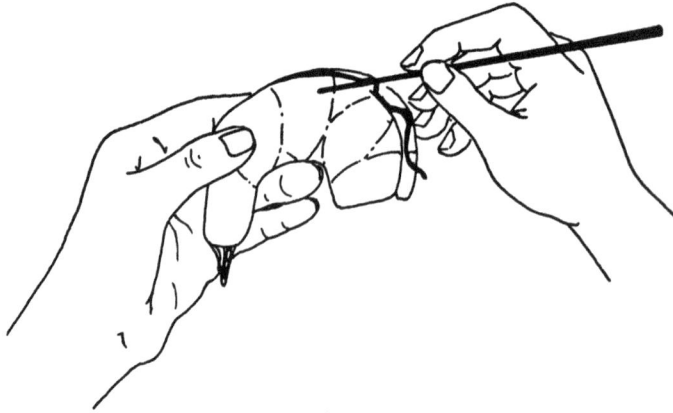

(2) Make a broth of six cups boiling water, two tablespoons salt, two tablespoons vinegar, two bay leaves, one teaspoon whole pickling spice (optional), and two stalks chopped celery. Add two pounds of shrimp, either in the shell or peeled and deveined, and bring to a boil. Cover and simmer until shrimp turn pink, usually about five minutes. You can cook frozen shrimp either of these ways without thawing them in advance.

Mussels: These delicate shellfish deteriorate rapidly, so cook as soon after gathering as possible. Scrub mussels in cold water, discarding any that are not tightly closed. Clip "whiskers" with scissors, if desired. Cover bottom of kettle with one inch of boiling water, drop in mussels and cook three to five minutes, or until shells open. Discard any that do not open.

Serving Seafood

You can make a fish dish more attractive by providing flavors, colors, and textures that contrast with those of the fish.

For flavor contrast, tart and acid foods such as lemon, sour sauces, cabbage slaw, pickles, and relishes are excellent with fish.

For color contrast, light colored vegetables go with red salmon, green and red ones with creamed or steamed white-fleshed fish.

For texture contrast, use crisp foods such as toast or celery with chowders, rich sauces with lean fish, and deep-fried potatoes or potato chips with canned salmon.

Choose a garnish from the following list to add the finishing touch to the fish dish you prepare.

Garnishes	*Suggested Preparation*
Beets	Cooked whole or sliced
Carrots	Tops, sticks, curls, or shredded
Celery	Tops, hearts, sticks, or curls
Chives	Chopped
Cucumbers	Slices or sticks
Dill	Sprigs or chopped
Green or red peppers	Sticks or rings
Hard-cooked eggs	Slices, wedges, deviled, or grated yolks
Lemons or limes	Slices, twists, or wedges
Lettuce	Leaves or shredded
Mint	Sprigs or chopped
Nut meats	Toasted whole, halved, slivered, or chopped
Olives	Whole, sliced, or chopped
Oranges	Slices, twists, or wedges
Paprika	Sprinkled sparingly
Parsley	Sprigs or chopped
Pickles	Whole, sliced, or chopped
Radishes	Whole, sliced, or roses
Watercress	Sprigs or chopped

Appetizers and Sauces

Broiled Seafood Canapés

White bread 6 slices
Butter ¼ cup
Fish or shellfish 1 cup
  cooked and flaked

Catsup or chili sauce ⅓ cup
Processed cheese ¼ pound,
  grated or sliced

Toast bread on one side; after trimming away crust, butter untoasted side. Cover with layer of fish, then catsup; top with cheese. Cut in half or thirds; place canapés on baking sheet and broil until cheese melts and canapés are heated through. Makes 12 to 18 canapés.

Seafood Pretties

**White, whole wheat, or
  rye bread** 6 thin slices
Cream cheese 2 3-ounce packages
**Whitefish, sardines, pickled herring,
  cooked lobster tail, king crab,**

**cooked shrimp, salmon caviar,
  rolled smoked salmon** 1 cup
Pimiento sliced
Green pepper sliced
Ripe or stuffed olives sliced

Quarter bread and cut into fancy shapes (stars, diamonds, circles, etc.); spread with cream cheese and top with seafood. Garnish with additional cream cheese put through pastry tube and with slices of pimiento, green pepper, or olive. Makes 24 appetizers.
Variation: Use your favorite cheese spread instead of cream cheese.

Nor'east Nibbles

Frozen fried fish sticks 16
Parmesan cheese ½ cup grated

Butter or margarine 2 tablespoons
Sea Sauce

Cut frozen fish sticks into thirds; roll each piece in cheese. Melt butter in 10 by 15 by 1-inch baking pan. Place fish in pan and bake at 450° for 8 to 10 minutes. Turn carefully and bake 8 to 10 minutes longer, or until crisp and brown. Drain on absorbent paper and serve with hot Sea Sauce. Makes 48 appetizers.

Sea Sauce

Tomato sauce 1 8-ounce can
Chili sauce ¼ cup
Garlic powder ¼ teaspoon
Oregano ¼ teaspoon

Liquid hot pepper sauce ¼ teaspoon
Thyme ¼ teaspoon
Sugar ⅛ teaspoon
Basil pinch

Combine all ingredients and simmer 10 to 12 minutes, stirring occasionally. Makes about 1 cup.

Pickled Fish

Fresh fish fillets 10 pounds,
  cut in pieces
Pickling salt 1 cup
Cold water 1 gallon
Pickling salt 2½ pounds
Cold water 1 gallon
White distilled vinegar
  2 quarts, 5% acidity
Water 2½ pints
White peppercorns 1 ounce

Whole allspice 1 ounce
Mustard seed 1 ounce or
  Whole mixed pickling
  spice 2 ounces
Bay leaves ½ ounce,
  save 1 for jar
Onions ½ pound, sliced
Hot peppers 1 ounce,
  dried whole or ground (optional)
Lemon 1 slice (optional)

Soak fish in weak salt and water brine (1 cup salt, 1 gallon water) for 1 hour; drain. Pack in a deep glass, heavy plastic, or enamel container and cover with second, stronger salt and water brine (2½ pounds salt, 1 gallon water); keep refrigerated at 40 to 45° for 12 hours. Rinse fish in fresh water. Combine next 6 ingredients in large kettle; boil and add fish. Simmer 10 minutes, or until fish is easily pierced with a fork. Remove fish from liquid and place in single layer on flat pan; refrigerate, cooling rapidly to prevent spoilage. Pack cold fish in a large clean glass jar along with a bay leaf, onions, peppers, and lemon. Strain vinegar solution, bring to a boil, and cover fish with it; seal jar with canning lid immediately. This fish must be stored at 40 to 45° and should be used within 4 to 6 weeks.

Note: For further information on pickling, see Index.

Seafood Cocktail

Halibut 6 ounces
  cooked and flaked
Salmon 6 ounces
  cooked and flaked
Small shrimp 6 ounces
  cooked and cleaned
Celery ½ cup finely diced
Cucumber ½, diced
Salt ¼ teaspoon

Lemon juice of 1 lemon
Catsup 1 14-ounce bottle
Prepared horseradish 2 teaspoons
Worcestershire sauce
  2 teaspoons
Green pepper 2 teaspoons minced
Lemon juice 2 teaspoons
Lettuce leaves
Lemon wedges 6

Combine first 7 ingredients in bowl; mix and chill. Make a sauce by combining the next 5 ingredients; chill. Arrange fish mixture on lettuce leaves in 6 sherbet glasses. Top with sauce and serve with lemon wedges. Serves 6.

Halibut Dip

Halibut or other white fish 1½ cups cooked and flaked
Mayonnaise or salad dressing ½ cup

Stuffed olives ¼ cup finely chopped or
Sweet relish ¼ cup
Onion to taste, grated
Salt and pepper to taste

Blend all ingredients thoroughly. Chill at least 1 hour. Makes 2 cups.

Halibut Dunk

Halibut 1 cup cooked and flaked
Sour cream 2 cups

Onion soup mix 1 1¼-ounce envelope

Combine ingredients well; chill thoroughly. Makes 3 cups.

Busy-Day Canapés

Large cucumber 1
Ice water 3 cups
Salt 2 teaspoons
Party rye bread ½ 15-ounce loaf, thinly sliced

Butter or margarine 2 tablespoons, softened
Herring in sour cream 1 12-ounce jar
Paprika

Wash cucumber; score by running sharp-tined fork down its length from end to end. Cut crosswise into very thin slices. Place cucumber in bowl with ice water and salt, and let stand 30 minutes to crisp; drain on absorbent paper. Spread slices of bread with butter; overlap 2 cucumber slices on each slice. Top cucumber with 1 large or 2 small pieces of herring. Sprinkle with paprika. Makes about 24 canapés.

Favorite Pickled Herring or Salmon

Medium herring fillets 12 or
Salmon fillet 1½ to 2 pounds*
Cider vinegar 1 quart, at least 5% acidity
White vinegar 1 pint, at least 5% acidity

Brown sugar 3 cups
Whole pickling spice 3 ounces
Medium white onions 2, sliced
Bay leaves 4
Red chili peppers a few

If salt herring is used, place in crock and soak in fresh water until excess salt is removed. Prepare a pickling sauce by simmering vinegars, sugar, and pickling spice together for 2 to

3 hours. (If pickling salmon, add 1 tablespoon salad oil to pickling sauce.) Cut fish into 1-inch lengths or cubes. Using 4 sterilized pint jars, put a layer of sliced onion and a bay leaf on the bottom of each; add fish to within 1 inch of the top. Cover fish with pickling sauce and top filled jars with another layer of onion and some chili peppers. Seal. Let stand refrigerated at least 2 days before serving, longer if possible. Makes 4 pints.

*If salmon is used, wrap salmon in cheesecloth, place in kettle, cover with boiling water (add 1½ tablespoons salt per quart of water), cover and simmer for 25 to 30 minutes. Do not overcook; fish should remain firm. Drain and chill.

Note: For further information on pickling, see index.

Pickled Herring, Norwegian Style

Medium herring 8
Water 1 quart
Pickling salt ¼ cup
Onion 1, sliced
Lemon ¼, sliced
Bay leaves 2

Peppercorns 1 teaspoon
Ground allspice ¼ teaspoon
Whole cloves 6
White vinegar 1 pint,
    at least 5% acidity
Water 1 pint

Fillet herring, cover with brine made of water and salt, and soak for 30 minutes. Remove fish from brine and wipe dry. In a crock, alternate layers of herring and a mixture of onion, lemon, and spices. Cover with vinegar and water. Set crock in kettle of cold water; bring water to a boil, cover, and let mixture cook until meat drops from the bones. The herring is ready to use when cold. Store in a cool place. Serves 6.

Note: For further information on pickling, see Index.

Curried Salmon Balls

Smoked salmon 1 7¾-ounce can
Chutney 3 tablespoons
    chopped

Curry powder 2 teaspoons
Mayonnaise ¼ cup
Almonds ¾ cup chopped

Drain and flake salmon; combine with chutney, curry powder, and mayonnaise. Form into 1-inch balls; roll in almonds. Insert toothpick in each, and place on serving tray. Chill at least 1 hour before serving. Makes about 40 balls.

Dilly Salmon Spread

Salmon 1 15½-ounce can
Sour cream 1 cup
French-fried onions
 ¾ cup chopped
Lemon juice 2 tablespoons

Worcestershire sauce
 1 teaspoon
Dillweed ½ teaspoon
Salt ¼ teaspoon

Drain and flake salmon; add remaining ingredients. Mix thoroughly and chill. Makes about 2½ cups.

Salm-Olive Ball

Salmon 1 15½-ounce can
Cream cheese 1 8-ounce
 package, softened
Green pepper ¼ cup
 finely chopped
Stuffed green olives
 ¾ cup quartered
Lemon juice 1 teaspoon
Onion 2 teaspoons grated

Salt ¼ teaspoon
Liquid smoke ½ teaspoon
Seasoning salt pinch
Onion salt pinch
Nuts ⅔ cup chopped
Prepared horseradish
 1 teaspoon
Parsley ¼ cup chopped

Drain salmon and remove bones and skin. Combine all ingredients except parsley and blend well. Improvise by adding more seasonings, if you wish. Form mixture into ball; roll in parsley. Chill at least 1 hour, preferably longer, before serving. Serves 12.

Salmon-Avocado Spread

Avocado 1, peeled
Salmon 1 cup cooked
 and flaked or
 Salmon 1 7¾-ounce can,
 drained and skin removed
Lemon juice 1 tablespoon

Mayonnaise or salad
 dressing 1 tablespoon
Onion 1½ teaspoons grated
Liquid pepper sauce 4 drops
Salt ½ teaspoon
Paprika garnish

Grate avocado coarsely into a bowl. Add next 6 ingredients and mix lightly. Pour into small bowl and garnish with paprika; then chill. Makes about 1½ cups.

Salmon-Sour Cream Dip

Salmon 1 15½-ounce can
Salt ½ teaspoon
Liquid pepper sauce 3 drops
Onion 1 teaspoon grated

Sour cream 1 cup
Red caviar, chopped walnuts,
   or pecans garnish

Drain and mash salmon; blend in salt, pepper sauce, and onion. Fold in sour cream and chill. Garnish with caviar. Makes about 2 cups.

Smoked Salmon Dip

Smoked or kippered salmon
   1½ to 2 cups crumbled

Sour cream 1 cup
Garlic salt to taste

Blend ingredients; chill at least 1 hour before serving. Makes about 2½ cups.

Smoked Salmon-Cheese Dip

Smoked salmon 1 cup flaked or
   Smoked salmon 1 7¾-ounce
can, drained and flaked

Extra-sharp cheese
   spread ½ pound
Mayonnaise or salad
   dressing about ¼ cup

Beat salmon with rotary beater until light and fluffy; add cheese and blend thoroughly. Add mayonnaise until mixture is an appropriate dipping or spreading consistency, then chill. Makes about 2 cups.

Pickled Salmon

Mild cured (lightly smoked) salmon
Cold water to cover fish
Onions sliced

Mixed pickling spices
White vinegar at least 5% acidity
Water

Slice salmon in ¼- to ½-inch pieces, and soak overnight in cold water. Drain; then alternate layers of salmon, onion, and pickling spices in an airtight container until full. Add equal amounts of vinegar and water to fill container, packing contents down with a knife blade to avoid pockets of air. Seal and refrigerate 3 to 5 days. To serve, peel away skin and cut into bite-sized chunks.
Variation: Add extra vinegar when pickling for even more spice.

Note: For further information on pickling, see Index.

Pickled Salmon, Cooked

Salmon 3- to
4-pound piece
Water to cover fish
Pickling salt 1½ tablespoons
per quart of water
Cooking liquid 1 quart

White vinegar 2 quarts,
at least 5% acidity
Nutmeg 1½ teaspoons
Mace 6 blades
Peppercorns 1 ounce
Salad oil 1 tablespoon

Wrap salmon in cheesecloth and simmer, covered, in salted water for about 45 minutes. Do not overcook; fish should remain firm. Drain, saving 1 quart of the liquid, and chill. Combine cooking liquid, vinegar, nutmeg, mace, and peppercorns in saucepan; cover and simmer 5 minutes. Cool and add salad oil. Put salmon in deep ceramic or glass container and pour pickling mixture over it; cover, and store in cool place. This will keep for several months. Serves 6.

Note: For further information on pickling, see Index.

Salmon Cured in Olive Oil

Salmon fillets 2 pounds,
skinned
Salt 3 tablespoons

Sugar 2 tablespoons
Olive oil about 1 pint

Dry fillets with paper towels. Combine salt and sugar; press into salmon, thoroughly covering all fish. Fit fish snugly into a glass pan in a single layer. Put plastic wrap over fish and a board or platter over the plastic, weigh down on the salmon with a can of vegetables or a brick, and refrigerate. Occasionally spoon the juices which form, over fish. After 24 hours remove weights and dry salmon with paper towels again. Using a sharp knife, slice into thin diagonal slices. Pack slices firmly into small jars to within ½ inch of the tops. Completely cover salmon with olive oil, working the oil down with a knife in order to remove any air bubbles from the jars. Cover tightly and refrigerate at least a day before using. This will keep up to 2 weeks in refrigerator. To serve, press salmon between paper towels to remove excess oil. It resembles gravlax or lox and is good with rye bread. Makes 1½ pints.

Fast Cheese-Bread Ring with Kippered Salmon

**Refrigerated flaky baking powder
  biscuits** 1 10-ounce can
Instant minced onion ½ cup

Cheddar cheese ½ pound,
  grated
Kippered salmon ¼ pound,
  crumbled

Separate refrigerated biscuits and place on baking sheet in the shape of a double ring; let rest 10 minutes, or until dough comes to room temperature. Lightly work biscuits together to form one piece. Sprinkle onion and half the cheese on biscuit ring, and gently press into dough. Sprinkle half the remaining cheese on top. Bake at 400° for 8 minutes. Remove from oven and top with salmon and remaining cheese. Return to oven for 2 minutes, or until cheese melts and biscuits are golden. Pull apart or cut into wedges and serve hot. Makes 4 to 6 servings.

Salmon Flips

Salmon 1 15½-ounce can
Bacon slices 4
**Condensed cheddar cheese
  soup** ¾ cup

Prepared horseradish 1 teaspoon
Instant minced onion 1 teaspoon
Pepper pinch
Cheese Canapé Pastry

Drain and flake salmon. Fry bacon until crisp; drain on absorbent paper; crumble. Combine all ingredients except pastry. Roll pastry until very thin and cut into 2½-inch squares. Place a heaping teaspoonful of salmon mixture on one side of each square. Moisten edges and fold into triangular shapes; press edges together with a fork. Place turnovers on a 10 by 15 by 1-inch baking pan; prick tops. Bake at 450° for 10 to 12 minutes, or until lightly browned. Makes about 80 appetizers.

Cheese Canapé Pastry

Butter or margarine
  1 cup, softened
Cheese 1 cup grated

Flour 2 cups
Salt pinch
Cayenne pinch

Cream butter and cheese; add flour, salt, and pepper, and mix thoroughly. Shape dough into ball; chill 3 hours before rolling.

Salmon Nuggets

Salmon 1 15½-ounce can
Potatoes ½ cup
  cooked and mashed
Celery 1 tablespoon
  finely diced
Onion 1 tablespoon
  finely chopped
Butter 1 tablespoon, melted

Pepper pinch
Worcestershire sauce 1 teaspoon
Egg 1, beaten
Cheddar cheese about 1 cup
**Dry bread crumbs,
  cracker crumbs, or
  cornflakes** 1 cup
Oil for deep frying

Drain and flake salmon. Combine with next 7 ingredients; mix well. Shape into walnut-sized balls. Cut ⅜-inch cubes of cheese and insert one in each ball. Roll in crumbs and deep fry at 375° for 3 to 4 minutes, or until golden brown. Makes about 60 balls.

Salmon Snips

Salmon 1 15½-ounce can,
  drained and flaked
Mayonnaise ½ cup
Dill pickle ½ cup finely chopped
Sharp cheddar cheese 1 cup grated

English muffins 6, split
Parmesan cheese
  ½ cup grated
Stuffed green olives
  24, halved

Combine salmon, mayonnaise, dill pickle, and cheddar cheese; spread on muffin halves. Sprinkle generously with Parmesan cheese and arrange 4 pieces of olive on each muffin half. Place on cookie sheet and bake at 350° for 12 minutes; then broil 2 to 3 minutes, or until toasted. Cut into quarters and serve hot. Makes 48 wedges.

Note: You can assemble these in advance and bake when ready to serve.

Salmon Wrap-Arounds

White bread 12 slices
Salmon 1 15½-ounce can,
  drained and flaked
Ripe olives 3 tablespoons chopped

Lemon juice 1 tablespoon
Mayonnaise ⅓ cup
Monosodium glutamate ¼ teaspoon
Butter 3 tablespoons, melted

Remove crust from bread and flatten slices with rolling pin. Combine next 5 ingredients; blend until smooth and spread on bread. Roll up each slice and fasten with toothpicks; brush with butter. Place on baking sheet and bake at 400° for 15 minutes. Makes 12 servings.

Smoky Salmon

Salmon 1 7¾-ounce can*
Mayonnaise or salad dressing ¼ cup
Lemon juice 1 tablespoon
Prepared horseradish 1 teaspoon
Onion 1 teaspoon grated
Liquid smoke ¼ teaspoon
Pastry 1 9-inch crust portion
Paprika garnish

Drain and flake salmon; add next 5 ingredients; mix thoroughly. Divide pastry in half; roll into circles about 9 inches in diameter. Spread each circle with half the salmon mixture; cut each circle into 16 wedge-shaped pieces. Roll up from wide to pointed edges and place rolls on a 10 by 15 by 1-inch baking pan; prick tops. Sprinkle with paprika. Bake at 450° for 10 to 15 minutes, or until lightly browned. Makes 32 appetizers.
*Canned smoked salmon may be substituted for the canned salmon and liquid smoke.

Note: To avoid last-minute work, assemble in advance, cover with waxed paper, and refrigerate until ready to bake.

Caviar Crown

Cream cheese 2 8-ounce
  packages, softened
Lemon juice 2 tablespoons
Green onion 2 tablespoons chopped
Worcestershire sauce 1 teaspoon
Salmon caviar 1 4-ounce
  jar, drained
Whitefish caviar 1 3½-ounce
  jar, drained
Parsley garnish*

Cream the cheese and blend in lemon juice, onion, and Worcestershire sauce; place in center of serving plate and shape in a circle about 7 inches in diameter and 1 inch thick, similar to a layer cake. Cover a 4-inch-diameter circle in the center with salmon caviar. Cover the rest of the cheese with whitefish caviar. Place small sprigs of parsley around edge of salmon caviar; garnish base of cheese circle with parsley. Makes about 2 cups.
*A ring of overlapping slices of tiny stuffed olives or a ribbon of cream cheese put through a pastry tube may be substituted for the parsley that garnishes the salmon caviar circle.

Note: For large parties, make several small crowns, using ½ recipe for each one. With cheese mixture make two cheese circles, each about 3½ inches in diameter and 1 inch thick. Cover a 2-inch-diameter circle in the center of each with salmon caviar and the remaining surfaces with whitefish caviar. Continue decorating as you would the large crown.

Salmon Caviar

Fresh skein salmon eggs should
  yield 2 cups cleaned eggs

Salt ½ cup
Cold water 2 cups

Gently separate eggs individually from the skein; remove as much membrane as possible. Stir salt and water together in large dish until salt is thoroughly dissolved; add eggs and stir gently. Allow to stand 30 minutes; they will become firm and absorb some of the salt. Pick out membrane particles; these turn white so are easily seen. Drain water from the eggs by pouring into strainer. Rinse eggs gently in large dish of cold water and strain again. Pick out any remaining membrane. Chill and store tightly covered in refrigerator. Caviar will keep this way for several months; when it develops an off-flavor, discard it. Makes 2 cups.

Note: Caviar should be served ice cold. It is especially tasty on unsalted crackers or toast or, with a dollop of sour cream, as an addition to salads.

Fried Salmon Eggs

**Fresh skein immature salmon
  eggs*** 2 cups
**Corn meal or cracker
  crumbs** 1½ cups

Salt and pepper to taste
Oil for frying 1 cup
Butter ½ cup

Cut skeins into conveniently sized pieces leaving the eggs intact; roll in corn meal and season. Using a cover with open vents, fry in hot oil and butter, browning well on both sides so that skeins are cooked through.
*Never use ripe eggs as they explode like popcorn.

Down East Pâté

Maine sardines 2 3¾-ounce cans
Cream cheese 2 8-ounce
  packages, softened
Lemon juice 3 tablespoons
Onion 2 tablespoons grated

Parsley 2 tablespoons chopped
Prepared horseradish 1 tablespoon
Liquid pepper sauce 2 drops
Potato chips ½ cup crushed
Parsley ½ cup chopped

Drain and mash sardines. Cream the cheese in mixing bowl and add sardines; blend in next 5 ingredients, mixing thoroughly. Shape into mound on serving plate. Combine potato chips and parsley and cover mound completely; chill. Makes about 3 cups.

Sautéed Shad Roe

Large pairs shad roe 4 or
  Medium pairs shad roe 5 to 6
Flour ¼ cup
Salt 1½ teaspoons
Pepper ⅛ teaspoon

Butter 1 cup
Lemon juice 1 tablespoon
  (optional)
Bacon ½ pound,
  sliced and fried crisp

Carefully separate the pairs of roe; do not break the membrane. Dust lightly with flour and season. In frying pan, melt butter and sauté roe gently until golden brown on each side. For a tangy flavor, add lemon juice to butter during frying time. Serve on hot platter garnished with bacon. Serves 8.

Shad Roe Delights

Boiling water to cover shad roe
Salt 1 tablespoon
Vinegar 1 tablespoon
Shad roe 4 medium pairs
Lemon juice 2 tablespoons

Egg yolks 2 cooked and
  mashed fine
Parsley 1 teaspoon, chopped
Pepper ⅛ teaspoon
Butter ¼ cup
Toast

Add salt, vinegar, and shad roe to water; cook 20 minutes, then drain, cover with cold water, and let stand 5 minutes. Add lemon juice to roe, breaking up lightly with fork; add egg yolks, parsley, and pepper; stir until blended. Pan fry in butter (adding more butter if needed to prevent sticking) until golden brown and serve with toast.
Variations: Cooked, drained roe may be dipped in beaten egg, rolled in coarse ground whole wheat flour and fried; or may be sautéed with bacon; or may be placed in buttered pan, covered with tomato sauce and baked in hot oven for 20 minutes; or may be dipped in cornmeal and pan fried.

Smelt Pâté

Cream cheese 2 8-ounce
  packages, softened
Prepared horseradish 2 teaspoons
Onion 2 tablespoons grated
Lemon juice 3 tablespoons

Smelt 1 cup cooked,
  boned, and mashed
Parsley 2 tablespoons chopped
Potato chips ½ cup crushed

Cream the cheese. Add horseradish, onion, lemon juice, and smelt; mix thoroughly. Shape into mound on serving plate. Combine parsley and potato chips and cover mound completely. Makes 3 cups.

Tuna Nuggets

Tuna 2 6½-ounce cans
Cream cheese 2 3-ounce
  packages, softened
Lemon juice 1 tablespoon

Prepared horseradish 2 teaspoons
Liquid pepper sauce ¼ teaspoon
Parsley 1 cup chopped

Drain and flake tuna. Cream the cheese; add tuna, lemon juice, horseradish, and pepper sauce; mix thoroughly. Shape into small balls, roll in parsley, and chill at least 1 hour before serving. Makes about 40 balls.

Tuna-Tomato Teasers

Tuna 1 6½-ounce can
Cream cheese 1 3-ounce
  package, softened
Ripe avocado 1, peeled and mashed
Lemon juice 1 tablespoon

Chili powder 1 teaspoon
Salt ½ teaspoon
Liquid pepper sauce ½ teaspoon
Worcestershire sauce ½ teaspoon
Cherry tomatoes 2 pints

Drain and flake tuna. Cream the cheese and avocado; add tuna and next 5 ingredients; mix thoroughly. Chill at least 1 hour. Wash tomatoes and hollow out centers; turn upside down to drain. Fill each tomato with heaping teaspoonful of tuna mixture. Makes about 40 appetizers.

Tuna Puffs

Tuna 2 6½-ounce cans
Celery 1 cup finely chopped
Mayonnaise or salad dressing ½ cup
Onion 2 tablespoons chopped

Sweet pickle 2 tablespoons
  chopped
Salt to taste
Puff Shells

Drain and flake tuna. Combine all ingredients except puff shells; mix thoroughly. Cut tops from puff shells; fill each shell with about 2 teaspoons of tuna mixture and replace tops. Makes about 48 appetizers.

Puff Shells

Water ½ cup
Butter or margarine ¼ cup
Salt pinch

Flour ½ cup
Eggs 2

Combine water, butter, and salt in saucepan and bring to a boil. Add flour all at once and stir vigorously until mixture forms a ball and leaves sides of pan. Remove from heat; cool slightly. Add eggs, one at a time, beating thoroughly after each addition. Continue beating until stiff dough forms. Drop by level teaspoonfuls onto well-greased 16 by 14-inch cookie sheet. Bake at 450° for 10 minutes; reduce heat to 350° and continue baking about 10 minutes longer. Makes about 55 puffs.

Tuna Cheesies

Tuna 1 6½-ounce can
Cheese 1 cup grated
Butter or margarine ¼ cup, softened
Lemon juice 2 tablespoons

Onion 1⅓ tablespoons grated
Worcestershire sauce 1 teaspoon
Paprika ½ teaspoon
Liquid pepper sauce 3 drops
Melba toast rounds 30

Drain and flake tuna. Cream cheese and butter together; add tuna, and next 5 ingredients; mix thoroughly. Spread each toast round with about 2 teaspoonfuls of tuna mixture. Place on 10 by 15 by 1-inch baking sheet; broil about 4 inches from source of heat for 3 to 5 minutes, or until lightly browned. Makes about 30 canapés.

Great Lakes Dip

Smoked whitefish or other smoked fish ½ pound
Sour cream 1 cup
Lemon juice 2 tablespoons
Chives 2 teaspoons chopped
Instant minced onion 1 teaspoon

Salt ½ teaspoon
Rosemary ¼ teaspoon
Peppercorns 6, crushed
Ground cloves pinch
Parsley chopped

Remove skin and bones from fish; flake and combine with next 8 ingredients. Chill at least 1 hour to blend flavors. Sprinkle parsley over dip. Makes about 1¾ cups.

Clam Dip

Clams 1 7-ounce can minced
Heavy cream 1 cup, whipped until stiff

Cream cheese 1 3-ounce package
Onion to taste, grated
Salt and pepper to taste

Drain clams; blend thoroughly with remaining ingredients and chill. Makes 2 cups.

Clamdigger Dip

Clams 1 8-ounce can minced
Cream cheese 1 8-ounce
 package, softened
Lemon juice 1 tablespoon
Onion 1 tablespoon grated

Parsley 1 teaspoon chopped
Worcestershire sauce 1 teaspoon
Salt ¼ teaspoon
Liquid pepper sauce dash

Drain clams and reserve liquor. Cream the cheese; add last 6 ingredients and clams; mix thoroughly. If it is necessary to thin dip, add a little clam liquor. Chill at least 1 hour. Makes about 1¼ cups.

Clam Appetizers

Cream of celery soup
 1 10¾-ounce can
Clam nectar ¼ cup
Clams 1 cup chopped
Dry bread crumbs ¼ cup
Salt and pepper to taste

Cockle clam shells 24,
 2-inch widths
Parmesan chesse 1½ teaspoons
 grated
Parsley chopped
Paprika garnish

Combine first 5 ingredients; mix thoroughly. Spoon into scrubbed shells and sprinkle with Parmesan, parsley, and paprika. Place in shallow baking pan and bake at 325° for 20 minutes, or until bubbly. Makes 24 appetizers.

Clams Fried on the Half Shell

Butter clams 12, about
 2 inches across
Seasoned flour ¼ cup

Egg 1, slightly beaten
 with 2 teaspoons water
Cracker crumbs ¾ cup
Salad oil for frying

Cut clams completely in half from hinge so that you have half a clam on each half shell. Clean stomach, if desired. Dip clam side of shell in flour, then egg, then cracker crumbs. Fry, clam side down in ½ inch of oil until brown. Serve hot. Serves 8.

New Orleans Crab Spread

**Blue or other crab
  meat** ¾ pound or
  Crab meat 2 6½-ounce
  cans, drained
Tarragon vinegar ¼ cup
Mayonnaise or salad dressing ⅓ cup

Pimiento 3 tablespoons chopped
Green onion 2 tablespoons chopped
Salt 1 teaspoon
Freshly ground pepper ½ teaspoon
Capers 1 tablespoon, drained

Remove any shell or cartilage, and flake crab meat; add vinegar and chill for 30 minutes. Drain and add next 5 ingredients; mix thoroughly. Garnish with capers. Makes about 2 cups.

Crab in Blankets

Crab meat ½ pound, flaked
Cream cheese 1 8-ounce
  package, softened
Celery ⅓ cup finely chopped
Parsley 1 tablespoon minced

Lemon juice 1 tablespoon
Almonds ⅓ cup chopped
  and toasted
Salt and pepper to taste
Ham 12 thin slices

Blend all ingredients together except ham. Spread mixture on each ham slice and secure with a toothpick. Chill several hours; remove picks before serving. Makes 12 appetizers.

Crab on the Half Shell

Ripe avocados 2, halved
  lengthwise and pits removed
Lemon juice from 2 lemons
Crab meat 1 6½-ounce
  can, drained*
Seasoned salt ½ teaspoon
Lemon Pepper ¼ teaspoon
Celery stalks 2, chopped

Green onions 2, including
  tops, chopped
Parsley 1 tablespoon finely chopped
Water chestnuts 1 6½-ounce
  can, drained and chopped
Serving shells 4
Cocktail or chili sauce ¼ cup
Raw cashews garnish
Tortilla chips

Using a ¼-teaspoon measuring spoon, make avocado balls; toss them with lemon juice. Combine avocado with next 7 ingredients by tossing together lightly. Heap mixture into shells. Top each with cocktail sauce and cashews. Serve with chips. Serves 4.
*Instead of crab meat, try using sockeye salmon or other seafood native to the Northwest.

Crab Salad in Puff Shells

Crab meat or other seafood
  1 cup cooked and flaked
Mayonnaise or salad dressing   ¼ cup
Celery   ½ cup finely chopped
Sweet pickle or kelp
  relish   1 tablespoon

Onion   1 teaspoon grated
Egg   1, hard-cooked and chopped
Salt and pepper   to taste
Puff Shells (see Index)   36

Combine all ingredients except puff shells and mix thoroughly; chill. Cut tops from shells, fill with crab mixture, and replace tops. Makes 36 appetizers.

King Crab Canapés

King or other crab
  meat   6 ounces or
  Crab meat   1 6½-ounce
  can, drained
Flaky baking powder biscuits
  1 10-ounce can
Cheese   ½ cup grated

Mayonnaise or salad dressing
  2 tablespoons
Chives   1½ teaspoons chopped
Liquid pepper sauce   2 drops
Pepper   pinch
Salt   ¼ teaspoon
Egg whites   2

After removing any remaining shell or cartilage, drain and chop crab meat. Separate each biscuit into 2 thin ones and place in 10 by 15 by 1-inch baking pan. Bake at 400° for 6 to 8 minutes, or until lightly browned. Remove from oven and turn biscuits over on baking pan. Combine next 5 ingredients with crab meat; mix thoroughly. Add salt to egg whites and beat until stiff but not dry. Fold crab mixture into egg whites. Top each biscuit with a tablespoonful of crab mixture. Bake at 450° for 8 to 10 minutes, or until lightly browned. Serve hot. Makes 20 canapés.

Florida Stone Crab Claws à la Kennedy

When President Kennedy was in Florida, one of the popular dinner menus was stone crab claws followed by pompano. Both were flown, on occasion, to the White House in Washington.

Only the large claws of the stone crab are eaten. To preserve the species, Florida fishermen remove one claw from each stone crab they catch and then return the crab alive to the ocean; the claw is regenerated in two seasons. This recipe assumes you gather your own claws. If you buy them, they should already be cooked, and all you need do is crack them and serve with sauce.

Water 3 quarts
Salt 1 teaspoon
Lime juice 1 tablespoon

Florida stone crab
 claws 12 to 18
Sauce à la Kennedy

In large saucepan, combine water, salt, and lime juice; bring to boil. Add crab claws and simmer 20 minutes. Remove and chill claws. Crack shells in several places so meat can be removed easily. Serve with Sauce à la Kennedy. Serves 6.

Sauce à la Kennedy

Mayonnaise ½ cup
Steak sauce ¼ cup
Lemon juice 2 tablespoons

Prepared mustard 4 tablespoons
Liquid pepper sauce
 2 to 3 drops

Combine all ingredients and chill. Makes about 1 cup.

Crab Dabs

Dungeness or other crab
 meat ¾ pound or
 Crab meat 2 6½-ounce cans
Soft bread crumbs ⅓ cup
Dry sherry 2 tablespoons

Chives 1 teaspoon chopped
Dry mustard 1 teaspoon
Salt ¼ teaspoon
Bacon slices 10, cut into thirds

Remove any shell or cartilage from crab meat; drain and chop. Combine with next 5 ingredients; mix thoroughly and chill for 30 minutes. Shape tablespoonfuls of mixture into rolls; wrap a piece of bacon around each roll and secure with toothpick. Place rolls on broiler pan; broil about 4 inches from source of heat for 8 to 10 minutes, or until bacon is crisp. Makes 30 rolls.

Lil' Crab Cakes

Butter ½ cup, melted
Bread 6 slices, crust removed
Egg yolks 3, slightly beaten
Salt ¾ teaspoon
Liquid pepper sauce ⅛ teaspoon

Worcestershire sauce 2 teaspoons
Crab meat 1½ pounds, flaked
Egg whites 3, stiffly beaten
Butter ¼ cup

Pour butter over bread and let soak 15 minutes. Mash bread, adding egg yolks, salt, pepper sauce, and Worcestershire sauce; blend in crab meat and fold in egg whites. Shape into small cakes. Melt butter in a skillet and brown cakes on both sides, adding more butter if needed to prevent sticking. Serve hot. Makes 25 small cakes.

Hen House Homards

Lobster meat 1 pound
Mayonnaise or salad dressing ⅔ cup
Chili sauce 1 tablespoon
Green pepper 1 teaspoon chopped
Onion 1 teaspoon grated

Pimiento 1 teaspoon chopped
Eggs 16, hard-cooked and halved
  lengthwise with yolks removed*
Parsley garnish

After removing any shell or cartilage, drain and chop lobster meat; combine with next 5 ingredients. Fill each egg white half with 1 tablespoon lobster mixture; sprinkle with parsley and chill. Makes 32 appetizers.
*Use egg yolks in other recipes.

Lobster Boats

Lobster meat ½ pound
Fresh mushrooms 24, 1½-inch
  diameter
**Condensed cream of mushroom
  soup** ¼ cup
Soft bread crumbs 2 tablespoons

Mayonnaise or salad dressing
  2 tablespoons
Worcestershire sauce ¼ teaspoon
Liquid pepper sauce ⅛ teaspoon
Pepper pinch
Parmesan cheese grated

After removing any shell or cartilage, drain and chop lobster meat. Rinse mushrooms in cold water; dry and remove stems. Combine next 6 ingredients with lobster; mix thoroughly. Stuff each mushroom cap with a tablespoonful of the lobster mixture; sprinkle with cheese. Place mushrooms in well-greased 10 by 15 by 1-inch baking pan. Bake at 400° for 10 to 15 minutes, or until lightly browned. Makes 24 appetizers.

Oysters Rockefeller

Oysters Rockefeller originated in 1899 at Antoine's, the celebrated New Orleans restaurant. The richness of the recipe prompted its inventor to name it after the richest man he could think of — John D. Rockefeller.

Shucked oysters 18
Butter or margarine ¼ cup
Celery ¼ cup chopped
Green onion ¼ cup chopped
Parsley 2 tablespoons chopped
Frozen chopped spinach
    1 10-ounce package

Anisette 1 tablespoon
Salt ¼ teaspoon
Rock salt*
Baking shells or ramekins 18
Dry bread crumbs ¼ cup
Butter or margarine 1 tablespoon,
    melted

In small saucepan, melt butter; add celery, onion, and parsley. Cover and cook 5 minutes, or until tender. Combine cooked vegetables with spinach in blender container; add anisette and salt. Chop mixture in blender until almost puréed, stopping once or twice to push vegetables into cutting blades. If you have no blender, vegetables may be run through a food mill. Make layers of rock salt in 3 pie tins and sprinkle with water; place baking shells on top. Put an oyster in each shell and top with spinach mixture. Combine bread crumbs and melted butter; sprinkle over oysters. Bake at 450° for 10 minutes. Serve immediately in pie tins. Serves 6.
*This holds the baking shells upright and helps keep oysters hot when served.

Angels on Horseback

Shucked oysters 24
Bacon slices 12, cut into halves
Salt ½ teaspoon

Pepper ⅛ teaspoon
Paprika ⅛ teaspoon
Parsley 2 tablespoons chopped

Drain oysters and lay each across a piece of bacon. Sprinkle with seasonings and parsley. Roll bacon around oyster and fasten with toothpick. Place oysters on rack in shallow baking pan and bake at 400° for 10 to 15 minutes, or until bacon is crisp. Remove toothpicks and serve. Makes 24 appetizers.

Oyster Snaps

Small shucked oysters   24
Rice vinegar   ¼ cup
Soy sauce   2 tablespoons
Cashews   ½ cup finely ground
Mayonnaise   ½ cup
Lemon juice   1 teaspoon
Soy sauce   1 tablespoon

Curry powder   ½ teaspoon
Liquid pepper sauce   1 or 2 drops
Bacon slices   2, cut into
  1-inch pieces
Toast rounds or crackers
  24, buttered

Drain oysters and retain liquor in bowl; add vinegar and soy sauce to liquor. Marinate oysters in this for 10 minutes; drain again and roll in cashews. Arrange oysters slightly apart on shallow pan lined with lightly buttered aluminum foil. Blend next 5 ingredients. Top each oyster with a teaspoonful of this mixture and a piece of bacon. Broil 3 inches from source of heat for 5 minutes, or until oysters start to curl at edges and bacon sizzles. Serve on toast rounds. Serves 6.

Oysters San Juan

Butter or margarine   ½ cup
Green pepper   ½ cup coarsely chopped
Green onion   ½ cup coarsely chopped
Parsley   2 tablespoons minced

Small select rock oysters   16
Seasoning salt   pinch
Black pepper   pinch

Melt butter in skillet over medium heat; sauté green pepper, onion, and parsley no more than 3 to 4 minutes so vegetables remain crisp. Add oysters with their liquor and seasonings and cook no more than 5 minutes longer; avoid overcooking. Serve at once in small saucedishes along with pieces of bread with which to absorb the excellent sauce. Serves 4.

Nutty Oysters

Oysters   2 10-ounce jars
Blanched almonds   ¼ cup chopped
  and toasted
Soft bread crumbs   3 cups
Egg   1, beaten
Onion   1 tablespoon chopped
Parsley   1 tablespoon chopped

Salt   ¼ teaspoon
Nutmeg   pinch
Pepper   pinch
Dry bread crumbs   ½ cup
Oil   for deep frying
Cocktail Sauce (see Index)   1 cup

Drain oysters thoroughly and chop. Combine with next 8 ingredients and mix thoroughly. Drop by tablespoonfuls into crumbs; roll to form balls. Place in single layer in fry basket. Deep fry in oil at 350° for 2 to 3 minutes, or until golden brown. Drain on absorbent paper. Heat cocktail sauce and serve with oyster balls. Makes about 40 appetizers.

Scal-la-pops

Scallops 1 pound, rinsed
and drained
Water chestnuts 1 6½-ounce
can, drained

Marinade
Bacon slices 15, cut
into halves

Cut large scallops in half. Cut water chestnuts into thirds; place in bowl with scallops. Add marinade and let stand at least 2 hours, stirring occasionally. Drain. Place a scallop and a piece of water chestnut on each piece of bacon. Wrap bacon around scallop and chestnut and secure with toothpick. Place scallops on broiler pan. Broil about 4 inches from source of heat for 6 to 8 minutes. Turn and broil 4 to 5 minutes longer or until bacon is crisp. Makes 30 appetizers.

Marinade

Salad oil ¼ cup
Soy sauce ¼ cup
Catsup 2 tablespoons

Vinegar 1 tablespoon
Pepper ¼ teaspoon
Garlic cloves 2, crushed

Combine all ingredients and mix thoroughly. Makes about ¾ cup.

Skewered Scallops

Scallops 1 pound, rinsed
and drained
Large green peppers 2
Cherry tomatoes 1 pint
Lemon juice ⅓ cup

Honey 3 tablespoons
Prepared mustard 3 tablespoons
Oil 2 tablespoons
Curry powder 1½ teaspoons

Cut large scallops in half. Remove seeds from peppers and cut peppers into 1-inch squares. Alternate tomatoes, scallops, and pieces of pepper on 40 skewers or 3-inch long toothpicks. Place these kabobs on well-greased broiler pan. Combine remaining ingredients; brush kabobs with this sauce. Broil about 4 inches from source of heat for 5 to 7 minutes. Turn carefully and brush again with sauce. Broil 5 to 7 minutes longer, basting once. Makes 40 appetizers.

Scallop Rémoulade Appetizer

Water 1 cup
Dry white wine ½ cup
Onion slices 2
Parsley sprigs 2
Salt ½ teaspoon
Thyme ¼ teaspoon

Scallops 1½ pounds, rinsed
and dried
Lettuce shredded
Rémoulade Sauce
Egg 1, hard-cooked and
chopped (optional)

In saucepan combine first 6 ingredients; bring to boil. Place scallops in poaching liquid; cover and simmer 2 to 5 minutes, or until tender. Drain scallops and chill. Arrange on beds of lettuce in individual seafood shells or cocktail glasses. Spoon about 3½ tablespoons Rémoulade Sauce on top of each serving. Garnish with egg, if desired. Serves 6.

Rémoulade Sauce

Mayonnaise ½ cup
Tarragon vinegar ¼ cup
Prepared brown mustard
2 tablespoons
Catsup 1 tablespoon
Paprika 1½ teaspoons

Salt ½ teaspoon
Cayenne ¼ teaspoon
Salad oil ½ cup
Celery ¼ cup chopped
Green onion ¼ cup chopped
Parsley 1 tablespoon chopped

In small bowl combine first 7 ingredients; slowly add salad oil, beating constantly (may be done in a blender), until sauce is as thick as mayonnaise. Stir in celery, green onion, and parsley. Allow to stand 3 or 4 hours to blend flavors. Makes 1¾ cups.

Biloxi Butter

Shrimp ½ pound cooked, peeled
and deveined or
Shrimp 2 4½-ounce cans, drained
and rinsed*
Butter or margarine ½ cup, softened
Lemon juice 2 tablespoons

Prepared horseradish 2 teaspoons
Salt ¼ teaspoon
Nutmeg ⅛ teaspoon
Liquid pepper sauce ⅛ teaspoon
Tiny shrimp or chopped
parsley garnish

Grind shrimp and cream butter. Add shrimp to butter along with next 5 ingredients; mix thoroughly. Pack mixture into a 1½-cup mold or 2 6-ounce custard cups and chill. Remove from mold and arrange on serving plate. Garnish with tiny shrimp. Makes about 1½ cups.
*When using canned shrimp you do not need to grind them; omit the recipe's salt.

Shrimp Canapé Paste

Shrimp 2 cups cooked, peeled,
  and deveined
Catsup ¼ cup
Mayonnaise or salad dressing ¼ cup

Lemon juice 2 tablespoons
Salt ½ teaspoon
Dry mustard ⅛ teaspoon

Grind shrimp finely and combine with remaining ingredients; mix well; chill. Makes 2 cups.

Note: This spread becomes a dip when more mayonnaise is added.

Shrimp Paste Charleston

Shrimp ½ pound cooked and
  cleaned or
  Shrimp 2 4½-ounce cans, drained
  and rinsed
Butter or margarine ½ cup
Pale dry sherry 2 tablespoons

Lemon juice 1 tablespoon
Onion 1 tablespoon grated
Ground mace ¼ teaspoon
Dry mustard ¼ teaspoon
Cayenne ¼ teaspoon

Put shrimp through finest blade of food grinder or chop as finely as possible with knife. Cream butter; blend in next 6 ingredients; add shrimp and beat until smooth. Chill at least 1 hour before serving. Makes 1¾ cups.

Note: Shrimp paste may be placed in a simple mold and refrigerated until firm. To unmold, loosen edges with thin-bladed knife, dip bottom of mold in hot water, invert mold over serving plate, and shake gently.

Shrimp Dip

Sour cream 2 cups
Salad seasoning 1 teaspoon
Tomato cocktail sauce 2 teaspoons
Lemon juice ½ teaspoon
Liquid pepper sauce dash

Small shrimp ½ pound cooked
  and cleaned or
  Small shrimp 1 4½-ounce can,
  drained and rinsed

Combine first 5 ingredients; mix well. Stir in shrimp and chill several hours before serving. Makes about 2½ cups.

Mariner's Shrimp

Garlic clove 1, crushed
Salad oil ¼ cup

Shrimp 1 pound cooked, peeled,
  and deveined
Cocktail Sauce (see Index)

Place garlic in oil and let stand for ½ hour. Remove garlic and add shrimp; toss lightly to coat shrimp with oil. Chill 2 hours or longer. Serve cold on cocktail toothpicks with a cocktail sauce as a dip. Serves 6.

Pickled Rock Shrimp

Salad oil ½ cup
Lime juice ½ cup
Onion ½ cup sliced
Lemon slices 6
Capers 1 tablespoon with liquid
Parsley 1 tablespoon chopped

Salt ½ teaspoon
Dried dillweed ½ teaspoon
Liquid pepper sauce ⅛ teaspoon
Rock or other shrimp 2 pounds
  cooked, peeled, and deveined

Combine first 9 ingredients to make marinade; pour over shrimp and toss lightly. Cover and chill several hours, stirring occasionally. Drain. Serve on cocktail toothpicks or as individual portions on salad greens. Serves 12 to 15.

Pineapple-Boat Shrimp

Large pineapple 1
Dairy sour cream 1 cup
Brown sugar 1 cup
Cream cheese 1 8-ounce
  package, softened
Lime or lemon juice 1 tablespoon

Mayonnaise ½ cup
Pacific Northwest shrimp ½ pound
  cooked, peeled, and deveined
Cheddar cheese ⅓ cup grated
Walnuts ⅔ cup chopped

Cut pineapple in half lengthwise, leaving green top attached. Remove center core and discard. Remove fruit, leaving ¾-inch-thick shells. Cut pineapple into large cubes; dip each into sour cream and then into brown sugar. Set aside. Blend together cream cheese, lime juice, and mayonnaise; add chopped shrimp and cheese and form into walnut-sized balls. Roll in nuts and chill for 2 hours. To serve, pile pineapple cubes and shrimp balls into pineapple shells. Provide long toothpicks. Serves 8.

Shrimp-Avocado Cocktail

Lemon juice 2 tablespoons
Avocados 2, peeled and cubed
Shrimp 2 4½-ounce cans,
  drained and rinsed

Lettuce
Lemon Cream Dressing

Sprinkle lemon juice over avocado; chill avocado and shrimp. Line 6 cocktail glasses with lettuce; place avocado and shrimp on lettuce and top with Lemon Cream Dressing. Serves 6.

Lemon Cream Dressing

Sour cream ½ cup
Lemon juice 1 tablespoon
Parsley 1 tablespoon chopped

Prepared horseradish 1 teaspoon
Salt ¼ teaspoon

Combine all ingredients and chill to blend flavors. Makes ½ cup.

Shrimp Cocktail

Chili sauce ¾ cup
Lemon juice ¼ cup
Prepared horseradish 1 tablespoon
  (optional)
Onion 1 teaspoon minced

Worcestershire sauce 2 teaspoons
Liquid pepper sauce 4 drops
Salt pinch
Shrimp 1 pound cooked, peeled,
  and deveined

Combine all ingredients except shrimp to make sauce; chill thoroughly. Set aside about 24 shrimp for garnish; divide the rest evenly into 8 cocktail cups. Spoon sauce over shrimp and garnish cups by hooking several shrimp over each rim. Makes 1 cup sauce and serves 8.

Shrimp Noel

Salt ½ cup
Raw shrimp 3 pounds in shells
Boiling water 2 quarts
Curly endive 4 large bunches
Plastic foam cone 1, 2½ feet high

Plastic foam square 1, 12 by 12 by 1 inch
Round toothpicks 1 small box
Cocktail Sauce (see Index)

Place salt and shrimp in boiling water; cover and simmer for 3 to 5 minutes, or until shrimp are pink and tender. Drain. Peel shrimp, leaving on tail sections, remove sand veins, and rinse with cold water; chill. Separate endive leaves and wash; chill. Place plastic cone in center of the foam square and draw a circle around the base of the cone. Cut out circle and insert cone. Starting at the outside edges of the square, cover base and cone with overlapping leaves of endive; cover fully with greens so cone resembles a Christmas tree. Fasten endive to foam with toothpick halves. Attach shrimp to tree with toothpicks. Serve with cocktail sauce. Makes about 90 appetizers.

Crusty Shrimp

Shrimp ½ pound cooked, peeled, and deveined or
  Shrimp 2 4½-ounce cans, drained and rinsed
Mayonnaise or salad dressing 3 tablespoons
Lemon juice 2 tablespoons

Sweet pickle 1 tablespoon chopped
Prepared horseradish 1 teaspoon
Prepared mustard 1 teaspoon
Salt 1 teaspoon
Pastry 1 9-inch crust portion
Paprika

Grind shrimp. Combine shrimp with next 6 ingredients and mix thoroughly. Roll pastry very thin and cut into 2½-inch-diameter circles. Place a teaspoonful of shrimp mixture in center of each circle. Moisten edges with cold water, fold circles in half, over shrimp, and press edges together with a fork. Place turnovers on a 10 by 15 by 1-inch baking pan. Prick tops and sprinkle with paprika. Bake at 450° for 12 to 15 minutes, or until lightly browned. Makes about 40 appetizers.

Shrimp Party Puffs

Raw medium shrimp ¾ pound
  peeled and deveined
Bamboo shoots ⅔ cup minced
Ground ginger ¼ teaspoon
Ground coriander ¼ teaspoon
Uncooked bacon fat ¼ cup minced

Anise seed ⅛ teaspoon crushed
White pepper ⅛ teaspoon
Salt 1 teaspoon
Refrigerator crescent rolls
  2 8-ounce cans

Grind shrimp through medium blade of food chopper and mix with next 7 ingredients. Divide mixture into 32 equal portions. Separate crescent dough as package directs; cut each section in half. Place a portion of mixture in center of each triangle of dough; fold over dough and seal edges. Place on unbuttered cookie sheet; prick tops. Bake at 375° for 15 minutes or until puffs are golden. Makes 32 appetizers.

Boiled Shrimp Mutiny

Bay leaves 2
Salt 1 tablespoon
Water 2 quarts
Beer 1 11-ounce can

Raw shrimp 2 pounds in shells
Thousand Island dressing or
  Cocktail Sauce (see Index) or
  Mayonnaise seasoned with dillweed

Add bay leaves and salt to water and bring to full boil. Add beer and shrimp and simmer for 3 to 5 minutes or until shrimp turn pink. Drain shrimp and rinse in cold water. Peel and devein. Serve on toothpicks with dressing. Makes about 48 to 60 appetizers.

Skewered Shrimp

Raw shrimp 1 pound peeled
  and deveined
Large green peppers 2
Bacon slices 8, cut into sixths

Button mushrooms 3 4-ounce
  cans, drained
Oil ⅓ cup
Salt 1 teaspoon
Pepper pinch

Rinse shrimp with cold water; drain. Wash and seed peppers; cut into 1-inch squares. Thread on 48 skewers or 3-inch long toothpicks, alternating bacon, mushrooms, peppers, and shrimp. Place kabobs on well-greased broiler pan. Combine oil, salt, and pepper; brush kabobs with mixture. Broil about 4 inches from source of heat for 5 to 7 minutes. Turn carefully and brush again with oil. Broil 5 to 7 minutes longer, basting once. Makes about 48 appetizers.

Sweet Sea Pickles, Alaskan Style

Giant kelp 4 pounds	**Boiling water**
Pickling salt 1 cup	**Sugar** 3½ cups
Water 2 gallons	**White vinegar** 1 pint
Alum ½ teaspoon	**Oil of cloves** ½ teaspoon*
Water 2 quarts	**Oil of cinnamon** ½ teaspoon*

Cut kelp into 12-inch lengths and split bulbs. Remove dark surface layer with a vegetable parer. Soak kelp in brine solution (1 cup salt to 2 gallons water) for 2 hours. Care must be taken to keep kelp covered with brine. Remove kelp from brine and wash thoroughly with cold water. Cut kelp into 1-inch cubes and soak in solution of alum and 2 quarts water for 15 minutes. Drain and wash in cold water; drain again. Place kelp in enamel kettle and cover with boiling water. Simmer only until kelp can be pierced with a fork. Drain. Combine sugar, vinegar, and oils; boil 2 minutes and pour over cooked kelp. Let stand overnight in the enamel kettle or a crock. In the morning, drain off and save syrup; reheat kelp to boiling point. Pour syrup back over kelp and allow to stand 24 hours. The third morning, heat both kelp and syrup to boiling point; seal immediately in hot sterilized jars. Makes 3 pints. For further information on pickling, see Index.
*When oils instead of whole spices are used, kelp cubes remain clear and almost transparent. A small amount of green food coloring may be used to brighten kelp.

Note: The giant kelp is easily recognized by the floating bulb attached to a long hollow stem, which in turn is rooted to the bottom of a shallow bay or channel. Gather it during June, July, and August when the kelp is in its prime. Use only those rooted to the bottom.

Blender Béarnaise Sauce

Green onion 1 tablespoon chopped	**Chervil leaves** ¼ teaspoon
Lemon juice 2 teaspoons	**Egg yolks** 3
Dry white wine ¼ cup	**Cayenne** ⅛ teaspoon
Tarragon leaves ½ teaspoon	**Butter or margarine** ½ cup

In small saucepan, combine first 5 ingredients. Simmer until mixture is reduced to about 2 tablespoons; cool. Place egg yolks, cayenne, and herb mixture in blender container; cover. Quickly turn blender on and off. Heat butter over moderate heat until almost bubbling. Turn blender on high speed; slowly pour in butter, blending about 30 seconds or until thick and fluffy. Keep warm until ready to serve. Makes 1 cup.

Blender Hollandaise Sauce

Egg yolks 3
Lemon juice 2 tablespoons

Cayenne pinch
Butter or margarine ½ cup

Place egg yolks, lemon juice, and cayenne in blender container; cover. Quickly turn blender on and off. Heat butter over moderate heat until almost bubbling. Turn blender on high speed; slowly pour in butter, blending about 30 seconds or until thick and fluffy. Keep warm until ready to serve. Makes 1 cup.
Variation: *Caper Hollandaise Sauce:* Add 2 teaspoons chopped capers when ready to serve.

Caper Sauce

Plain yogurt 1 cup
Capers 2 tablespoons chopped
Lemon juice 1 tablespoon

Parsley 1 tablespoon chopped
Instant minced onion 2 teaspoons
Lemon rind 1 teaspoon grated

Combine all ingredients and mix thoroughly. Chill. Makes about 1¼ cups.

Celery-Mustard Sauce

**Condensed cream of celery
  soup** 1 cup

Prepared mustard 2 tablespoons
Milk ¼ cup

Combine ingredients in saucepan; heat and stir until smooth. Makes about 1¼ cups.

Cocktail Sauce I

Catsup or chili sauce ¾ cup
Mayonnaise or salad dressing ¼ cup
Vinegar or lemon juice
  2 tablespoons

Prepared horseradish 1 tablespoon
Onion 1 tablespoon chopped
Worcestershire sauce ¼ teaspoon
Hot pepper sauce 3 drops

Combine all ingredients; chill. Makes about 1 cup.

Cocktail Sauce II

Catsup ¾ cup
Lemon juice ¼ cup*
Celery ¼ cup minced
Liquid pepper sauce 4 to 6 drops

Salt ¼ teaspoon
Cayenne pinch
Prepared horseradish 1 tablespoon
(optional)

Combine all ingredients; chill. Makes about 1 cup.
*You may want to use 2 tablespoons vinegar and 2 tablespoons lemon juice.

Cocktail Sauce III

Catsup ½ cup
Worcestershire sauce 1 teaspoon
Lemon juice 2 tablespoons

Onion juice 1 teaspoon
Liquid pepper sauce 2 or 3 drops
Salt pinch

Combine all ingredients; chill. Makes about ½ cup.

Lemon Basting Sauce

Lemon juice from 1 lemon
Garlic salt ½ teaspoon

Pepper ¼ teaspoon
Butter ¼ cup, melted

Combine all ingredients and brush over fish steaks (especially salmon) while cooking. Makes about ½ cup.

Wine Basting Sauce

Olive oil ¼ cup
Tomato ½ cup diced
Rosemary 1 teaspoon

Lemon juice 1 tablespoon
Dry white wine 1 cup
Salt and pepper to taste

Combine all ingredients and brush over fish steaks (especially halibut) while cooking. Extra sauce may be heated and served with fish. Makes about 1½ cups.

Quick Mushroom Sauce

Onion ⅓ cup sliced
Butter or margarine 2 tablespoons
**Condensed cream of mushroom
  soup** 1 10¾-ounce can

Milk 1 cup
Thyme ¼ teaspoon (optional)
Salt ¼ teaspoon

In saucepan, sauté onion in butter until tender and golden. Gradually stir in soup, then milk; add thyme and salt. Continue stirring and heat thoroughly. Serve with broiled, fried, or baked fish. Makes about 2 cups.

Salmon Steak Sauce

Stuffed olives ½ cup
Green onion 1 tablespoon diced
Sweet cucumber chip pickles
  1 tablespoon chopped

Lemon juice 2 tablespoons
Currant or apple jelly
  1 tablespoon
Water 2 tablespoons

In saucepan, combine all ingredients and heat. Serve warm over salmon steaks. Makes about ½ cup.

Sherried Shrimp Sauce

Sliced mushrooms 1 4-ounce can
Evaporated milk ¾ cup
Water ¼ cup
Eggs 3, slightly beaten
Butter ¼ cup
Flour ¼ cup
Salt ½ teaspoon
Pepper ¼ teaspoon

Dry sherry ¼ cup
Water ¼ cup
Shrimp 1 cup cooked, peeled,
  and deveined or
  Tiny shrimp 2 4½-ounce
  cans, drained
Chives 1 tablespoon finely chopped

Drain mushroom liquid into milk; add water and eggs and set aside. In saucepan, melt butter over moderate heat and blend in flour, salt, and pepper. Gradually add milk mixture and cook gently, stirring constantly, until smooth and thick. Do not boil or eggs will curdle. Remove from heat; add sherry and water and beat until smooth. Add shrimp, mushrooms, and chives and heat thoroughly. Serve over baked fish. Makes about 2 cups.

Shrimp-Pea Sauce

Butter or margarine 2 tablespoons
Flour 2 tablespoons
Salt ½ teaspoon
Paprika ¼ teaspoon
Dry mustard ¼ teaspoon

Milk 1 cup
Shrimp ¼ pound cooked, peeled,
  and deveined
Peas 1 cup, cooked

In saucepan, melt butter; blend in flour, and seasonings. Add milk gradually and cook, stirring constantly, until thick and smooth. Add shrimp and peas; heat thoroughly. Serve over boiled or steamed fish. Makes enough for 6 servings of fish.

Spiced Tomato Sauce

Tomatoes 1 16-ounce can
Onion ¼ cup chopped
Parsley sprigs 2
Salt 1 teaspoon
Whole peppercorns 2

Whole cloves 2
Whole allspice 1
Butter 3 tablespoons
Flour 3 tablespoons

Simmer first 7 ingredients together for 10 minutes; remove whole spices. In saucepan, melt butter and blend in flour. Gradually add tomato mixture and cook, stirring constantly, until thick. Use as a sauce in which to bake fish or serve separately as a fish accompaniment. Makes about 2 cups.

Tartar Sauce

Mayonnaise or salad dressing 1 cup
Onion 3 tablespoons finely chopped
Sweet pickle 3 tablespoons
  chopped and drained

Parsley 3 tablespoons chopped
Stuffed olives 3 tablespoons chopped

Combine all ingredients and mix well. Chill. Makes about 1½ cups.

Quick Tartar Sauce

Mayonnaise or salad dressing 1 cup

Sweet pickle relish ½ cup
  undrained

Combine and chill. Makes about 1½ cups.

Tomato Sauce

Butter 2 tablespoons
Onion 1, diced
Flour 2 tablespoons

Tomato juice 1½ cups
Salt ½ teaspoon
Pepper pinch

In saucepan, melt butter and sauté onion until tender. Blend in flour and cook until golden. Add tomato juice, and seasonings, stirring constantly; simmer for 3 to 4 minutes. Serve hot over fish. Makes 1¼ cups.

Whipped Cream Dressing

Salt ½ teaspoon
Mayonnaise or salad dressing
  2 tablespoons

Heavy cream ½ cup, stiffly
  whipped

Fold salt and mayonnaise into whipped cream; chill. Serve with molded fish salads. Makes about ¾ cup.

White Sauce

Butter 2 tablespoons
Flour 2 tablespoons
Salt ¼ teaspoon

Pepper pinch
Milk 1 cup

In saucepan, melt butter and blend in flour, salt, and pepper. Gradually add milk and cook, stirring constantly, until thickened. Makes 1 cup.
Variations:
Cheese Sauce: Add ½ cup grated cheese to thickened sauce.
Almond Sauce: Brown ¼ pound sliced blanched almonds in butter before adding other ingredients.
Egg Sauce: Add 1 sliced or chopped hard-cooked egg and 1 teaspoon butter to thickened sauce.

Seasoned Butters

Butter or margarine ¼ cup
Lemon juice 1 tablespoon
Parsley 1 tablespoon minced

Salt ½ teaspoon
Cayenne pinch

To serve hot: Melt butter; add remaining 4 ingredients.
Pour over piping hot fish.
To serve cold: Whip softened butter until creamy. Gradually stir in remaining 4 ingredients. Form into small balls and chill.

Variations:

Mustard Butter: Add 2 tablespoons prepared mustard.

Dilled Wine Butter: Substitute 3 tablespoons white wine for lemon juice and add 2 tablespoons fresh dillweed, minced.

Black Butter: Slowly heat butter until frothy and brown before adding other ingredients.

Soy Butter: Add 1 tablespoon soy sauce.

Chili Butter: Add 1 tablespoon chili sauce.

Supreme Butter: Make hot lemon butter; let it cool. Whip ¼ cup cream and stir into butter.

Thyme Butter: Add ½ teaspoon each thyme and basil.

Soups, Stews, and Chowders

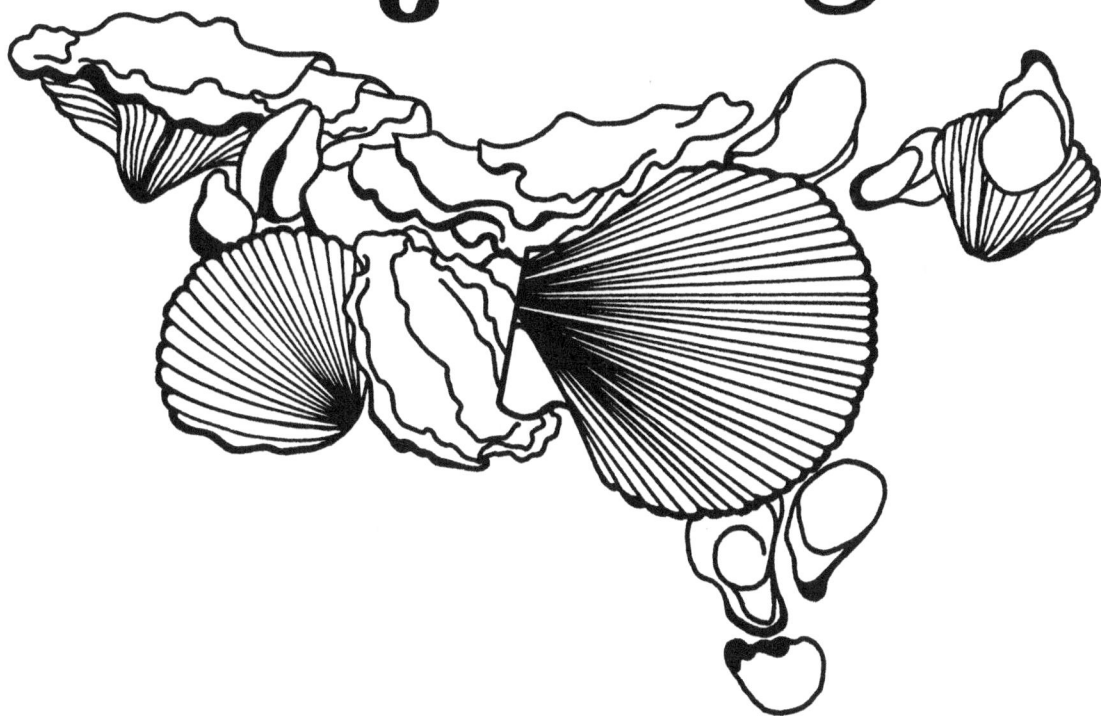

Dinner-Bell Fish Soup-Stew

Fish fillets 1 pound
Water 2 cups
Elbow macaroni 1 cup
Carrots 1 cup sliced
Onion 1½ cups chopped
Salt 1 teaspoon

Ground cloves pinch
Pepper pinch
Condensed split pea with ham soup 1 11½-ounce can
Milk 2 cups

Cut fillets into 1-inch pieces. Combine next 7 ingredients in large saucepan or Dutch oven; bring to boil. Cover and cook slowly for 15 minutes or until carrots and macaroni are tender. Add soup and milk; heat and stir until blended. Add fish, cover, and cook for 10 minutes or until fish flakes easily. Makes about 8 cups; serves 4 to 6.

Manhattan Fish Soup-Stew

Fish fillets 1 pound
Carrots 1½ cups sliced
Water 1 cup
Condensed cream of potato soup 1 10¾-ounce can

Frozen cut green beans 1 10-ounce package, thawed
Stewed tomatoes 1¼ cups
Evaporated milk 1 cup
Onion salt 1½ teaspoons
Thyme ¼ teaspoon

Cut fillets into 1-inch pieces. In covered saucepan, simmer carrots in water for 15 minutes or until almost tender. Stir in next 6 ingredients and heat until simmering; add fish, cover, and simmer for 10 minutes or until fish flakes easily and beans are tender. Serve with biscuits, crackers, or bread. Makes about 7 cups; serves 4 for dinner.

New England Fish Chowder

Fish fillets or steaks 1 pound
Bacon or salt pork 2 tablespoons chopped
Onion ½ cup chopped
Potatoes 2½ cups diced
Boiling water 1½ cups

Salt 1 teaspoon
Pepper pinch
Milk 2 cups
Butter 1 tablespoon
Parsley chopped

If fish is in steaks, remove bones and skin. Cut fish into 1-inch pieces. In heavy saucepan, fry bacon until crisp; add onion and cook until tender. Add potatoes, water, seasonings, and fish; cover and simmer for 15 minutes or until potatoes are tender. Add milk and butter; heat thoroughly and sprinkle with parsley. Serves 6.

Washington Codfish Chowder

Large potatoes 3, or 5 medium, peeled and diced
Medium onions 2, chopped
Celery stalks 3, cut into ½-inch pieces
Water 2 cups
Evaporated milk 1 cup

Savory ½ teaspoon
Tarragon 1 teaspoon
Thyme 1 teaspoon
Salt and pepper to taste
Cod fillets 1 pound
Butter or margarine 1 tablespoon

Combine first 9 ingredients in saucepan and simmer for 15 minutes or until potatoes are nearly done. Cut fish into small pieces while other ingredients are cooking. Add to soup and simmer 5 minutes or until fish flakes easily. Add butter and serve. Serves 4.

Halibut-Tomato Soup

Bacon ¼ cup diced
Onion ½ cup chopped
Celery ½ cup chopped
Water 2 cups
Salt 1½ teaspoons
Pepper pinch

Rice ⅓ cup
Halibut or other white-fleshed fish fillets 1 pound, cut into 1-inch cubes
Tomato juice 2 cups

Fry bacon until crisp; add onion and celery and cook until tender. Add water, salt, pepper, and rice; cover and simmer for 10 minutes. Add fish and simmer until rice is tender and fish flakes easily. Add tomato juice and heat thoroughly; serve immediately. Serves 6.

Seafood Soup

Halibut 1 pound
Shucked oysters 1 cup
Shucked clams 1 cup or
  Chopped clams 1 8-ounce can
Shrimp ½ cup cooked, peeled,
  and deveined or
  Shrimp 1 4½-ounce can, drained
Large onions 2, chopped
Celery ribs 4, cut diagonally
  into pieces
Green pepper 1, coarsely chopped
Small garlic clove 1, crushed
Butter ½ cup
Water 2 quarts

Chicken-flavored stock base
  2 teaspoons
Salt 1 teaspoon
Pepper ½ teaspoon
Bay leaves 2
Thyme ¼ teaspoon
Flour ½ cup
Cold water 1 cup
Evaporated milk 1 13-ounce can
Cream-style corn 1 17-ounce can
Medium potatoes 2, cooked and cubed
Pimiento 1 2-ounce jar,
  drained and chopped
Parsley chopped

Snip halibut, oysters, clams, and shrimp (if large) into pieces with scissors and reserve any liquor from oysters and clams. In a large kettle, sauté onion, celery, green pepper, and garlic in butter over low heat until soft. Add next 6 ingredients plus any seafood liquor; simmer 20 minutes. Make a paste of flour and cold water; stir it into stock with a whisk. When stock thickens, add raw seafood and cook 5 minutes. Add milk, corn, potatoes, pimiento, shrimp, and canned seafood, if used; simmer 10 minutes longer. Pour into a large soup tureen and sprinkle with parsley. Serve with hot garlic-herb bread. Serves 8.

Cioppino

Halibut, sole, bass, or other
  firm fish fillets 3 pounds
Large Dungeness crab
  1 pound, cooked
Shrimp 1 pound in shells, cooked
Littleneck clams 2 dozen or
  Shucked clams 1 pint, liquor
  drained and reserved
Onion 1½ cups chopped
Green pepper 1 cup chopped
Olive oil ¼ cup
Bay leaf ¼

Parsley sprig 1
Basil pinch
Salt 1 teaspoon
Stewed tomatoes 3½ cups
Red table wine 2 cups
Tomato juice 2 cups
Combined clam and oyster
  liquor 2 cups
Shucked oysters 1 pint,
  liquor drained and reserved
Parsley ¼ cup minced

Cut fish into serving-size pieces. Crack and clean crab, leaving some of the legs in the shell. Split each shrimp shell along the back and remove sand veins. Scrub clams. Soak in salt water for 15 minutes and drain; repeat. Cover the bottom of large kettle with ½ inch of boiling water. Add clams; cover and steam until shells partially open. Save liquor from clams as you remove the top shell of each; strain liquor through cheesecloth to remove any sand. In large saucepan, sauté onion and green pepper in olive oil. Tie bay leaf, parsley, and basil in a cheesecloth bag; place in saucepan. Add next 5 ingredients; simmer 10 minutes. Arrange fish in a large kettle; add sauce and simmer for 20 minutes or until fish flakes easily. Remove herb bag. Add oysters (and clams, if shucked) and cook for 3 minutes or until edges curl. Add crab, shrimp, and clams; cook for 1 minute. Serve in deep bowls — shells and all — garnished with parsley. Complement the dish with crusty bread and red wine. Serves 8-10.

Note: This popular stew may be varied by using many different combinations of fish and shellfish.

Gulf Court Bouillon

Red drum or other fish fillets or steaks 2 pounds
Butter or margarine ⅓ cup
Flour ½ cup
Onion 1½ cups chopped
Celery 1 cup chopped
Green onion ½ cup chopped
Green pepper ½ cup chopped
Parsley 2 tablespoons chopped
Garlic clove 1, minced

Tomato sauce with tomato bits 2 15-ounce cans
Dry red wine ¾ cup
Lemon juice 2 tablespoons
Salt ½ teaspoon
Thyme leaves ½ teaspoon crushed
Marjoram leaves, ¼ teaspoon crushed
Cayenne ¼ teaspoon
Whole allspice 6
Bay leaf 1
Lemon slices

Remove skin and bones from steaks. Cut fish into 6 portions. In heavy 4- or 5-quart Dutch oven, melt butter and blend in flour; cook over moderate heat, stirring constantly, until flour is light brown. Add next 6 ingredients; cover and cook over low heat for 5 minutes or until tender. Gradually stir in tomato sauce Add next 8 ingredients and bring to boil; simmer for 30 minutes. Add fish to stock; cover and simmer very gently for 5 to 10 minutes or until fish flakes easily. To serve, place fish in 6 soup bowls and pour 1 cup of court bouillon into each. Garnish with lemon slices. Serves 6.

Creole Bouillabaisse

Red drum or other fish fillets 1 pound
Sea trout or other fish fillets 1 pound
Butter or margarine 2 tablespoons
Olive oil 2 tablespoons
Flour ¼ cup
Onion 1 cup chopped
Celery ½ cup chopped
Garlic clove 1, minced
Water 5 cups
Dry white wine ¼ cup

Tomatoes 1 16-ounce can, chopped and juice included
Parsley 2 tablespoons chopped
Lemon juice 1 tablespoon
Bay leaf 1
Salt ½ teaspoon
Saffron ¼ teaspoon
Cayenne ¼ teaspoon
Raw shrimp ½ pound peeled and deveined
Shucked oysters 1 pint
Crab meat 1 6½-ounce can drained and cartilage removed

Remove skin and bones from fish. Cut each fish into 6 or 8 portions each. In a 4- or 5-quart Dutch oven, melt butter; add olive oil and blend in flour. Cook, stirring constantly, until flour is light brown. Add onion, celery, and garlic; cook and stir until vegetables begin to brown. Gradually stir in water. Add next 8 ingredients and ¼ of the fish; simmer, covered, for 20 minutes. Add remaining fish, cover, and simmer 5 to 8 minutes. Add shrimp, oysters, and crab meat; cover and simmer 3 to 5 minutes longer or until all seafood is done. Serves 8.

Salmon Stew

Salmon 1 15½-ounce can, liquid drained and reserved
Butter 4 tablespoons
Onion 1 tablespoon chopped (optional)

Milk 1 quart
Salt 1½ teaspoons
Pepper ⅛ teaspoon
Paprika (optional)

Remove bones and skin and break salmon into chunks. In large saucepan, melt butter and add onion and salmon; cook about 3 minutes. Add milk, salmon liquid, salt, and pepper; simmer about 5 minutes but do not boil. Serve at once, garnished with paprika. Serves 3 to 4.

Fish and Vegetable Bisque

Salmon or halibut 2 pounds
Boiling water 1 quart
Bay leaf 1, crushed
Vinegar 1 tablespoon
Pepper ¼ teaspoon
Corn 2 ears or
   Whole-kernel corn 1 8½-ounce
   can, drained
Bacon slices 2, diced
Medium carrots 2, diced

Onion 1, diced
Celery stalks 2, sliced
Red cabbage 1 cup shredded
Large potato 1, diced
Garlic clove 1, minced
Dill seeds 1 teaspoon
Vegetable stock or water 1 cup
Parsley ½ teaspoon
Paprika pinch
Salt 2 teaspoons

Cut fish into small chunks and drop into boiling water; cook for 3 minutes. Remove fish and return the skin and bones to water with bay leaf, vinegar, pepper, and corn cobs from which corn has been removed and reserved. Cover pan and boil stock for 15 minutes; strain and set aside. Fry bacon in soup kettle. Add next 7 ingredients and corn; sauté until vegetables are almost tender. Pour in fish stock and vegetable stock and simmer for 10 minutes. Add fish, parsley, paprika, and salt just before serving. Serves 4 to 6.

Salmon Bisque I

Butter or margarine ¼ cup
Onion ¼ cup chopped
Celery ¼ cup chopped
Flour 3 tablespoons
Milk 3 cups*

Tomato juice 1 cup
Salt 1½ teaspoons
Salmon 2 cups cooked and
   coarsely flaked
Parsley 1 tablespoon chopped

In saucepan, melt butter over low heat; add onion and celery and cook until tender. Stir in flour and gradually add milk; cook and stir until slightly thickened. Blend in tomato juice; add salt and salmon. Heat thoroughly but do not boil. Garnish with parsley and serve piping hot with crackers. Serves 6.
*If canned salmon is your fish, use its liquid in place of part of the milk.

Salmon Bisque II

Butter 4 tablespoons
Green onions and tops
   ⅓ cup finely chopped
Celery and leaves ½ cup
   finely chopped
Flour 2 tablespoons
Milk 1 cup

Half-and-half 1 cup
Salmon 2 cups cooked and flaked or
   Salmon 1 15½-ounce can,
   drained and flaked
Salt ½ teaspoon
Pepper ⅛ teaspoon
Cooking sherry 2 tablespoons

In medium-sized saucepan, melt butter over low heat; add onions and celery and cook for 5 minutes, stirring constantly. Blend in flour; gradually add milk and half-and-half and cook, stirring constantly, until mixture thickens slightly. Add salmon, seasonings, and sherry; stir well. Simmer for 5 minutes, stirring frequently. Serve with crackers, hot rolls, or toast. Serves 3 to 4.

Salmon Chowder

Chicken bouillon cube 1
Boiling water 1 cup
Onion ¾ cup chopped
Green pepper ½ cup chopped
Garlic clove 1, finely chopped
Butter or margarine ¼ cup
Salmon 1 15½-ounce can,
   in large chunks and drained

Salmon liquid ⅓ cup
Tomatoes 1 16-ounce can
Whole-kernel corn 1 8½-ounce can
Okra 1 cup sliced (optional)
Salt ½ teaspoon
Thyme ¼ teaspoon
Pepper pinch
Bay leaf 1

Dissolve bouillon cube in boiling water. In large saucepan, sauté onion, green pepper, and garlic in butter until tender. Add bouillon and remaining 9 ingredients; simmer for 15 minutes or until vegetables are tender. Remove bay leaf and serve. Serves 6.

Tuna Chowder

Bacon slices 1½, diced
Tuna 1 6½-ounce can, in chunks
Thyme ¼ teaspoon
Onion ¼ cup chopped
Potatoes 1 cup diced
Salt 1 teaspoon

Pepper pinch
Tomatoes 1 16-ounce can
Milk 4 cups
Butter 2 teaspoons
Parsley 1 teaspoon minced

In deep skillet, fry bacon until crisp. Drain oil from tuna into skillet; stir in thyme and onion and cook until tender. Add potato, seasonings, and tomatoes. Cover and cook for 15 minutes or until potatoes are tender. Add milk and tuna; bring to a simmer, dab with butter, sprinkle with parsley, and serve. Serves 3 to 4.

Tuna-Corn Chowder

Condensed cream of potato soup
  1 10¾-ounce can
Milk 3 cups
Butter or margarine 1 tablespoon
Onion 1 tablespoon grated
Small bay leaf 1

Pepper pinch
Whole-kernel corn
  1 8½-ounce can
Tuna 2 6½-ounce cans,
  drained and in chunks
Parsley chopped

Combine first 6 ingredients; heat to simmering point, stirring occasionally. Add corn and tuna; heat thoroughly and remove bay leaf. Serve garnished with parsley. Serves 6.

Abalone Chowder

Bacon slices 4, diced
Abalone 6 slices, pounded and diced
Medium potato 1, peeled and diced
Small onion 1, minced

Hot water 1½ cups
Hot milk 3 cups
Butter or margarine 1 tablespoon
Salt and pepper to taste

In 2-quart saucepan, fry bacon until brown; drain all but 2 tablespoons of drippings from pan. Add abalone, potato, and onion to bacon; sauté until onion is golden brown. Add water and simmer until potato is tender. Stir in milk and butter and season to taste. Serves 4 to 6.

Clam and Onion Soup

Bacon slices 4, diced
Onion 3 cups sliced and
  separated into rings
Minced clams 2 8-ounce cans,
  with liquor
Milk 3 cups

Celery salt ½ teaspoon
Salt ½ teaspoon
Hard toast 6 slices
Parmesan cheese ¼ cup grated
  (optional)

Fry bacon until crisp; add onion and cook until tender. In a saucepan, combine clams, milk, celery salt, and salt; heat but do not boil. Place toast in 6 heated soup bowls; cover with bacon and onions. Pour in clam mixture and sprinkle with cheese; serve immediately. Serves 6.

Souper Clam Dandy

Frozen baby lima beans
1 10-ounce package
Boiling water 1 cup
Savor Salt ½ teaspoon
Minced clams 2 8-ounce
cans, drained

Condensed cream of chicken soup
2 10¾-ounce cans
Milk 1½ cups
Onion powder 1 tablespoon
Liquid pepper sauce 2 or 3 drops
Bacon slices 4, fried and crumbled

In a covered 3-quart pan, simmer lima beans in water and Savor Salt for 10 to 15 minutes or until tender. Stir in next 5 ingredients; cover and heat thoroughly. Pour into bowls and garnish with bacon. Serves 6.

Clam and Tomato Bisque

Shucked clams 1 quart
Cold water 1½ cups
Onion ½, chopped
Butter ⅓ cup
Flour ⅓ cup

Cream or evaporated milk 2 cups
Stewed tomatoes 1 cup
Baking soda ⅛ teaspoon
Salt and pepper to taste

Rinse and drain clams. Finely chop hard parts of clams and add to water. Heat slowly to simmering point and cook for 20 minutes; strain and reserve broth. In saucepan, sauté onion in butter for 5 minutes; blend in flour and gradually add clam broth. Stir until thickened. Add cream and both cooked and raw parts of clams; bring to a simmer. Combine tomatoes and baking soda; add to clam mixture just as it begins to simmer. Heat thoroughly and season to taste; serve at once. Serves 6.

Alaska Clam Chowder

Butter or margarine 3 tablespoons
Onion ½ cup chopped
Garlic clove ½, finely chopped
Flour ¼ cup
Bay leaf ½
Boiling clam liquor
plus water 2 cups

Bouillon cube 1
Milk 1 cup
Minced clams 1 8-ounce
can, drained
Noodles 1 cup, cooked
Paprika garnish

In saucepan, melt butter and sauté onion and garlic until tender; blend in flour and add bay leaf. Dissolve bouillon cube in clam liquor plus water; gradually add liquid to saucepan and cook, stirring constantly, until thickened. Add milk, clams, and noodles; heat thoroughly. Serve garnished with paprika in heated bowls. Serves 6.

Bonaparte Chowder*

Bacon ½ cup diced
Onion ¾ cup chopped
Potatoes 2 cups chopped
Clam liquor plus water 1 cup
Milk 2 cups
Evaporated milk 1 cup
Salt 1 teaspoon
Pepper ⅛ teaspoon
Paprika ¼ teaspoon

Shucked clams 1 cup chopped,
 liquor reserved or
 Minced clams 1 8-ounce can,
 liquor reserved
Small Pacific shrimp 1 cup or
 Shrimp 2 4½-ounce cans, drained
Butter 2 tablespoons

In heavy saucepan, fry bacon until crisp; remove with a slotted spoon and reserve. Sauté onion in drippings until tender but not brown; add potatoes and clam liquor plus water and simmer, covered, over low heat until potatoes are tender. Add milk and evaporated milk; bring to simmering point. Add seasonings, clams, and shrimp. When hot, taste for seasonings. Just before serving, add bacon bits and butter. Serve with oyster crackers. Serves 6.
*Named for the little shrimp.

Chuckanut Chowder

Potatoes 1 cup diced
Turnips ½ cup diced
Onion ⅓ cup diced
Clam liquor 1 pint*
Evaporated milk 1 5⅓-ounce can
Parsley 2 tablespoons chopped
Chives 2 tablespoons chopped

Green pepper 2 tablespoons chopped
Shucked clams 1 cup chopped
Margarine 3 tablespoons
Salt ½ teaspoon
Sugar 1 teaspoon
Bacon slices 3, fried and
 crumbled

In saucepan, boil potatoes, turnips, and onion in clam liquor until tender. Add next 8 ingredients; remove from heat and allow to stand for 20 minutes so flavors blend. Reheat but do not boil; garnish with bacon and serve. Serves 3 to 4.
*If you do not have a full pint of clam liquor, use some water.

Clam and Corn Chowder

Bacon 3 slices, diced
Onion 1 cup chopped
Potatoes 2 cups diced
Clam liquor plus water 1 cup
Whole-kernel corn 1½ cups
Milk 3 cups
Flour 2 tablespoons

Butter or margarine 1 tablespoon
Celery salt 1 teaspoon
Pepper pinch
Minced clams 2 8-ounce cans,
  liquor reserved
Salt to taste
Cracker crumbs ½ cup (optional)

In large saucepan, fry bacon until crisp. Add onion and cook until tender. Add potatoes and clam liquor plus water; simmer until potatoes are tender. Add corn and milk. Blend flour into butter and add to mixture in saucepan, stirring until thickened. Add celery salt, pepper, and clams; taste for seasoning and simmer for 5 minutes. Top with cracker crumbs and serve hot. Serves 6.

Easy Clam Chowder

Water 2¼ cups
Butter 3 tablespoons
Salt ¼ teaspoon
Dehydrated mixed vegetable flakes 3 tablespoons
Dehydrated green pepper
  3 tablespoons
Dehydrated chopped onion
  3 tablespoons
Bacon bits 2 tablespoons
Potato flakes 2¼ cups
White port 3 tablespoons

Condensed tomato soup
  1 10¾-ounce can
Garlic cloves 2 teaspoons pressed
Pepper ¾ teaspoon
Salt 1¼ teaspoons
Milk or milk plus clam liquor
  2 cups
Puget Sound butter clams
  1 cup minced
Whipped cream unsweetened,
  for garnish (optional)

In large saucepan, heat water, butter, and salt to boiling point; add vegetable flakes, green pepper, onion, and bacon bits. Simmer for 4 minutes, stirring occasionally; remove from heat. Add potato flakes and stir until mixture is fluffy. Blend in port, soup, and seasonings; stir in milk and clams. Return to heat and simmer for 5 minutes, stirring constantly. Pour into soup bowls; top each with a dollop of whipped cream and heat under the broiler until cream is bubbling and brown. Serves 6 to 8.

Note: This is a "quickie" dinner, and because the ingredients are easy to carry, it is a good one to make when camping. Unless you can keep fresh clams cold, substitute canned clams.

Manhattan Clam Chowder

Bacon ½ cup diced
Medium onion 1, chopped
Potatoes 1 cup diced
Water 2 cups
Bay leaf ½

Shucked clams 1 pint with liquor
Tomatoes 1 16-ounce can
Salt 1 teaspoon
Pepper ⅛ teaspoon
Thyme ⅛ teaspoon

In large saucepan, fry bacon until crisp; add onion and sauté for 5 minutes or until tender. Add potatoes, water, and bay leaf; cover and simmer for 10 to 15 minutes or until potatoes are tender. Add remaining ingredients; heat thoroughly but do not boil. Serves 6.

New England Clam Chowder

Bacon or salt pork
  2 tablespoons diced
Onion ½ cup chopped
Potatoes 1 cup diced
Water 2 cups

Shucked clams 1 pint, including liquor
Evaporated milk 1 13-ounce can
Butter 3 tablespoons
Salt 1 teaspoon
White pepper ¼ teaspoon

In a deep saucepan, fry bacon until crisp; remove from pan with a slotted spoon and reserve for garnish. Add onion to drippings and sauté until tender but not brown. Add potatoes and water, cover, and simmer gently for 15 minutes or until potatoes are tender. Stir in remaining ingredients. Heat until piping hot but do not boil; garnish with bacon bits. Serves 6.

Crab Meat Soup

Condensed green pea soup
  1 11¼-ounce can
Condensed tomato soup
  1 10¾-ounce can

Milk 1 cup
Evaporated milk ½ cup
Crab meat 1 cup flaked
Sherry ¼ cup

In saucepan, combine soups, milk, and evaporated milk; blend thoroughly. Add crab meat; cook and stir over low heat until hot. Add sherry and remove from heat just before soup boils. Serves 4.

Crab, Shrimp, and Okra Gumbo

Blue crab meat   1 pound
Raw shrimp   1 pound peeled
  and deveined
Butter or margarine   6 tablespoons
Flour   6 tablespoons
Onion   1 cup chopped
Green pepper   ½ cup chopped
Green onion   2 tablespoons chopped
Garlic clove   1, minced
Chicken broth   1 quart
Tomato sauce with tomato bits
  1 15-ounce can

Parsley   1 tablespoon chopped
Salt   ½ teaspoon
Thyme leaves   ½ teaspoon crushed
Cayenne   ¼ teaspoon
Bay leaf   1
Liquid pepper sauce   2 or 3 drops
  (optional)
Cut okra   1 14½-ounce can, drained
Lemon   1, sliced
Rice   3 cups cooked

Remove any shell or cartilage from crab meat. Cut large shrimp in halves. In heavy 4- or 5-quart Dutch oven, melt butter and blend in flour. Cook over moderate heat, stirring constantly, until flour is medium brown. Add onion, green pepper, green onion, and garlic; continue stirring and cook until vegetables are lightly browned. Gradually stir in chicken broth. Add next 7 ingredients and bring to a boil; cover and simmer 30 minutes. Add okra, lemon slices, crab meat, and shrimp; cover and simmer for 5 minutes or until shrimp are tender and pink. Remove lemon. Serve by ladling gumbo over mounds of cooked rice in deep soup bowls. Serves 6.

Alaska Crab Stew

Crab meat or combination of
  cooked seafood   1 pound
Onion   ½ cup chopped
Garlic clove   1, finely chopped
Celery   ¼ cup chopped
Butter or margarine   ¼ cup

Tomatoes   1 16-ounce can
Pepper   ¼ teaspoon
Paprika   ¼ teaspoon
Chili powder   ½ teaspoon
Spaghetti   1 quart cooked
Parmesan cheese   grated

Keeping crab in large pieces, remove any shell or cartilage. In large saucepan, sauté onion, garlic, and celery in butter until tender. Add tomatoes and seasonings; simmer for 1 hour. Add crab meat and simmer 10 minutes longer. Stir in spaghetti; heat thoroughly and serve with cheese sprinkled over the top. Serves 6.

Shellfish Stew

Crab meat 2 cups
Lobster meat 1 5-ounce can
Shrimp 1 4½-ounce can,
 rinsed and drained
Oysters 12, drained
Butter ¼ cup
Minced clams 1 8-ounce can,
 with liquor

Condensed shrimp soup
 1 10¾-ounce can
Steak sauce 1 teaspoon
Milk 3½ cups
Cream ½ cup
Salt and pepper to taste
Dry sherry ¼ cup
Paprika or chopped parsley

In large saucepan, sauté lobster, crab, shrimp, and oysters in butter for 5 minutes. Add next 6 ingredients; bring to a simmer and add sherry. Sprinkle with paprika and serve with French bread. Serves 6.

King Crab Chowder

Large onion ½, chopped
Green pepper 2 tablespoons minced
Celery ½ cup chopped
Bacon drippings or cooking oil
 3 tablespoons
Potato ½ cup diced
Salt ½ teaspoon
Pepper pinch

Paprika pinch
Water 1½ cups
Whole-kernel corn 1½ cups
King or other crab meat
 1 cup flaked
Milk 2 cups
Flour 1½ teaspoons (optional)
Butter 1½ tablespoons (optional)

In large saucepan, sauté onion, green pepper, and celery in bacon drippings for 5 minutes. Add potato, seasonings, and water; cover and simmer until potato is soft. Add corn, crab meat, and milk; bring to a simmer. Blend flour into butter; stir into chowder and serve when thickened. Serves 8.

Crawfish Bisque

Live crawfish 8 pounds
Salt 1½ cups
Water 3 gallons
Bacon drippings ¼ cup
Butter or margarine ¼ cup
Flour ½ cup
Onion 2 cups finely chopped
Celery 1 cup finely chopped
Green pepper ½ cup finely chopped
Garlic clove 1, minced
Hot water 4 cups

Tomato sauce with tomato bits
    2 15-ounce cans
Parsley ¼ cup chopped
Lemon juice 2 tablespoons
Bay leaves 2
Thyme leaves 1 teaspoon crushed
Salt 1 teaspoon
Cayenne ¾ teaspoon
Whole allspice 8
Stuffed Heads 48
Rice 3 cups cooked

Wash crawfish in cold water. In large container, dissolve salt in 3 gallons of water and soak crawfish in it for 15 minutes. In 10-quart pot, bring 6 quarts of water to a boil; with tongs, drop crawfish into water and boil for 5 minutes. Remove and cool crawfish. Shell as follows: break off tail, snap it in half lengthwise, lift out meat in 1 piece, and discard tail shell; snap off large claws (if desired, break claws with nutcracker and remove bits of meat) and smaller legs and discard; cut off top of head just behind eyes and discard; scoop body shell clean, carefully removing and reserving yellow fat; discard digestive tract. Wash 48 of the body shells, which in Louisiana are called crawfish "heads." Put all the crawfish meat through the finest blade of a food grinder; reserve 2 cups for Stuffed Heads. Use what is left, about 1 cup, in bisque. In 4- or 5-quart Dutch oven, melt bacon drippings and butter; blend in flour. Cook over moderate heat, stirring constantly, until brown. Add onion, celery, green pepper, and garlic; cover and cook for 5 minutes or until tender. Gradually stir in water; add next 8 ingredients. Stir in crawfish meat and fat; cover and simmer for 1 hour. To serve, ladle into soup plates over rice and 5 or 6 Stuffed Heads. Serves 6 to 8.

Stuffed Crawfish Heads

Butter or margarine ½ cup
Onion 1 cup finely chopped
Celery ½ cup finely chopped
Garlic clove 1, minced
Parsley ¼ cup chopped
Salt 1 teaspoon

Cayenne ¼ teaspoon
Ground crawfish meat 2 cups
Soft bread crumbs 2 cups
Crawfish body shells 48
Flour ½ cup
Oil for deep frying

In 10-inch frying pan, melt butter and add onion, celery, and garlic. Cover and cook for 5 minutes or until tender. Stir in parsley, seasonings, and crawfish meat; remove from heat and add bread crumbs. Stuff mixture into shells and roll shells in flour. Place in single layer in fry basket; fry in deep fat at 350° for 3 minutes or until lightly browned. Drain on absorbent paper and keep warm until ready to serve. Makes 48 "heads."

Quick Oyster Pick Up

Shucked oysters 1 pint
Oyster liquor plus water 2 cups
Cream of leek soup mix
  1 1¾-ounce package

Milk 1 cup
Parsley garnish

Drain oysters. In a saucepan, combine oyster liquor plus water and soup mix; bring to a boil, stirring constantly. Reduce heat and simmer for 10 minutes. Add milk and heat thoroughly, stirring occasionally. Add oysters and simmer 3 to 5 minutes or until edges begin to curl. Sprinkle with parsley. Serves 6.

Oyster Stew

Shucked oysters 1 pint
Evaporated milk 1 13-ounce can
Water 1⅔ cups
Salt 1 teaspoon

Pepper pinch
Worcestershire sauce 1 tablespoon
Butter 2 tablespoons
Paprika garnish

In saucepan, simmer oysters in their liquor for 3 minutes or until edges curl. Add milk, water, salt, and pepper; heat to a simmer but do not boil. Add Worcestershire sauce and remove from heat. Stir in butter and garnish with paprika. Serves 6.

Oyster Chowder

Onion 3 tablespoons chopped
Butter 3 tablespoons
Water 1 cup
Celery ⅔ cup diced
Potatoes 2 cups diced

Salt 1 tablespoon
Pepper ½ teaspoon
Milk 1 quart
Shucked oysters 1 pint
Parsley chopped

In large saucepan, fry onion in butter until slightly browned; add water, celery, potatoes, and seasonings. Cover and simmer until vegetables are tender. Add milk and bring to a simmer again. Simmer oysters in their liquor for 5 minutes or until edges curl; drain. Add oysters to chowder and serve immediately with parsley sprinkled over the top. Serves 6.

Rosy Seafood Gumbo

Crab meat   ½ pound
Butter or margarine   ⅓ cup
Green onion   ⅔ cup chopped,
   including tops
Celery   ½ cup chopped
Garlic cloves   2, finely chopped
Fresh okra   2 cups sliced or
   Frozen sliced okra
   1 10-ounce package
Salt   1½ teaspoons

Pepper   ½ teaspoon
Sugar   ¼ teaspoon
Thyme   ¼ teaspoon crushed
Bay leaf   1
Liquid pepper sauce   6 drops
Tomatoes   2 16-ounce cans
Raw shrimp   ½ pound
   peeled and deveined
Rice   6 servings

Remove any shell or cartilage from crab meat. Combine next 11 ingredients in a 3-quart saucepan. Cook for 10 minutes, stirring occasionally. Add tomatoes, shrimp, and crab; cover; cook 10 minutes longer, or until shrimp turn pink, stirring occasionally. Remove bay leaf. Serve gumbo over rice in soup bowls. Serves 6.

Shrimp Bisque

Butter or margarine   4 tablespoons
Celery   2 tablespoons chopped
Onion   2 tablespoons chopped
Flour   2 tablespoons
Salt   1 teaspoon
Paprika   ¼ teaspoon

Pepper   pinch
Milk   1 quart
Shrimp   3 4½-ounce cans,
   drained and rinsed
Parsley   chopped

In saucepan, melt butter; add celery and onion and cook until tender. Blend in flour and seasonings. Add milk gradually and cook, stirring constantly, until thickened. Add chopped shrimp and heat thoroughly; do not boil. Garnish with parsley. Serves 6.

Salads
and
Sandwiches

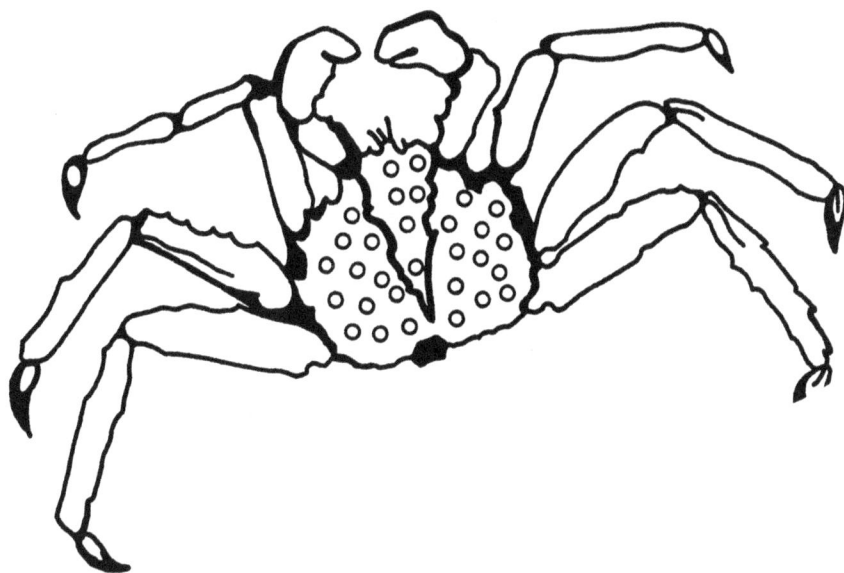

Plantation Fish in Aspic

**Grouper or other fish
   fillets** 2 pounds
Boiling water 2 cups
Sauterne 1 cup
Medium onion 1, quartered
Celery stick 1, quartered
Bay leaves 2
Salt 1½ teaspoons
Thyme leaves ¼ teaspoon crushed
Lemon 1, washed
Cold water ½ cup

Unflavored gelatin 2 tablespoons
Tarragon vinegar ¼ cup
Lemon juice 2 tablespoons
Dry mustard 1 teaspoon
Celery ¼ cup chopped
Green onion ¼ cup chopped
Green pepper ¼ cup chopped
Pimiento 2 tablespoons chopped
Parsley 2 tablespoons chopped
Salad greens
Mayonnaise

Place fillets in well-buttered 10-inch frying pan; add next 7 ingredients. Cut lemon in half; squeeze juice over fish and drop peel into pan. Cover and simmer for 5 to 10 minutes or until fish flakes easily. Remove fish and set aside to cool; strain poaching liquid. In 4-cup measuring container, put cold water; stir in gelatin to soften. Add hot poaching liquid; stir to dissolve gelatin. Add vinegar, lemon juice, and enough water to make 4 cups liquid. Make a paste of mustard and small amount of liquid; stir paste into liquid. Chill to unbeaten egg white consistency. Remove skin and bones from fish; flake fish into small pieces. Mix together fish, celery, green onion, green pepper, pimiento, and parsley. Fold together fish mixture and gelatin. Pour into lightly oiled 5 by 9 by 3-inch loaf pan. Chill until firm. Unmold onto serving dish lined with salad greens. Serve with mayonnaise. Serves 6.

Halibut Layer Salad

Lemon gelatin 1 3-ounce package
Boiling water 1¾ cups
Orange 1, peeled and sectioned
Unflavored gelatin ½ tablespoon
Cold water 2 tablespoons
Mayonnaise ¼ cup
Lemon juice ¼ cup
Halibut 2 cups cooked and flaked

Blanched slivered almonds ¼ cup
Celery ½ cup chopped
Cucumber ½ cup chopped
Green or ripe olives
   1 tablespoon chopped
Lettuce leaves
Mayonnaise garnish
Slivered almonds garnish

Stir lemon gelatin into boiling water until dissolved; set aside ¾ cup in small bowl and keep at room temperature. Place orange sections in the bottom of 5- or 6-cup mold. Pour remaining lemon gelatin over orange sections and chill until firm. Place unflavored gelatin and cold water in top of double boiler; when gelatin is softened, dissolve over boiling water, stirring constantly. Add mayonnaise, lemon juice, halibut, and almonds. Spread on top of firm orange layer; chill until second layer is firm. Add celery, cucumber, and olives to ¾ cup reserved lemon gelatin. Pour on top of fish layer; chill until firm. Gently unmold onto platter of lettuce leaves. Garnish with dabs of mayonnaise and sprinkle with almonds. Serves 4 to 6.

Jellied Halibut Salad

Lemon gelatin 2 3-ounce packages
Boiling water 1½ cups
Vinegar ¼ cup
Salt ½ teaspoon
Carrots 1 cup grated
Celery 1 cup diced

Green pepper ¼ cup chopped
Green onions 4, finely chopped
Mayonnaise 1 cup
Halibut 2 cups cooked and flaked
Lettuce leaves

Dissolve gelatin in boiling water. Add vinegar and salt; chill until almost congealed. Fold in next 6 ingredients. Pour into 6 individual molds and chill until firm. Unmold onto lettuce leaves. Serves 6.

Summer Seagarden

Mackerel or sardines 4 3¾-ounce cans, drained and flaked or
Salmon or other fish 2 cups cooked and flaked
Celery 1 cup chopped
Onion 2 tablespoons chopped
Sweet pickle 2 tablespoons chopped

Eggs 3, hard-cooked and chopped
Mayonnaise or salad dressing ½ cup
Medium tomatoes 6, tops and pulp removed
Salt ¼ teaspoon
Lettuce

Combine first 6 ingredients; chill. Sprinkle insides of tomatoes with salt; stuff with fish mixture. Serve in lettuce cups. Serves 6.

Rockfish-Tomato Salad

Rockfish 1½ cups cooked and flaked
Onion 1 teaspoon grated
Green pepper 1 teaspoon chopped
Celery 2 tablespoons chopped
Salt 1 teaspoon

Potato chips or crackers ¼ cup crushed
Mayonnaise ¼ cup
Medium tomatoes 6, tops and pulp removed
Lettuce

Combine first 7 ingredients; chill. Fill tomatoes with mixture and serve on lettuce. Serves 6.

Rockfish Sea Slaw

Rockfish fillets 1½ pounds
Salt 1 tablespoon
Boiling water 1 quart
Salad dressing ¼ cup
Onion 1 tablespoon chopped
Sweet pickle relish 2 tablespoons

Lemon juice 1 tablespoon
Salt 1 teaspoon
Green cabbage 1 cup shredded
Red cabbage 1 cup shredded
Lettuce cups 6
Lemon wedges 6

Place fillets and salt in water; cover and simmer for about 10 minutes or until fish flakes. Do not overcook. Drain and flake fish. Combine with next 5 ingredients; chill for 1 hour to blend flavors. Add green and red cabbage and toss lightly. Spoon into lettuce cups and garnish with lemon wedges. Serves 6.

Aloha Salmon Platter

Salmon 2 cups cooked
Small pineapple 1
Avocado 1, peeled and sliced
  lengthwise
Lemon juice from 1 lemon
Papaya 1, peeled, seeded, and sliced

Mandarin oranges 2 11-ounce
  cans, drained
Dairy sour cream 1 cup
Lime 1, juice and grated rind
Chutney ¼ cup finely chopped
Macadamia nuts 1 cup chopped

Make a row of salmon chunks down the center of a 12 by 18-inch tray. Peel, remove eyes, and slice pineapple into rounds; halve the slices and remove core. Arrange pineapple along the left side of salmon. Dip avocado in lemon juice; arrange along right side of salmon. Make a row of papaya beside the pineapple and a row of oranges beside the avocado. Cover tray with plastic wrap and chill. Combine sour cream, lime juice and rind, and chutney; chill. When serving, pass sour cream dressing and macadamia nuts in small bowls. Serves 6.
*Tuna or shellfish may be substituted for salmon.

Easy Salmon-Cabbage Salad

Salmon 2 cups cooked and flaked
Onion 2 tablespoons finely chopped
Parsley 2 tablespoons chopped
Cabbage 1 quart shredded

Eggs 2, hard-cooked and chopped
**Sour Cream Dressing or
  other dressing** 1 cup

Combine all ingredients and serve at once. Serves 6.

Sour Cream Dressing

Dairy sour cream 1 cup
Wine vinegar 2 tablespoons
Sugar 1 teaspoon
Seasoning salt ½ teaspoon

Dillweed ½ teaspoon
Salad Elegance or other
 salad seasoning ½ teaspoon

Combine all ingredients and blend well. Makes about 1 cup.

Elegant Salmon-Cabbage Salad

Mayonnaise or salad dressing ¾ cup
Dry mustard ½ teaspoon
Parsley 1 tablespoon chopped
Tarragon ¼ teaspoon
Garlic clove ½, crushed
Dillweed ½ teaspoon
Onion 1 to 2 tablespoons finely chopped
Anchovy paste 1 teaspoon (optional)

Eggs 2, hard-cooked and chopped
Cabbage 4 cups shredded
Salmon 2 15½-ounce cans, drained
Lettuce
Egg 1, hard-cooked and sliced
Pitted ripe olives ½ cup sliced
Tomatoes 2, cut into wedges

Combine first 9 ingredients and blend well; toss cabbage with this dressing. Break salmon into pieces and toss with cabbage. Arrange on lettuce; garnish with egg, olives, and tomatoes. Serves 6.

Festive Salmon Mousse

Unflavored gelatin 1 tablespoon
Cold water 2 tablespoons
Chicken bouillon cube 1
Boiling water 1 cup
Lemon juice 1 tablespoon
Salmon 3 7¾-ounce cans,
 liquid drained and reserved
Mayonnaise or salad dressing ½ cup
Parsley 2 tablespoons chopped
Lemon juice 1 tablespoon

Onion 1 tablespoon grated
Prepared horseradish 1 teaspoon
 (optional)
Salt ¼ teaspoon
Pepper pinch
Unflavored gelatin 2 tablespoons
Salmon liquid plus water ½ cup
Whipping cream 1 cup, whipped
Salad greens
Egg 1, hard-cooked and sliced

Soften 1 tablespoon gelatin in cold water for 5 minutes. Dissolve bouillon cube in boiling water; add bouillon and lemon juice to gelatin and stir until gelatin dissolves. Pour into 1½-quart mold; chill until firm. Combine next 8 ingredients and mix well. Soften 2 tablespoons gelatin in salmon liquid plus water for 5 minutes; place over boiling water and stir until dissolved. Add to salmon mixture and blend thoroughly, using an electric mixer or blender. Fold whipped cream into salmon mixture. Spread over congealed aspic; chill until firm. Unmold onto a serving platter and garnish with greens and egg. Serves 6.

Jellied Salmon-Stuffed Tomatoes

Lemon gelatin 1 3-ounce package
Boiling water 1 cup
Mayonnaise ½ cup
Lemon juice 2 tablespoons
Worcestershire sauce ½ teaspoon
Salt ½ teaspoon or to taste
Firm tomatoes 6

Salmon 1½ cups cooked and flaked or
  Salmon 1 15½-ounce can,
  drained and flaked
Onion 1 teaspoon minced
Cucumber ½ cup seeded and grated
Lettuce
Mayonnaise and paprika garnish

Dissolve gelatin in boiling water. Add mayonnaise, lemon juice, Worcestershire and salt; chill until consistency of unbeaten egg whites. Scald tomatoes in boiling water for 1 minute; peel, cut slices from top, and scoop out pulp. Invert and chill. Fold salmon, onion, and cucumber into gelatin; chill until almost firm. Fill tomatoes with gelatin mixture and chill until gelatin is firm. Serve whole or cut crosswise in slices on crisp lettuce with additional mayonnaise. Sprinkle with paprika. Serves 6.

Plain Salmon Salad

Lettuce
Salmon 2 cups cooked
Ripe olives ¼ cup

Eggs 2, hard-cooked and sliced
Tomatoes 2, cut into wedges
Thousand Island or other dressing

Make beds of lettuce in 4 individual salad bowls. Arrange ½ cup of salmon chunks in each and garnish with olives, eggs, and tomatoes. Serve with dressing. Serves 4.

Salmon-Apple Salad

Lemon juice 1 tablespoon
Red apple 1, unpeeled, cored,
  and diced
Salmon 2 cups cooked and in
  chunks or canned equivalent

Celery 1 cup chopped
Salted peanuts ½ cup shelled
Mayonnaise or salad dressing ½ cup
Lettuce cups 4

Sprinkle lemon juice over apple; combine with salmon, celery, peanuts, and mayonnaise. Toss lightly and serve in lettuce cups. Serves 4.

Salmon-Fruit Salad

Lemon juice 1 tablespoon
Salmon 2 cups cooked and in
   chunks or canned equivalent
Oranges 2, peeled and cut
   into chunks
Banana 1, sliced

Red apple 1, unpeeled, cored,
   and diced
Lettuce leaves 3 cups torn
Mayonnaise or salad dressing ¼ cup
Blanched almonds ¼ cup, toasted
Lettuce cups 6

Sprinkle lemon juice over salmon. Toss lightly with next 6 ingredients. Serve at once in lettuce cups. Serves 6.

Salmon-Macaroni Salad

Macaroni 8 ounces, cooked, rinsed
   in cold water, and drained
Onion 2 tablespoons finely chopped
Celery 4 tablespoons chopped
Parsley 2 tablespoons chopped
Medium cucumber 1, sliced

Salmon 1 15½-ounce can,
   drained and flaked
Salt 1 teaspoon
Salad dressing ½ cup
Salad greens
Egg 1, hard-cooked and sliced
Pitted ripe olives 6, sliced

Combine first 8 ingredients and mix well. Line large salad bowl with salad greens; spoon macaroni mixture onto greens. Garnish with egg and olives; chill. Serves 6.

Smoked Salmon and Tomato Salad

Smoked salmon 1 7¾-ounce can,
   drained and flaked
Eggs 2, hard-cooked and chopped
Celery ¾ cup chopped
Cucumber ¼ cup chopped
Onion 1 tablespoon grated

Lemon juice 1 tablespoon
Mayonnaise or salad dressing ⅓ cup
Medium tomatoes 6, tops
   and pulp removed
Salt ¼ teaspoon
Lettuce cups 6

Combine first 7 ingredients. Salt insides of tomatoes and fill with salmon mixture. Serve in lettuce cups. Serves 6.

Baked Salmon Salad

Salmon 1 15½-ounce can, drained
Rice 2 cups cooked
Celery 1 cup thinly sliced
Parsley ½ cup chopped
Pitted ripe olives ¼ cup sliced
Mayonnaise or salad dressing ½ cup

French dressing 2 tablespoons
Lemon juice 2 tablespoons
Curry powder 1 teaspoon
Mayonnaise or salad dressing
2 tablespoons
Paprika garnish

Combine salmon chunks, rice, celery, parsley, and olives. In separate bowl, combine mayonnaise, French dressing, lemon juice, and curry powder. Add mayonnaise mixture to salmon mixture; toss lightly. Spoon into 6 well-buttered 6-ounce casseroles or custard cups. Top each with a teaspoon of mayonnaise; sprinkle with paprika. Bake at 400° for 15 to 20 minutes or until heated. Serves 6.

Sea Garden Antipasto

Maine sardines 3 3¾-ounce cans,
drained, oil reserved*
Button mushrooms
2 4-ounce cans, drained
Marinade
Cucumber slices 24

Celery sticks 18
Radish roses 12
Tomato wedges 12
Green pepper rings 6
Large lettuce leaves 6

Arrange sardines and mushrooms in shallow dish; pour marinade over them and chill for 30 minutes. Chill next 5 ingredients. Drain sardines and mushrooms; arrange on lettuce leaves with other vegetables. Serve remaining marinade separately. Serves 6.
*Lobster, tuna, crab, pickled herring, or shrimp may also be used.

Marinade

Sardine oil
French dressing ½ cup
Soy sauce ¼ cup
Wine vinegar 2 tablespoons

Water 2 tablespoons
Garlic clove 1, crushed
Powdered ginger pinch
Pepper pinch

Combine all ingredients and mix thoroughly. Makes about 1¼ cups.

California Tuna Salad

Orange sections 2 cups
Avocado 1
Lemon juice 1 tablespoon
Celery 1 cup chopped
Blanched slivered almonds
  ½ cup, toasted

Tuna 2 6½-ounce cans,
  drained and flaked
Curry powder 1½ teaspoons (optional)
Mayonnaise or salad dressing ½ cup
Salad greens

Reserve 12 orange sections for garnish; cut remaining sections into halves. Cut avocado in half lengthwise and remove seed. Peel and slice avocado; sprinkle with lemon juice. Reserve 6 slices avocado for garnish; cut remaining slices into fourths. Combine orange, avocado, celery, almonds, and tuna. Combine curry powder and mayonnaise; pour over tuna mixture and toss lightly. Chill. Serve on salad greens; garnish with orange sections and avocado slices. Serves 6.

Molded Tuna Salad

Unflavored gelatin 1 tablespoon
Cold water ¼ cup
Lemon juice 2 tablespoons
Prepared mustard 1 teaspoon
Salt ¼ teaspoon
Paprika ¼ teaspoon

Tuna 2 6½-ounce cans,
  drained and flaked
Celery 1 cup chopped
Mayonnaise ½ cup
Lettuce
Cucumber Dressing

Soften gelatin for 5 minutes in cold water. Place over boiling water and stir until dissolved; add lemon juice, mustard, salt, and paprika. Chill until partially set. Add tuna, celery, and mayonnaise. Rinse a 1-quart mold; fill with tuna mixture and chill until firm. Unmold onto crisp lettuce and serve with Cucumber Dressing. Serves 6 to 8.

Cucumber Dressing

Mayonnaise 1 cup
Vinegar or sweet pickle juice
  1 tablespoon

Cucumber ½ cup unpeeled
  and finely diced

Thin mayonnaise with vinegar; mix in cucumber.

Simple Seafood Salad

Tuna 2 6½-ounce cans, drained or
  Salmon 1 15½-ounce can, drained
Celery 1 cup chopped
Mayonnaise or salad dressing ⅓ cup

Eggs 2, hard-cooked and chopped
Onion 2 tablespoons chopped
Sweet pickle 2 tablespoons chopped
Salad greens

Break fish into large pieces; combine with next 5 ingredients. Toss lightly and chill. Serve on salad greens. Serves 6.

Tuna-Macaroni Salad

Syrup from pineapple 2 tablespoons
Salad dressing ½ cup
Curry powder ½ teaspoon (optional)
Salt ¼ teaspoon
Elbow macaroni 1 cup cooked,
  rinsed in cold water, and drained
Pineapple chunks or tidbits
  1 8-ounce can, drained

Tuna 1 6½-ounce can,
  drained and flaked
Celery ¾ cup sliced
American cheese ½ cup cubed
Sweet pickle ½ cup chopped
Salad greens (optional)

Combine syrup, salad dressing, curry powder, and salt and pour over macaroni; mix well. Chill at least 1 hour. Add remaining ingredients; mix well. Chill thoroughly. Serve plain or on salad greens. Serves 6.

Tuna Toss

Tuna 2 6½-ounce cans,
  drained and flaked
Carrots 3 cups shredded
Pineapple chunks 1 13¼-ounce
  can, drained

Celery ½ cup sliced
Mayonnaise or salad dressing ½ cup
Seedless raisins ¼ cup
Salad greens
Carrot curls

Combine first 6 ingredients and mix lightly. Serve, garnished with carrot curls, on salad greens. Serves 6.

Tuna Waldorf Salad

Apple 1 cup unpeeled, cored,
  and diced
Lemon juice 1 tablespoon
Tuna 1 6½-ounce can,
  drained and flaked

Celery 1 cup sliced
Seedless raisins ½ cup
Salad dressing ⅓ cup
Lettuce cups 4 or 5
Walnuts ¼ cup shelled

Sprinkle apple with lemon juice; toss with tuna, celery, raisins, and salad dressing. Fill lettuce cups and top with walnuts. Serves 4 to 5.

Clam-Potato Salad

Shucked clams 1 pint, drained or
  Clams 2 8-ounce cans, drained
Butter or margarine 2 tablespoons
Potatoes 1 cup cooked and diced
Eggs 2, hard-cooked and chopped
Celery 1 cup chopped
Onion 1 tablespoon grated

Pimiento 2 tablespoons chopped
Salt 1 teaspoon
Pepper pinch
Thyme ¼ teaspoon
Mayonnaise or salad dressing ½ cup
Lettuce cups 6

Cook clams in butter until edges curl; chop. Combine with next 9 ingredients and chill. Serve in lettuce cups. Serves 6.

Chef's Salad Chesapeake

Crab meat 1 pound, drained
  and flaked or
  Crab meat 2 6½-ounce cans,
  drained and flaked
Asparagus spears 18, cooked and chilled

Lettuce cups 6
Lemon-Caper Dressing
Eggs 3, hard-cooked and sliced
Paprika garnish

Remove any shell or cartilage from crab. Arrange 3 asparagus spears in each lettuce cup. Divide crab among cups. Add Lemon-Caper Dressing and top with egg slices; sprinkle with paprika. Serves 6.

Lemon-Caper Dressing

Mayonnaise or salad dressing ½ cup
Capers 1 tablespoon drained
Lemon juice 1 tablespoon

Prepared mustard ½ teaspoon
Worcestershire sauce ½ teaspoon
Liquid pepper sauce 2 drops

Combine all ingredients; chill. Makes about ⅔ cup.

Hawaiian Salad

Shrimp ½ pound cooked, peeled, and deveined
Crab meat ½ pound
Celery ½ cup finely chopped
Green pepper ½ cup chopped
Green onions ½ cup chopped

Sweet pickle juice 2 teaspoons
Salt ¼ teaspoon
Pepper ¼ teaspoon
Mayonnaise 1 cup
Papayas 4, halved lengthwise and seeds removed

Mix together first 5 ingredients. Blend pickle juice and seasonings into mayonnaise; pour over salad and mix gently. Spoon into papaya halves and serve immediately. Serves 8.

Neptune's Salad

Sandwich bread 1 loaf, sliced
Butter ¼ cup, softened
Medium onion 1, diced
Eggs 4, hard-cooked and chopped
Shrimp 2 cups cooked, peeled, and deveined

Crab meat 2 cups
Celery 1 cup diced
Salad dressing 3 cups
Lettuce leaves

The day before serving, remove crusts from bread, butter slices, and cut into ½-inch cubes. In large bowl, toss bread with onion and eggs; cover with plastic wrap and store overnight in refrigerator. Three hours before serving, add shrimp, crab meat, celery, and salad dressing to bread cubes. Mix thoroughly and chill for 3 hours. Serve on lettuce leaves. Serves 12.

Seafood Louis

Any variety lettuce 1 head, shredded
Salt to taste
Crab meat or cooked shrimp
 1 pound or
 Halibut, cod, or rockfish
 2 cups cooked and flaked

Tomatoes 2, cut into wedges
Eggs 3, hard-cooked and cut into wedges
Louis Dressing

Arrange lettuce in large shallow salad bowl; sprinkle with salt. Arrange seafood over lettuce. Place tomato and egg wedges alternately around edge of bowl. Spread Louis Dressing over seafood just before serving. Serves 6.

Louis Dressing

Mayonnaise or salad dressing 1 cup
Catsup 3 tablespoons
Onion 1 tablespoon chopped

Sweet pickle or Alaska Sweet Sea Relish (see Index) 2 tablespoons

Combine all ingredients and chill. Makes about 1¼ cups.

Crab-Celery Victor

Chicken bouillon cubes 2
Boiling water 3 cups
Celery hearts 2 5 inches long,
    cut into thirds lengthwise

French Dressing 1 cup
King crab meat 1 pound
Large lettuce cups 6
Pepper to taste

In 10-inch frying pan, dissolve bouillon cubes in boiling water. Add celery, cover pan and simmer for 10 to 15 minutes or until celery is barely tender. Set pan aside until celery is cool, then drain and place in shallow dish. Pour dressing over celery and chill for two hours. Drain celery, reserving dressing. Cut crab meat into 1-inch pieces. Arrange celery in lettuce cups; sprinkle with pepper. Add crab and serve with remaining dressing. Serves 6.

Lobster Salad

Spiny lobster meat 1 pound cooked
Salad oil ½ cup
Egg yolks 6, hard-cooked and mashed
Sugar 1 tablespoon
Dry mustard 1 teaspoon
Salt 1 teaspoon
Cayenne ¼ teaspoon

Vinegar ½ cup
Celery 1½ cups chopped
Egg whites 6, hard-cooked
    and chopped
Green onions 1½ cups chopped
Capers 2 tablespoons with liquid
Salad greens

Cut lobster meat into ½-inch cubes. Gradually blend oil into egg yolks. Stir sugar, mustard, salt, and cayenne into vinegar; combine with oil and yolks. In separate bowl, combine lobster meat, celery, egg whites, green onion, and capers. Pour yolk dressing over lobster mixture and toss lightly. Serve on salad greens. Serves 6.

Scallop-Vegetable Salad

Scallops 1½ pounds
Salt 2 tablespoons
Boiling water 1 quart
Cut green beans 1 16-ounce
   can, drained
Celery 1 cup sliced

Onion ¼ cup chopped
Green pepper ¼ cup chopped
Pimiento 1 tablespoon chopped
Marinade
Lettuce cups 6

Rinse scallops, put in saucepan with salt and boiling water; cover and simmer for 3 minutes or until scallops are tender. Drain, cool and slice scallops. Combine with next 6 ingredients. Cover and chill for at least 1 hour; drain. Serve in lettuce cups. Serves 6.

Marinade

Cider vinegar ½ cup
Sugar 1 tablespoon
Salt ¼ teaspoon

Pepper pinch
Salad oil ¼ cup

Combine vinegar, sugar, salt, and pepper. Add oil gradually and blend thoroughly. Makes about ¾ cup.

Fisherman's Salad Bowl

Garlic clove 1, cut in half
Lettuce 1 head, chopped
Celery stalks 4, diced
Tomatoes 2, diced
Eggs 3, hard-cooked and sliced
Pitted ripe olives 15, sliced
Red peppers 1 9-ounce jar,
   drained and diced

Green onions 4, chopped
Blue cheese dressing ½ cup
Crab meat 1 6½-ounce can,
   drained and flaked
Shrimp 2 4½-ounce cans,
   drained and rinsed

Rub wooden bowl with cut garlic. In bowl, combine next 7 ingredients; add dressing and toss lightly. Scatter crab and shrimp over top. Serves 4.

Gulf Shrimp Salad

Shrimp 3 4½-ounce cans, drained and rinsed
Rice 2 cups cooked
Celery 1 cup sliced
Parsley ½ cup chopped
Pitted ripe olives ¼ cup sliced

Mayonnaise or salad dressing ½ cup
French dressing 2 tablespoons
Lemon juice 2 tablespoons
Curry powder 1 teaspoon
Salad greens

Cut large shrimp into halves. Combine first 5 ingredients; set aside. Combine mayonnaise, French dressing, lemon juice, and curry powder; mix thoroughly. Toss lightly with shrimp mixture; chill. Serve on salad greens. Serves 6.

Hood Canal Shrimp Salad

Raw Hood Canal shrimp 1 pound (24 to 26 shrimp) peeled and deveined
Extra-dry champagne ½ cup
Large cucumber 1, diced
Crushed pineapple 1 20-ounce can, juice drained and reserved
Freshly ground pepper ½ teaspoon
Lemon 1, unpeeled and sliced
Tartar sauce 1 6-ounce jar
Cream cheese 1 8-ounce package, softened

Stuffed olives 1 6-ounce jar, drained and sliced
Lemon 1, peeled, segments slivered, membrane removed
Extra-dry champagne ½ cup
Egg white 1, stiffly beaten
Parsley ½ cup chopped
Watercress 1 bunch
Sliced pineapple 2 rings, cut into thirds
Egg yolk 1, poached

Marinate shrimp in ½ cup champagne for 15 minutes. Dry cucumber on paper towels. In saucepan, combine pineapple juice, pepper, lemon slices, and shrimp; simmer until shrimp are pink. Remove shrimp and reserve 6 for garnish. Cut remaining shrimp into bite-size pieces. Blend together tartar sauce and cream cheese; fold in shrimp, cucumber, crushed pineapple, olives, lemon segments, and remaining champagne. Chill until ready to serve. Dip rims of 6 champagne glasses into egg white and then into parsley until each rim is well coated. Line each glass with watercress leaves; chill. Force egg yolk through a coarse sieve. Fill glasses with shrimp salad. Place ⅓ of a pineapple ring and 1 shrimp on rim of each glass and garnish salad with egg yolk. Serve with a glass of champagne. Serves 6.

Jellied Shrimp and Orange Salad

Shrimp 2 4½-ounce cans, drained and rinsed
Unflavored gelatin 1 tablespoon
Cold water ¼ cup
Mayonnaise ¾ cup
Lemon juice 1 tablespoon

Orange juice ¼ cup
Orange 1, peeled and sectioned or cut into pieces
Almonds ¼ cup chopped and toasted
Salt ¼ teaspoon
Heavy cream ½ cup, whipped

Cut shrimp into halves if large. Soften gelatin in cold water; stir over low heat or boiling water until dissolved. Blend with mayonnaise and lemon and orange juice; add shrimp, orange sections, and almonds. Add salt to whipped cream and fold into shrimp mixture. Spoon into 4-cup mold; chill until set. Serves 8.

Mixed Seafood Salad

Shrimp 2 4½-ounce cans, drained and rinsed
Tuna 1 6½-ounce can, drained and flaked
Crab 1 6½-ounce can, drained and flaked
Salmon 1 7¾-ounce can, drained and flaked
Lettuce 1 head, shredded
Cherry tomatoes 1-pint box

Large carrot 1, thickly sliced
Celery stalk 1, thickly sliced
Radishes 5, sliced
Cauliflower 1 head, broken into florets
Cucumber 1, coarsely cubed
Alfalfa sprouts 1 cup
Dressing ¾ cup
Eggs 2, hard-cooked and sliced
Paprika garnish

Combine first 12 ingredients; toss lightly with your choice of dressing. Garnish with egg and paprika. Serves 8 to 10.

Molded Shrimp Salad

Lemon gelatin 1 3-ounce package
Boiling water 1 cup
Heavy cream ½ cup, whipped
Mayonnaise ½ cup
Tiny shrimp 1 cup cooked, peeled, and deveined or
 Shrimp 2 4½-ounce cans, drained and rinsed

Celery 1 cup finely diced
Stuffed olives ½ cup
Onion juice 1 teaspoon
Eggs 2, hard-cooked and sliced
Lettuce leaves

Dissolve gelatin in boiling water; chill until slightly thickened. Add next 6 ingredients; mix well. Gently fold in eggs. Pour into 1½-quart mold and chill until firm. Unmold onto lettuce leaves. Serves 8.

Patio Shrimp Plate

Shrimp 3 4½-ounce cans, drained
Large cucumber 1, sliced

Lettuce
Patio Shrimp Sauce

Cover shrimp with ice water and let stand for 5 minutes; drain. Arrange shrimp and cucumber slices on lettuce. Serve with Patio Shrimp Sauce. Serves 6.

Patio Shrimp Sauce

Dairy sour cream 1 cup
Prepared horseradish 1 tablespoon
Onion 1 tablespoon grated

Paprika ½ teaspoon
Salt ½ teaspoon

Combine all ingredients and blend well. Makes about 1 cup.

Sea Fare Shrimp Salad

Small shrimp 3 cups cooked,
  peeled, and deveined
Oil and Vinegar Dressing
Green onions 1 cup chopped
Avocado 1, peeled and diced
Papaya 1, peeled, seeded, and diced

Fresh coconut 1 cup shredded
Medium tomato 1, peeled and diced
Iceberg lettuce several large
  outer leaves
Iceberg lettuce 3 cups shredded

Place shrimp in bowl and pour Oil and Vinegar Dressing over them; marinate in refrigerator for at least 1 hour. Reserve 1 cup of marinated shrimp. Add next 5 ingredients to remaining shrimp and dressing; toss gently. Line shallow salad bowl with lettuce leaves. Arrange shredded lettuce over leaves and heap shrimp mixture on top of lettuce. Garnish with reserved shrimp and serve. Serves 4.

Oil and Vinegar Dressing

Olive oil ¼ cup
Salad oil ¼ cup
White wine vinegar ¼ cup
Lemon juice 2 tablespoons

Seasoned salt 1 teaspoon
Liquid pepper sauce 2 or 3 drops
Lemon Pepper ⅛ teaspoon

In jar, combine olive oil, salad oil, and vinegar; add remaining ingredients. Shake until well blended. Makes about ¾ cup.

Seafood Salad with Pineapple

Lettuce 1 head, shredded
Shrimp ¾ pound cooked,
  peeled, and deveined or
  **Crab meat, halibut, cod, or
  rockfish** 1½ cups cooked and flaked

Pineapple 1 20-ounce can,
  drained and diced
Celery 1 cup chopped
Mayonnaise or salad dressing ¼ cup

Arrange lettuce in a large shallow salad bowl. Combine seafood, pineapple, celery, and mayonnaise; spoon over lettuce. Serves 6.

Shrimp and Apple Salad

Shrimp ¾ pound cooked,
  peeled, and deveined
Red apples 2 cups unpeeled,
  cored, and diced
Lemon juice 1 tablespoon

Celery ½ cup chopped
Salt 1 teaspoon
Mayonnaise or salad dressing ⅓ cup
Lettuce cups 6

Combine first 6 ingredients; chill. Spoon into lettuce cups. Serves 6.

Shrimp and Macaroni Salad

Shrimp 3 4½-ounce cans,
  drained and rinsed
Shell macaroni 2 cups cooked
Cauliflower 1 cup chopped
Celery 1 cup chopped
Parsley ¼ cup chopped
Sweet pickle ¼ cup chopped or
  Sweet pickle relish ¼ cup drained
Mayonnaise or salad dressing ½ cup

French dressing 3 tablespoons
Lemon juice 1 tablespoon
Onion 1 teaspoon grated
Celery seed 1 teaspoon
Salt 1 teaspoon
Pepper ¼ teaspoon
Salad greens
Egg 1, hard-cooked and sliced

Cut large shrimp into halves. Combine with next 5 ingredients; set aside. Combine mayonnaise with next 6 ingredients and mix thoroughly. Add mayonnaise mixture to shrimp mixture and toss lightly; chill. Spoon onto salad greens; garnish with egg slices. Serves 6.

Shrimp-Melon Gloriatta

Melons or cantaloupe 2
Lemon-gelatin 1 3-ounce package
Boiling water 1 cup
Shrimp 1 cup cooked, peeled, and deveined

Whipping cream 1 cup, whipped
Mayonnaise ¼ cup
Green onion 1½ teaspoons finely minced
Endive

Cut off top ¼ of melons; remove seeds. With melon ball cutter, scoop out 1 cup of melon balls. Scrape out remaining melon to within ½ inch of rind. Dissolve gelatin in boiling water; chill until slightly set. Combine melon balls, shrimp, cream, mayonnaise, and green onion; mix with gelatin and spoon into melon shells. Replace tops and chill for 12 hours. To serve, carefully quarter melons and arrange on endive-lined plates. Serves 8.

Shrimp Slaw

Cabbage 3 cups shredded
Green pepper 1, finely chopped
Small shrimp 1 4½-ounce can, drained and rinsed
Green onions 2, finely chopped
Mayonnaise ½ cup
Lemon juice 1 teaspoon

Salt and pepper to taste
Lettuce cups 4
Tomato 1, cut into wedges
Eggs 2, hard-cooked and cut into wedges
Green olives ¼ cup sliced

Combine first 7 ingredients by tossing together lightly; chill thoroughly. Spoon into lettuce cups and garnish with tomato, eggs, and olives. Serves 4.

Hot Shrimp Salad

Mayonnaise 1 cup
Prepared mustard 1 tablespoon
Parsley flakes 1 tablespoon
Green onion 1 tablespoon sliced
Shrimp 2 cups cooked, peeled, and deveined
Whole almonds ½ cup

Pimiento ¼ cup chopped
Celery 1 cup finely chopped
Crushed pineapple 1 8¼-ounce can, drained
Herb-seasoned croutons 1½ cups
Paprika garnish

Blend together mayonnaise, mustard, parsley, and onion. Cut shrimp into halves and add with almonds, pimiento, celery, and pineapple. Pour into 6 by 10-inch baking dish; cover with croutons. Bake at 350° for 30 minutes or until bubbling. Just before serving, stir mixture and sprinkle paprika on top. Serves 6 to 8.

Seafood Hot Dogs

Egg   1, slightly beaten
Water   1 tablespoon
Salt   ½ teaspoon
Pepper   pinch
Small fish fillets   6

Flour   ½ cup
Dry bread crumbs   ½ cup
Cooking oil   4 tablespoons
Hot dog buns   6, split and toasted
Hot dog relishes

In shallow bowl, stir together egg, water, salt, and pepper. Dip fish into flour, then into egg mixture; roll in crumbs. In heavy frying pan, fry fish in oil over moderate heat for about 5 minutes on each side, or until browned. Drain on absorbent paper and serve in hot dog buns accompanied with hot dog relishes. Serves 6.

Haliburgers

Halibut   2 cups cooked and flaked
Mayonnaise   ½ cup
Salt   ½ teaspoon
Worcestershire sauce   ½ teaspoon
Onion   2 tablespoons finely chopped

Lemon juice   2 teaspoons
Hamburger buns   6, split, buttered,
   and heated
Lettuce leaves   6
Tomato slices   6

Combine first 6 ingredients. Spread on buns; add a leaf of lettuce and a slice of tomato to each. Serves 6.

Salmon Sandwich Spread I

Salmon   1 cup cooked and flaked
   or canned equivalent
Lemon juice   1 teaspoon
Crushed pineapple   ¼ cup drained

Peanuts or other nuts
   2 tablespoons finely chopped
Mayonnaise   2 tablespoons

Blend all ingredients thoroughly. Makes about 1 cup; enough for 3 or 4 sandwiches.

Salmon Sandwich Spread II

Salmon   2 cups cooked and flaked
Cabbage   1 cup chopped
Carrot   ⅓ cup grated

Catsup   1½ teaspoons
Mayonnaise   ⅓ cup
Salt   to taste

Combine first 5 ingredients. Taste; add salt if necessary. Chill. Makes about 3½ cups; enough for 6 sandwiches.

Take-Me-Along Seafood Sandwich

Salmon 2 15½-ounce cans, drained and flaked
Celery 2 cups chopped
Walnuts 1 cup chopped
Mayonnaise or salad dressing ¾ cup

French bread 1-pound long loaf
Dill pickles 3, sliced lengthwise
Bermuda onion 1, sliced and separated into rings
Lettuce leaves

Combine salmon, celery, walnuts, and mayonnaise; chill. Cut bread in half lengthwise and remove a small amount of crumb along full length of both halves. Spread each half with salmon mixture; cut each half crosswise into 12 slices. Serve with pickle slices, onion rings, and lettuce. Serves 12.

Salmon Alaska

Mayonnaise or salad dressing 1 cup
Lemon juice 2 tablespoons
Parsley flakes 1½ teaspoons
Cayenne pinch
Egg whites 2, stiffly beaten but not dry

Tomato slices 6
White bread 6 slices, toasted
Salmon 1 15½-ounce can, drained and flaked

Combine mayonnaise, lemon juice, parsley, and cayenne; fold into egg whites. Place a tomato slice on each piece of toast. Cover tomato with salmon. Place toast on 10 by 16-inch bake-and-serve platter. Spoon mayonnaise mixture over each sandwich. Broil about 12 inches from source of heat for 6 to 8 minutes or until lightly browned. Serves 6.

Salmonburgers

Onion ½ cup chopped
Butter or margarine ¼ cup
Salmon liquid ⅓ cup
Dry bread crumbs ⅓ cup
Eggs 2, beaten
Parsley ¼ cup chopped
Dry mustard 1 teaspoon
Salt ½ teaspoon

Salmon 1 15½-ounce can, drained and flaked
Dry bread crumbs ½ cup
Cooking oil
Round buns 6, split, buttered, and heated
Lemon wedges

In saucepan, sauté onion in butter until tender. Add next 7 ingredients; mix well. Shape into 6 cakes and coat with crumbs. Pour ⅛-inch layer of oil into heavy frying pan. When oil is hot but not smoking fry cakes over moderate heat for about 3 minutes on each side, or until brown. Drain on absorbent paper. Place salmon cakes in buns and serve with lemon wedges. Serves 6.

Tuna Sandwich Spread I

Tuna 1 6½-ounce can,
  drained and flaked
Dill pickle or cucumber chips
  2 tablespoons chopped
Cucumber ½ cup chopped

Corn chips ½ cup crushed
Mayonnaise 4 tablespoons
Lemon juice 2 tablespoons
Hot pepper sauce 2 or 3 drops
Salt to taste

In bowl, combine tuna, pickle, cucumber, and corn chips. Blend together mayonnaise, lemon juice, and hot pepper sauce; add to tuna mixture. Taste; add salt if necessary. Makes about 1½ cups; enough for 4 to 6 sandwiches.

Tuna Sandwich Spread II

Tuna 2 6½-ounce cans,
  drained and flaked
Pitted ripe olives ¼ cup chopped
Cashews ¼ cup chopped

Lemon juice 1 tablespoon
Mayonnaise 3 tablespoons
Salt and pepper to taste

Combine all ingredients and store in covered container in refrigerator until ready to spread on sandwiches. Makes about 2 cups; enough for 6 to 8 sandwiches.

Danish Tuna Sandwiches

Tuna 2 6½-ounce cans,
  drained and flaked
Cabbage 1 cup coarsely grated
Carrot 1 cup coarsely grated
Mayonnaise 3 tablespoons
Catsup 1 tablespoon

Lemon juice 1 tablespoon
Salt ½ teaspoon
Pepper pinch
Lettuce leaves 6
Bread 6 slices, toasted and buttered
Cucumber 1, sliced

Combine tuna, cabbage, and carrot. Mix together next 5 ingredients; add to tuna mixture and toss lightly. Arrange lettuce on toast; spread ⅓ cup of tuna mixture over each lettuce leaf. Top with cucumber slices. Serves 6.

Broiled Tuna-Cheese Sandwiches

American cheese ¼ pound, grated
Eggs 3, hard-cooked and chopped
Tuna 1 6½-ounce can,
  drained and flaked
Mayonnaise ½ cup

Green pepper 2 tablespoons chopped
Sweet pickle relish 1 tablespoon
Salt ¾ teaspoon
Bread 6 slices, toasted

Combine first 7 ingredients and spread on toast. Broil about 4 inches from source of heat until cheese begins to melt. Serve immediately. Serves 6.

C and C on the Rocks*

Shucked clams ¾ cup drained
Dungeness crab meat ¾ cup
Blue cheese ¼ cup crumbled
Caraway cheese ¼ cup cubed
Condensed cream of mushroom soup
  1 10¾-ounce can

Chablis ¾ cup
Mushrooms ¼ cup diced
Garlic paste 2 tablespoons
Butter or margarine 2 tablespoons
English muffins 3, split
Bacon bits garnish

Put clams and crab together through fine blade of meat grinder. In saucepan, melt cheeses over low heat; add soup, Chablis, and mushrooms and blend. Stir in clams and crab and simmer for 5 minutes. Combine garlic paste and butter and spread over muffins; toast under broiler. Pour saucepan ingredients over muffins, sprinkle with bacon, and serve. Serves 6.
*Clams, crab—and muffins for rocks—of course.

Clamburgers

Minced clams 1 7-ounce can, drained
Egg 1, beaten
Lemon juice 1 tablespoon
Parsley 1 tablespoon chopped
Onion 1 tablespoon grated

Salt ½ teaspoon
Pepper pinch
Dry bread crumbs ½ cup
Cooking oil 3 tablespoons
Large buns 6, split and toasted

Combine first 7 ingredients; form into 6 flat cakes. Roll in crumbs. In heavy frying pan, fry cakes in oil over moderate heat for 5 minutes on each side, or until brown; serve in buns. Serves 6.

French-Toasted Seafood Sandwiches

Crab, shrimp, or fish 2 cups
  cooked and flaked
Celery ½ cup chopped
Onion 2 tablespoons finely chopped
Worcestershire sauce 1 teaspoon
Prepared mustard ½ teaspoon
Mayonnaise or salad dressing ½ cup

Salt and pepper to taste
Bread 12 slices, buttered
Eggs 2, beaten
Milk ½ cup
Salt ¼ teaspoon
Butter or margarine 3 tablespoons

Combine first 6 ingredients; taste and add salt and pepper if necessary. Spread 6 slices of bread with fish mixture; cover with remaining bread slices. Combine eggs, milk, and salt; dip sandwiches in egg mixture. In heavy frying pan, fry sandwiches in butter over moderate heat until filling is hot and egg crust is golden brown on each side. Serves 6.

Note: The spread may be chilled and used on conventional sandwiches.

Oyster Club Sandwiches

Bacon slices 6, cut in halves
Flour ½ cup
Salt ½ teaspoon
Pepper pinch
Shucked oysters 1 pint, drained

Bread 18 slices, toasted
  and buttered
Mayonnaise or salad dressing ½ cup
Lettuce leaves 12
Tomato slices 6

In heavy frying pan, fry bacon until crisp; drain on absorbent paper. Combine flour, salt, and pepper. Roll oysters in flour mixture and fry in bacon drippings over moderate heat for about 2 minutes. Turn and fry 2 minutes longer or until brown and edges curl; drain on absorbent paper. Spread toast with mayonnaise. Arrange lettuce and tomato on 6 toast slices; add another slice of toast, then oysters and bacon to each. To complete sandwiches, top oysters and bacon with remaining toast slices and secure layers with toothpicks; cut into quarters. Serves 6.

Note: Seafood spreads (see Index) also may be used successfully as one layer of a club sandwich.

Oyster Loaf

Shucked oysters 1 pint
Salt ½ teaspoon
Pepper ⅛ teaspoon
Eggs 2, beaten
Milk ¼ cup
French bread 2 loaves, 15 inches
long and 3 inches wide

Flour ¾ cup
Soft bread crumbs 2 cups
Butter or margarine ½ cup, melted
Oil for deep frying
Tartar sauce ½ cup
Lettuce 1½ cups shredded
Thin tomato slices 18

Drain oysters and dry between pieces of absorbent paper; season. Combine eggs and milk. Slice bread loaves in half horizontally; pull out the inside soft crumb from bottom and top halves and use in making soft bread crumbs. Roll oysters in flour, dip in egg mixture, and roll in soft crumbs to coat evenly. Refrigerate at least 30 minutes to firm coating. Brush inside of bread shells with melted butter. Place on cookie sheet and bake at 350° for 3 to 5 minutes to warm and crisp. Place oysters in single layer in fry basket. Fry in deep fat at 350° for 2 to 3 minutes; drain on absorbent paper. Spread inside of bread shells with tartar sauce. Place shredded lettuce in bottom halves of loaves; arrange tomato slices on lettuce and fried oysters on top of tomatoes. Cover with top halves of bread. Cut each loaf into 3 portions. Serves 6.

Shrimp Tropicana

Shrimp 2 4½-ounce cans, drained,
rinsed, and chopped
Cottage cheese 1 cup, drained
Crushed pineapple ½ cup drained
Mayonnaise or salad dressing ⅓ cup

Lemon juice 2 teaspoons
Salt ½ teaspoon
Cracked-wheat bread 12 slices,
buttered
Lettuce leaves 6

Combine first 6 ingredients and chill. Spread 6 slices of bread with shrimp mixture; cover with lettuce, then remaining bread. Serves 6.

Curried Shrimp Sandwiches

Shrimp   3 4½-ounce cans, drained, rinsed, and chopped
Butter or margarine   ¼ cup
Egg   1, beaten
Milk   ¼ cup

Salt   ¼ teaspoon
Curry powder   pinch
Bread   6 slices
Paprika

In frying pan, sauté shrimp in butter over moderate heat for 3 minutes. Combine egg, milk, salt, and curry powder. Pour over shrimp and cook, stirring constantly, until thickened. Toast bread under broiler on one side; spread shrimp mixture on untoasted side. Broil about 3 inches from source of heat for 2 to 4 minutes or until lightly browned. Sprinkle with paprika. Serves 6.

Sunny Shrimp Sandwiches

Shrimp   3 4½-ounce cans, drained and rinsed
Mayonnaise or salad dressing   ⅓ cup
Lemon juice   1 tablespoon
Lemon peel   1½ teaspoons grated

Rye bread   6 large slices, toasted
Romano cheese   6 tablespoons grated
Butter or margarine   2 tablespoons
Parsley sprigs   garnish

Combine shrimp, mayonnaise, lemon juice and peel; mix thoroughly. Spread shrimp mixture on toast; sprinkle with cheese and dot with butter. Broil about 6 inches from source of heat for 8 minutes or until lightly browned. Garnish with parsley. Serves 6.

Entrées and Stuffings

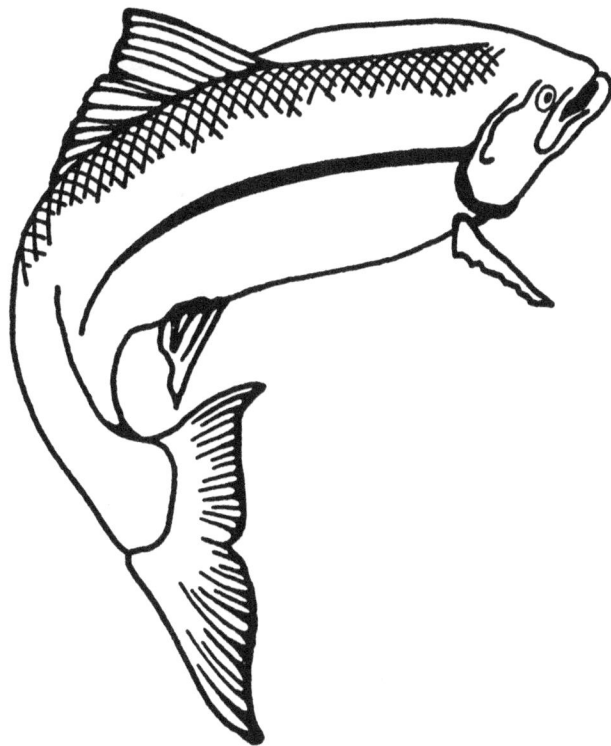

Baked Fillets or Steaks

Fish fillets or steaks 2 pounds   **Onion** 1 teaspoon grated
Salt 1 teaspoon   **Butter or other fat**
Pepper ⅛ teaspoon   4 tablespoons melted
Lemon juice 2 tablespoons   **Paprika** garnish

Cut fish into serving-size portions and sprinkle with salt and pepper. Add lemon juice and onion to butter; dip each piece of fish into this mixture and place in buttered shallow baking pan. Pour remaining butter over fish. Bake at 350° for 25 minutes or until fish flakes easily. Sprinkle with paprika and serve hot. Serves 6.

Baked Fillets in Spanish Sauce

Fish fillets 2 pounds   **Tomatoes** 1 16-ounce can
Onion ¼ cup chopped   **Salt** 1 teaspoon
Green pepper ¼ cup chopped   **Pepper** pinch
Butter or other fat 3 tablespoons   **Bay leaf** 1
Flour 2 tablespoons   **Whole clove** 1

Cut fillets into serving-size portions. Place in single layer in well-buttered shallow baking pan. Cook onion and green pepper in butter until tender. Blend in flour; add next 5 ingredients and cook until thickened, stirring constantly. Remove bay leaf and clove. Cover fish with sauce and bake at 350° for 25 to 30 minutes. Serves 6.

Chipper Fillets

Fish fillets 2 pounds skinned   **Potato chips** 1 cup crushed
Caesar salad dressing ½ cup   **Sharp cheddar cheese** ½ cup grated

Cut fillets into 6 portions; dip in salad dressing. Arrange on 8 by 12-inch bake-and-serve platter. Combine potato chips and cheese; sprinkle over fish. Bake at 350° for 15 to 20 minutes or until fish flakes easily. Serves 6.

Baked Fish

Fish 1 3- to 4-pound dressed   **Butter or other fat**
Salt 1½ teaspoons   4 tablespoons, melted
                                                      Bacon 3 slices (optional)

Wash and dry fish; sprinkle inside and out with salt and place in buttered baking pan. Brush with butter and lay bacon over top. Bake at 350° for 40 to 60 minutes or until fish flakes easily. Baste occasionally with drippings. Serve plain or with a sauce. Serves 6.

Baked Fish and Oysters

White-fleshed fish steaks
  6 1-inch-thick
Butter 2 tablespoons
Salt 1 teaspoon
Pepper pinch
Paprika pinch
Eggs 2, slightly beaten

Milk 4 tablespoons
Shucked oysters 12
Dry bread crumbs 1 cup
Worcestershire sauce 1 teaspoon
Butter ¼ cup, melted
Parsley and lemon slices garnish

Place steaks in buttered shallow baking dish; dot with butter and sprinkle with salt, pepper, and paprika. Combine eggs and milk. Dry oysters between paper towels; dip in egg mixture and then in bread crumbs. Place 2 oysters on each fish steak and bake at 350° for about 20 minutes or until fish flakes easily. Do not overbake. Add Worcestershire sauce to butter and pour over fish just before serving. Garnish with parsley and lemon. Serves 6.

Baked Stuffed Fish

Fish 1 3- to 4-pound dressed
Salt 1½ teaspoons
Bread stuffing (see Index)

Butter or other fat 4 tablespoons, melted
Bacon 3 slices (optional)

Wash and dry fish; sprinkle inside and out with salt. Stuff loosely and sew the opening with needle and string or close with skewers. Place in buttered baking pan, brush with butter, and lay bacon over top. Bake at 350° for 40 to 60 minutes or until fish flakes easily. If fish seems dry while baking, baste occasionally with drippings or additional melted butter. Remove string or skewers and serve hot. Serves 6.

Fish Portions Oriental

Frozen breaded fish portions
  1 12-ounce package
Pineapple chunks 1 15¼-ounce can
Pineapple syrup plus water ¾ cup
Sugar 2 tablespoons
Vinegar 2 tablespoons

Soy sauce 1 tablespoon
Cornstarch 1 tablespoon
Garlic salt ½ teaspoon
Medium green pepper ½, seeded
  and cut in strips
Rice 4 servings

Prepare fish portions as directed on package label. Drain pineapple chunks; save syrup. In saucepan, combine liquid with the next 5 ingredients; cook, stirring constantly, until sauce is thick and clear. Add pineapple chunks and green pepper. When pineapple is hot, serve fish portions on rice and spoon sauce over fish. Serves 4.

Fish Portions with Tomato Sauce

Frozen breaded fish portions
1 12-ounce package
Celery 1 cup sliced
Onion 1 cup thinly sliced
Margarine or vegetable oil
2 tablespoons
Flour 1 tablespoon
Garlic salt 1 teaspoon

Tomatoes 1 16-ounce can
Liquid pepper sauce 5 drops or to taste
Margarine or vegetable oil
2 tablespoons
Cabbage 6 cups shredded
(about 1 pound)
Salt ½ teaspoon

Prepare fish portions as directed on package label; keep warm. In saucepan cook celery and onion in margarine until onion is tender but not brown. Stir in flour and garlic salt, then tomatoes and pepper sauce; cover and simmer 15 minutes or until sauce is thick and flavors blended. Heat remaining margarine in large skillet; add cabbage, sprinkle with salt, and stir. Cover and cook slowly for 7 minutes or until cabbage is done to your taste, stirring several times. Serve fish portions on cabbage and spoon sauce over fish. Serves 4.

Planked Fish

Fish fillets or steaks 2 pounds
Cooking oil 2 tablespoons
Lemon juice 2 tablespoons

Salt 1 teaspoon
Paprika ½ teaspoon
Pepper pinch

Cut fillets into 6 portions. Place in single layer, skin side down, on preheated, greased plank or 13 by 18-inch bake-and-serve platter. Combine next 5 ingredients and pour over fish. Bake at 350° for 20 minutes or until fish flakes easily. Remove from oven; to serve arrange mashed potatoes and 2 or more vegetables (asparagus, broccoli, carrots, cauliflower, onions, peas, or tomatoes) around the fish. Serves 6.

Note: A dressed 3-pound fish requires about 50 minutes baking time when planked.

Broiled Fillets or Steaks

Fish fillets or steaks 2 pounds
Butter or other fat 2 tablespoons,
melted
Lemon juice 2 tablespoons

Salt 1 teaspoon
Paprika ½ teaspoon
Pepper pinch

Cut fillets into 6 portions; place in single layer, skin side down, in well-buttered 10 by 15-inch baking pan. Combine remaining 5 ingredients and pour over fish. Broil about 4 inches from source of heat for 10 minutes or until fish flakes easily. Baste once during broiling with sauce in pan. Serves 6.

Broiled Pan-Dressed Fish

Fish 1 3-pound pan-dressed
Butter or other fat ¼ cup, melted
Lemon juice ¼ cup

Salt 1½ teaspoons
Paprika ¾ teaspoon
Pepper pinch

Wash and dry fish; place in a well-buttered shallow 10 by 15-inch baking pan. Combine remaining 5 ingredients. Brush fish inside and out with this sauce. Broil about 4 inches from source of heat for 5 to 8 minutes; turn carefully and baste with sauce. Broil 5 minutes longer or until fish flakes easily. Serves 6.

Fish Fillets Amandine

White-fleshed fish fillets 2 pounds
Butter ½ cup, melted
Flour ½ cup
Paprika 1½ tablespoons*
Salt 1 teaspoon
Pepper ⅛ teaspoon

Blanched slivered almonds ½ cup
Parsley garnish
Peaches 1 16-ounce can,
  drained (optional)
Lemon juice 2 tablespoons
Liquid pepper sauce 2 dashes

Dip fillets in butter and dredge in flour which has been seasoned with paprika, salt, and pepper. Place fillets in greased broiler pan and broil 4 inches from source of heat for 8 minutes or until fish flakes easily. Place fish on warm platter and garnish with almonds and parsley. Arrange hot or cold peach halves at the edge of the platter. Mix any remaining butter with lemon juice and pepper sauce; serve over fish. Serves 6.
*Paprika will give a red color to the fillets, which is desired in this recipe.

Deep-Fried Fillets or Steaks

Fish fillets or steaks 2 pounds
Milk ¼ cup
Egg 1, beaten
Salt 1 teaspoon

Pepper pinch
**Dry bread, cereal, or cracker
  crumbs** 1½ cups
Oil for deep frying

Cut fillets into 6 portions. Combine milk, egg, and seasonings; dip fish in milk and roll in crumbs. Place in single layer in fry basket. Fry at 350° in deep fat for 3 to 5 minutes or until fish is brown and flakes easily. Drain on absorbent paper. Serves 6.

Note: Fry pan-dressed fish in 10-inch fry pan for 4 minutes on each side, or until fish flakes easily.

Oven-Fried Fish

Fish	2 pounds	**Cereal crumbs or toasted dry**	
Milk	1 cup	**bread crumbs** 1½ cups	
Salt	1 teaspoon	**Melted fat or oil** ¼ cup	

Cut fish into 6 portions. Combine milk and salt; dip fish into milk and roll in crumbs. Place in single layer, skin side down, on well-buttered 10 by 15-inch baking pan. Pour fat over fish. Bake at 500° for 10 minutes or until fish flakes easily. Serves 6.

Oven-Fried Pan-Dressed Fish

Fish	1 3-pound pan-dressed	**Cereal crumbs or toasted dry**	
Milk	½ cup	**bread crumbs** 1½ cups	
Salt	2 teaspoons	**Oil** ¼ cup	

Wash and dry fish. Combine milk and salt; dip fish in milk and roll in crumbs. Place fish on well-buttered 10 by 15-inch baking pan and brush with oil. Bake at 500° for 15 minutes or until fish is brown and flakes easily. Serves 4.

Poached Fish with Egg Sauce

Fish fillets or steaks 2 pounds		**Peppercorns** 3	
Boiling water 2 cups		**Parsley sprigs** 2	
Lemon juice ¼ cup		**Bay leaf** 1	
Small onion 1, thinly sliced		**Egg Sauce**	
Salt 1 teaspoon		**Paprika** garnish	

Remove skin and bones from fish; cut into 6 portions and place in well-buttered 10-inch frying pan. Add next 7 ingredients, cover, and simmer for 5 to 10 minutes or until fish flakes easily. Carefully remove fish to hot platter. Pour Egg Sauce over the fish and sprinkle with paprika. Serves 6.

Egg Sauce

Butter or margarine ¼ cup
Flour 2 tablespoons
Dry mustard ¾ teaspoon
Salt ½ teaspoon

Pepper pinch
Milk 1¼ cups
Eggs 2, hard-cooked and chopped
Parsley 1 tablespoon chopped

Melt butter and stir in flour, mustard, salt, and pepper. Add milk gradually and cook until thick and smooth, stirring constantly. Add eggs and parsley. When eggs are hot, remove from heat. Makes about 1½ cups.

Striped Bass with Low-Cal Stuffing

Striped bass or other fish
  3 pounds dressed
Salt 1½ teaspoons
Low-Cal Stuffing

Melted butter or cooking oil
  2 tablespoons
Lemon wedges

Wipe bass dry and sprinkle, inside and out, with salt. Loosely stuff fish and close opening with small skewers and string. Place fish on greased bake-and-serve platter and brush with butter. Bake at 350° for 40 to 60 minutes or until fish flakes easily. Remove skewers and serve with lemon wedges. Serves 6.

Low-Cal Stuffing

Onion ¾ cup chopped
Butter or margarine 1½ tablespoons
Apple 2¼ cups peeled,
  cored, and chopped
Celery ⅓ cup chopped

Parsley ⅓ cup chopped
Lemon juice 2 tablespoons
Salt ¼ teaspoon
Thyme ⅛ teaspoon

Sauté onion in butter until tender. Combine with remaining ingredients and mix thoroughly. Makes about 3 cups.

Succulent Sea Bass

Sea bass or other fish fillets
2 pounds skinned
Pineapple juice ½ cup

Steak sauce ¼ cup
Salt 1 teaspoon
Pepper pinch

Cut fillets into serving-size portions and arrange in single layer in shallow baking dish. Combine remaining ingredients; pour over fish. Let stand for 30 minutes, turning fish once. Remove fish and arrange on well-greased broiler pan. Broil about 4 inches from source of heat for 4 to 6 minutes; turn carefully and brush with marinade. Broil 4 to 6 minutes longer or until fish flakes easily. Serves 6.

Black Drum with Zesty Sauce

When swimming, the black drum makes a humming sound by rapid and repeated contraction of a specialized muscle. It is said that when a whole shoal of fish began "drumming" together, the Indians believed it was the ghosts of persons drowned.

Catsup ½ cup
Salad oil ¼ cup
Lemon juice ¼ cup
Onion 1 tablespoon grated
Worcestershire sauce 1 teaspoon

Prepared mustard 1 teaspoon
Garlic salt ½ teaspoon
Salt ¼ teaspoon
**Black drum or other fish
  fillets** 2 pounds

Combine first 8 ingredients in shallow bowl. Add fillets, turning to moisten both sides with sauce; cover bowl and place in refrigerator to marinate for 1 hour. Remove fish from marinade and reserve sauce for basting. Place fish in single layer in foil-lined 10 by 15-inch shallow baking pan. Broil about 4 inches from source of heat for 10 to 15 minutes or until fish flakes easily. Fish need not be turned, but baste it once during broiling. Serves 6.

Fast Catfish Broil

Catfish or other fish fillets
2 pounds skinned
Garlic French dressing ¼ cup

Soy sauce 3 tablespoons
Ground ginger ¾ teaspoon
Lime slices

Place fillets in single layer, skinned side down, on a greased 10 by 16-inch bake-and-serve platter. Combine French dressing, soy sauce, and ginger; pour over fillets and let stand for 10 mintues. Broil, without turning, about 4 inches from source of heat for 10 to 15 minutes or until fish flakes easily. Baste once during broiling with sauce from pan. Garnish with lime slices. Serves 6.

Cod Creole

Onion 2 tablespoons chopped
Green pepper ¼ cup minced
Butter 2 tablespoons
Tomatoes 1½ cups cooked
Mushrooms ¼ cup sliced

Olives ¼ cup sliced
Salt ¼ teaspoon
Pepper pinch
Sherry 2 tablespoons
Cod fillets 2 pounds

Cook onion and green pepper in butter until tender. Add tomatoes, mushrooms, and olives and cook 2 minutes; add seasonings, and sherry and remove from heat. Arrange fillets in shallow baking pan, pour sauce over fish, and bake at 400° for 20 minutes or until fish flakes easily. Serves 6.

Cod Curry

Cod fillets 2 pounds
Celery 1 cup finely sliced
Onion ½ cup sliced
Butter or vegetable oil 1 tablespoon
Curry powder ½ teaspoon
Salt 1 teaspoon

Pepper pinch
Milk ¾ cup
Paprika garnish
Parsley garnish
Lemon wedges garnish

Place fillets in single layer in buttered shallow baking dish. Cook celery and onion in butter for 5 minutes; add curry powder, salt, pepper, and milk. Spread mixture over fish and bake at 350° for 25 to 30 minutes. Sprinkle with paprika and garnish with parsley and lemon. Serves 6.

Broiled Oriental Fish Fillets

Soy sauce 1 tablespoon
Ground ginger ¼ teaspoon
Brown sugar 2 tablespoons

Salad oil 3 tablespoons
Cod or flounder fillets 1 pound

Combine soy sauce, ginger, brown sugar, and salad oil; pour over fillets. Cover and marinate for 2 hours in the refrigerator. Remove fish from the sauce and place in greased shallow baking pan. Broil, without turning, about 4 inches from source of heat for 5 minutes or until fish flakes easily and is nicely browned. Serves 4.

Lemon-Garlic Croaker

Lemon juice ¼ cup
Salt 1 teaspoon
Garlic clove 1, minced

Croaker or other firm fish
 fillets 2 pounds
Cornmeal 1½ cups
Margarine

Combine lemon juice, salt, and garlic in shallow dish. Add fillets, turning once and placing them skin side up. Cover and marinate for 30 minutes in refrigerator. Remove fish from marinade and roll in cornmeal. In heavy frying pan, over moderate heat, fry fish in hot but not smoking margarine until fish is brown on both sides. Cooking time is about 8 minutes, depending on thickness of fish. Drain on absorbent paper and serve immediately on hot platter. Serves 6.

Flounder à la Orange

Flounder fillets 2 pounds
Frozen orange juice concentrate
  ½ cup, thawed

Butter 2 tablespoons, melted
Salt ½ teaspoon
Nutmeg pinch

Place fillets, skin side down (or skin may be removed) in single layer in buttered shallow baking pan. Combine remaining ingredients and pour over fish. Bake at 350° for 20 minutes or until fish flakes easily. Serves 4.

Flounder in Wine Sauce

Flounder or other fish fillets
  2 pounds skinned
Salt 1½ teaspoons
Pepper pinch
Tomatoes 3, sliced
Salt ½ teaspoon
Pepper pinch

Butter or margarine 2 tablespoons
Flour 2 tablespoons
Milk ½ cup
Dry white wine ⅓ cup
Basil ½ teaspoon crushed
Parsley garnish

Sprinkle both sides of fillets with salt and pepper; arrange in single layer in buttered 8 by 12 by 2-inch baking dish. Arrange tomato slices over fillets; sprinkle with salt and pepper. In saucepan, melt butter and blend in flour; add milk gradually and cook, stirring constantly, until thick and smooth. Remove from heat and stir in wine and basil. Pour sauce over tomatoes. Bake at 350° for 25 minutes or until fish flakes easily. Sprinkle with parsley. Serves 6.

Planked Flounder

Flounder 1 3- to 4-pound piece boned
Salt 1 teaspoon
Pepper ¼ teaspoon
Butter 3 tablespoons
Lemon ½, for juice
Potatoes 3 cups cooked and mashed

Green peas 1½ cups cooked
Tomatoes 6 halves, broiled
Whole carrots 8, cooked and broiled
Parsley garnish
Lemon wedges

Heat a fish plank in the oven for a few minutes and then grease it. Lay fish flat on plank, skin side down. Season, dot with bits of butter, and squeeze lemon juice over it. Bake at 400° for 12 to 15 minutes, depending on thickness of fish. Then place plank about 4 inches from source of heat. Broil fish until it is browning nicely and almost done. Remove from oven and pile hot potatoes around it in a high border. Return to oven and broil until fish flakes easily and potatoes are lightly browned. Arrange spoonfuls of hot peas, tomato halves, and carrots around the fish and garnish with parsley and lemon wedges. Place plank on a platter and serve. Serves 6.

Faster Flounder

Flounder fillets 2 pounds skinned
Onion 2 tablespoons grated
Salt 1½ teaspoons
Pepper ⅛ teaspoon

Large tomatoes 2, cut into
  small pieces
Butter or margarine ¼ cup, melted
Swiss cheese 1 cup grated

Place fillets in single layer on well-greased 10 by 16-inch bake-and-serve platter. Sprinkle fish with onion, salt, and pepper; cover with tomatoes. Pour butter over tomatoes. Broil about 4 inches from source of heat for 10 minutes or until fillets flake easily. Remove from heat and sprinkle with cheese; return to broiler only long enough to melt cheese. Serves 6.

Tasty Flounder

Flounder fillets 2 pounds
Cooking oil
Garlic salt ½ teaspoon
Instant mashed potato flakes
  ½ cup plus 2 teaspoons

Chicken broth 1 cup
Green onion 1 tablespoon chopped
Parsley 2 teaspoons chopped

In heavy skillet, over moderate heat, fry fish in hot oil for 4 to 5 minutes on each side or until fillets flake easily and are nicely browned. Drain on absorbent paper and keep warm while making sauce. Add garlic salt, potato flakes, and broth to the pan and simmer for 1 to 2 minutes or until thick, stirring constantly. Pour sauce over fish and garnish with green onion and parsley. Serves 6.

Savory Baked Haddock

Haddock or other fish fillets
  2 pounds skinned
Lemon juice 2 teaspoons
Pepper pinch

Bacon slices 6, chopped
Soft bread crumbs ½ cup
Parsley 2 tablespoons chopped
Onion ¾ cup thinly sliced

Place fillets in single layer in buttered 8 by 12 by 2-inch baking dish; sprinkle with lemon juice and pepper. Fry bacon until crisp; remove from drippings with slotted spoon and combine with bread crumbs and parsley. Drain all but 2 tablespoons of bacon drippings from pan and sauté onion in pan until tender. Spread onion over fish; sprinkle crumb mixture over onion. Bake at 350° for 25 minutes or until fish flakes easily. Serves 6.

Baked Halibut

Halibut 1 3- to 4-pound piece
Salt 1½ teaspoons
Pepper pinch

Bread Stuffing (see Index)
Butter or other fat ¼ cup, melted
Bacon slices 4 (optional)

Clean, wash, and dry fish; sprinkle inside and out with salt and pepper. Stuff the fish loosely and either sew up opening or close it with skewers. Place fish in greased shallow baking pan; brush with melted butter and lay bacon over top. Bake at 350° for 35 to 45 minutes or until fish flakes easily. Baste occasionally with pan juices if fish seems dry while baking. Serves 6.

Halibut Hawaiian

Salt 1 teaspoon
Halibut steaks 2, about 1
  pound each*
Rice 1 cup cooked
Bread 1 cup cubed
Lemon juice 2 tablespoons

Crushed pineapple 1 cup drained
Salt ¾ teaspoon
Butter or margarine 3 tablespoons,
  melted
Bacon slices 3 (optional)
Pineapple juice ½ cup

Sprinkle salt over steaks. Combine next 5 ingredients. Place one steak in a well-buttered shallow baking pan; cover with rice mixture and place remaining steak over top. Brush with butter, arrange bacon on top, and pour pineapple juice around fish. Bake at 350° for 40 to 45 minutes or until fish flakes easily. Serves 6.
*Halibut cheeks may be used instead of steaks.

Halibut Mexicana

Halibut steaks or fillets 2 pounds
Butter 3 tablespoons
Green pepper 1, chopped
Tomatoes 3, chopped, or canned
  equivalent
Salt 2 teaspoons
Oregano ½ teaspoon

Garlic clove 1, minced
Cumin powder ½ teaspoon
Chili powder 2 teaspoons
Parsley 2 tablespoons minced
Green olives ¼ cup sliced
Capers 1 tablespoon
Port or red table wine 1 cup

Melt butter in skillet; add green pepper and sauté until soft. Add next 9 ingredients and simmer for 5 minutes; add port and heat 1 to 2 minutes longer. Pour sauce into shallow baking dish. Arrange halibut in dish, spooning some sauce over it. Bake at 350° for 15 minutes or until fish flakes easily. Serves 6.

Halibut and Pineapple Packages

Halibut fillets 2 pounds
Salt 2 teaspoons
Pepper ¼ teaspoon
Ground ginger ¼ teaspoon

Pineapple chunks 1 20-ounce
  can, drained
Green pepper 1, cut into
  24 strips
Tomato slices 6

Cut fillets into 6 portions and season. Cut 6 12-inch squares of aluminum foil; grease them. On each square, place a portion of halibut, 6 pineapple chunks, 4 strips of green pepper, and 1 slice of tomato. Seal the foil with a double fold, making it steamtight. Place packages in shallow baking pan. Bake at 450° for 20 to 25 minutes, depending on thickness of fish. Serve unopened on individual plates. Serves 6.

Halibut Pot Roast

Halibut 1 3-pound piece, boned
  and skinned
Flour 1 cup
Cooking oil 3 tablespoons
Carrots 6
Medium onions 6
Celery 2 cups chopped

Medium potatoes 6
Garlic cloves 2, finely chopped
Salt 2 teaspoons
Pepper ½ teaspoon
Water 2 cups
Butter 1 tablespoon
Flour 1 tablespoon

Roll fish in flour; in large heavy frying pan or Dutch oven, over moderate heat, brown it on all sides in hot oil. Place carrots, onions, celery, and potatoes around fish and add seasonings. Add water, cover, and bake at 350° for 45 minutes or until fish flakes easily. Remove fish and vegetables to a hot platter. Make a paste of butter and flour and thicken liquid in pan with it; serve over fish and vegetables. Serves 6.

Hearty Halibut

Halibut steaks 2 pounds
Onion ⅔ cup thinly sliced
Mushrooms 1½ cups chopped
Tomato ⅓ cup chopped
Green pepper ¼ cup chopped
Parsley ¼ cup chopped
Pimiento 3 tablespoons chopped

Dry white wine ½ cup
Lemon juice 2 tablespoons
Salt 1 teaspoon
Dillweed ¼ teaspoon
Pepper ⅛ teaspoon
Lemon wedges garnish

Cut steaks into serving-size portions. Arrange onion in bottom of buttered 8 by 12 by 2-inch baking dish. Place fish on top of onion. Combine next 5 ingredients and spread over fish. Combine wine, lemon juice, salt, dillweed, and pepper; pour over vegetables. Bake at 350° for 25 minutes or until fish flakes easily. Garnish with lemon wedges. Serves 6.

Quick Halibut Bake

Halibut steaks or fillets 2 pounds
Salt and pepper to taste
Butter 2 tablespoons
Small onion 1, chopped

Bay leaf 1, crumbled
Butter 2 tablespoons
Flour 3 to 4 tablespoons
Milk plus liquid from casserole 1 cup

Place fish in buttered baking dish; sprinkle with salt and pepper, and dot with butter, onion, and bay leaf. Bake at 350° for 30 minutes or until fish flakes easily. Drain and reserve liquid; keep fish warm while preparing sauce. Melt butter in saucepan over low heat; blend in flour, and stir until smooth. Add milk and fish liquid, stirring constantly. Cook until thick, then pour over fish. Serves 4 to 6.
Variations: Pour one 10¾-ounce can of condensed cream of mushroom soup over fish and bake or bake fish and pour your favorite barbecue sauce over fish for last ten minutes of baking.

Seattle Baked Halibut

Halibut steaks or fillets 2 pounds
Salt 1 teaspoon
Butter 2 tablespoons
Mushrooms ¼ pound sliced or
  Mushrooms 1 4-ounce can, drained

Dairy sour cream 1 cup
Sherry ¼ cup
Paprika garnish

Place halibut steaks in buttered shallow baking dish; sprinkle with salt. Bake at 425° for 10 minutes. Meanwhile, melt butter in saucepan and sauté mushrooms until golden brown; remove from heat and add sour cream and sherry. Pour sauce over halibut; sprinkle with paprika. Return to oven and bake at 375° for 10 minutes or until steaks flake easily. Serves 4 to 6.

Halibut Skillet Dinner

Medium potatoes 3, cubed
Carrots 3, sliced
Chicken broth 1 cup
Salt 1 teaspoon

Pepper ¼ teaspoon
Halibut 1½ pounds
Chives 2 tablespoons chopped

Arrange potatoes and carrots in large skillet. Add broth, season, and cover; bring to boil and simmer 15 minutes. Place halibut in center of skillet, pushing vegetables aside; sprinkle fish with chives. Cover and simmer 10 to 15 minutes or until fish flakes easily and vegetables are tender. Serves 4.

Broiled Halibut Steaks with Mushroom Sauce and Cheese

Halibut steaks 2 pounds,
  (½-inch thick)
Salt and pepper to taste
Butter or other fat ¼ cup, melted

Thin cheese slices 6
Bread 6 slices, toasted
Condensed cream of mushroom soup
  2 10¾-ounce cans, heated

Cut fish into 6 portions; season to taste. Place fish in greased shallow baking pan and brush with butter. Broil about 2 inches from source of heat for 5 to 8 minutes; baste with butter and turn carefully. Brush again with butter and broil 5 to 8 minutes longer or until fish flakes easily. Cover fish with cheese and continue broiling only until cheese melts. Place fish pieces on toast and cover with hot soup. Serves 6.

Golden Broiled Halibut Steaks

Halibut steaks 2 pounds
Butter 4 tablespoons, melted
Onion 1 tablespoon grated
Lemon juice 2 tablespoons
Salt 1 teaspoon

Pepper pinch
Thyme ¼ teaspoon
Paprika garnish
Parsley garnish
Lemon wedges garnish

Place steaks on greased broiler pan. Combine next 6 ingredients; baste steaks with half of this mixture. Preheat oven to 500°; broil steaks 2 to 4 inches from source of heat for 5 minutes. Turn, baste with remaining sauce, and continue broiling until fish flakes easily. Garnish with paprika, parsley, and lemon. Serves 6.

Halibut Kabobs Aloha

Halibut fillets 2 pounds
Pineapple chunks 1 15½-ounce can
Soy sauce 4 teaspoons
Lemon juice 1 tablespoon
Garlic salt ¼ teaspoon
Ground ginger ¼ teaspoon

Vegetable oil 3 tablespoons
Pineapple syrup 2 tablespoons
Sesame seeds ½ cup, toasted
Stuffed green olives 1 8-ounce can
Rice 6 servings
Sweet-Sour Sauce

Cut halibut into 1-inch cubes. Drain pineapple; reserve syrup. Combine next 6 ingredients and pour over halibut; marinate for 1 hour. Drain, and roll fish in sesame seeds. Arrange halibut on skewers alternately with pineapple chunks and green olives. Place on rack over broiler pan; broil 4 inches from source of heat for about 7 minutes. Serve with steamed rice and Sweet-Sour Sauce. Serves 6.

Sweet-Sour Sauce

Cornstarch 1 tablespoon
Brown sugar ½ cup
Soy sauce 2 teaspoons

Vinegar ⅓ cup
Pineapple syrup ½ cup

In saucepan, combine cornstarch and brown sugar; stir in other ingredients. Bring to a boil and simmer until thick and clear. Makes about 1 cup.

Hurry Up Halibut

Halibut steaks 2 pounds
Hickory smoke-flavored barbecue sauce ⅓ cup
Salad oil 3 tablespoons

Frozen pineapple juice concentrate 2 tablespoons, thawed
Lemon juice 1 tablespoon
Instant minced onion 1 tablespoon
Salt ¼ teaspoon

Place steaks in single layer on well-buttered 10 by 16-inch bake-and-serve platter. Combine remaining 6 ingredients; brush steaks with this sauce. Broil about 4 inches from source of heat for 10 to 15 minutes or until steaks flake easily. Baste once with sauce during broiling. Serves 6.

Deep-Fried Halibut

Halibut fillets 2 pounds
Salt 1 teaspoon
Pepper pinch
Egg 1, slightly beaten

Milk 1 tablespoon
Dry bread or cracker crumbs, or cornmeal 1 cup
Oil for deep frying

Cut fish into serving-size pieces; sprinkle top and bottom with salt and pepper. Combine egg and milk; dip fish into egg mixture and roll in crumbs. Fry, a single layer at a time, in deep fat at 375° for 3 to 5 minutes or until golden brown. Drain on absorbent paper and serve immediately. Serves 6.

Fried Halibut Supreme

Thick halibut steaks 2 pounds
Flour ½ cup
Salt and pepper to taste

Cooking oil 2 tablespoons
Butter or margarine ½ cup
Water ½ cup

Wipe halibut dry, dust with flour, season to taste, and fry in oil over medium heat until well browned on each side. Add butter and water; simmer, uncovered, for 30 minutes. Serve with mashed or boiled potatoes. Serves 6.

Halibut Fish and Chips

Halibut fillets 2 pounds
Salt to taste

Crispy Batter or Tender Batter
Oil for deep frying

Cut halibut into serving-size chunks and sprinkle lightly with salt; dip into batter. Fry at 375° for 3 to 4 minutes or until golden brown. Drain on absorbent paper and serve immediately with French fried potatoes. Serves 6.

Crispy Batter

Flour 1 cup
Baking powder 2 teaspoons
Salt 1¼ teaspoons

Sugar 2 teaspoons
Salad oil 1 tablespoon
Water 1 cup

Sift together flour, baking powder, salt, and sugar. Add oil to water. Make a well in the dry ingredients and slowly pour in liquid, stirring until well blended. Coats 2 pounds of fish.

Tender Batter

Flour 1½ cups
Baking powder 1 tablespoon
Salt 1 teaspoon

Eggs 2, beaten
Milk 1 cup

Sift together flour, baking powder, and salt. Combine eggs and milk. Add liquid to flour mixture and stir until smooth. Coats 2 pounds of fish.

Poached Halibut with Shrimp Sauce

Halibut steaks or fillets 2 pounds*
White wine 1 cup
Water 1 cup
Bay leaf 1
Thyme pinch
Salt 1 scant teaspoon
Butter 2 tablespoons

Flour 2 tablespoons
Reserved fish stock 2 cups
Egg yolks 2, slightly beaten
Lemon juice 1 tablespoon
Parsley 1 tablespoon minced
Shrimp 1 4½-ounce can,
  rinsed and drained

Place halibut in saucepan. Add next 5 ingredients. Bring to boil; reduce heat and poach for 10 to 15 minutes or until fish flakes easily. Remove halibut from stock and keep warm. In a clean saucepan, melt butter and add flour, stirring until smooth. Slowly add fish stock; cook until thick and creamy. Combine egg yolks, lemon juice, and parsley. Stir slowly into sauce; do not boil. Add shrimp and simmer 5 minutes. Spoon some sauce over halibut and serve the rest in a sauceboat. Serves 6.
*Salmon may be used instead of halibut.

Note: All the shrimp sauce may be poured over poached fish and baked at 325° for 20 minutes.

Herring Roe à la Meunière

Herring roe 1½ pounds
Salt ¾ teaspoon
Pepper pinch

Butter or margarine ½ cup
Lemon juice 2 tablespoons

Wash roe and dry on absorbent paper; remove membrane. If it is difficult to remove, parboil roe 8 minutes in 1 quart of water and 1 tablespoon vinegar or lemon juice; drain and then remove membrane. Sprinkle both sides of roe with salt and pepper. Fry in butter over moderate heat until brown on each side. Cooking time will be about 12 minutes, depending on the thickness of roe. Remove roe to heated platter. Add lemon juice to butter in pan and pour over roe. Serves 6.

King Mackerel Steaks with Sauce Provençale

King mackerel steaks 2 pounds
Butter or margarine
  2 tablespoons, melted
Salt 1 teaspoon

Pepper ⅛ teaspoon
Paprika pinch
Sauce Provençale

Place mackerel in single layer in well-greased shallow 10 by 15-inch baking pan. Brush with butter and season. Broil about 4 inches from source of heat for 10 to 15 minutes or until fish flakes easily. Steaks need not be turned during broiling. Serve with Sauce Provençale. Serves 6.

Sauce Provençale

Medium tomatoes 4, peeled,
  cut into wedges, and seeded
Sugar ½ teaspoon
Butter or margarine 2 tablespoons
Green onion ¼ cup chopped
Garlic clove 1, minced

Dry white wine ½ cup
Butter or margarine ½ cup
Parsley 2 tablespoons chopped
Salt ¼ teaspoon
Pepper ⅛ teaspoon

Sprinkle tomatoes with sugar; set aside. In small saucepan, melt 2 tablespoons butter. Add green onion and garlic, cover, and cook 2 to 3 minutes. Add wine and cook, stirring constantly, until liquid is slightly reduced. Add tomatoes and remaining ingredients. Heat, stirring gently, just until butter melts. Makes about 2 cups.

Sweet-and-Pungent Mahimahi

Mahimahi or other fish fillets
  2 pounds skinned
Flour ¼ cup
Onion ⅔ cup thinly sliced
Butter or cooking oil
  3 tablespoons

Green pepper ¼ cup thinly sliced
Vinegar ¾ cup
Water ¾ cup
Sugar ½ cup
Powdered ginger 1½ teaspoons
Salt 1 teaspoon

Cut fillets into serving-size portions and roll in flour. In 10-inch frying pan, sauté onion in butter until lightly browned. Remove onion from pan. Fry fish in same butter over moderate heat for 4 minutes or until brown on one side; turn carefully. Spread green pepper and onion over fish. Combine remaining 5 ingredients and pour into pan. Simmer, covered, for 10 to 15 minutes or until fish flakes easily. Serves 6.

Broiled Sesame Mullet

Mullet or other fish fillets 2 pounds
Salt 1 teaspoon
Pepper ⅛ teaspoon

Butter or margarine ¼ cup
Lemon juice 2 tablespoons
Sesame seeds 2 tablespoons, toasted

Cut fillets into 6 portions. Place in single layer, skin side down, in well-greased shallow 10 by 15-inch baking pan. Sprinkle with salt and pepper. Heat butter and lemon juice together. Baste fish with sauce and sprinkle with sesame seeds. Broil about 4 inches from source of heat, without turning, for 10 to 15 minutes or until fish flakes easily. Baste with any remaining sauce during cooking time. Serves 6.

Key Lime Mullet

Mullet or other fish fillets
  2 pounds skinned
Salt 1 teaspoon
Pepper pinch
Lime juice ¼ cup

Butter or margarine 3 tablespoons,
  melted
Paprika to taste
Lime wedges garnish

Cut fillets into serving-size portions and arrange in single layer in shallow dish; sprinkle with salt and pepper. Pour lime juice over fish and let stand for 30 minutes, turning fish once. Remove fish and arrange on well-greased broiler pan. Pour juice into butter. Brush fish with butter mixture and sprinkle with paprika. Broil about 4 inches from source of heat for 8 minutes or until fish flakes easily. Garnish with lime wedges. Serves 6.

Pompano en Papillote

When the Brazilian balloonist Alberto Santos-Dumont visited New Orleans in 1901, Antoine's honored him with a dish made to look like a turn-of-the-century flying balloon— a dish that became one of Antoine's most famous creations. The fish is baked in a rich, wine-flavored shrimp sauce inside a closed envelope made of baking parchment. A marvelous aroma fills the room when the *papillote* (paper bag) is cut open at the table.

Shrimp   ¼ pound cooked, peeled, and deveined
Water   3 cups
Salt   1 teaspoon
Lemon slices   2
Bay leaf   1
Thyme leaves   ⅛ teaspoon crushed
Pompano fillets   6, about 2 pounds
Cooking oil   2 tablespoons

Butter or margarine   2 tablespoons
Green onions   ½ cup chopped
Garlic clove   1, minced
Flour   3 tablespoons
Salt   ¼ teaspoon
Egg yolks   2, slightly beaten
Dry white wine   3 tablespoons
Crab meat   1 6½-ounce can, drained, flaked, and cartilage removed

Chop shrimp. In 10-inch frying pan, add next 5 ingredients and bring to a boil; add pompano. Cover and simmer, very gently, for 10 minutes or until fish flakes easily. Carefully remove fish from stock and skin from fish. Strain and reserve 1½ cups of stock. Cut 6 10 by 12-inch pieces of parchment or brown paper into heart shapes; brush paper with oil. Place a fillet on one side of each paper heart. In saucepan, melt butter; add onion and garlic and cook until tender. Blend in flour and salt; add reserved stock gradually and cook, stirring constantly, until thickened. Stir a small amount of hot mixture into egg yolks; add yolks to saucepan. Continue stirring the mixture and heat, without boiling, until thickened. Stir in wine, crab meat, and shrimp; heat but do not boil. Spoon about ½ cup of sauce over each fillet. Fold uncovered half of each paper heart over fish and sauce to form individual cases. Seal, starting at the top of the heart, by turning edges up, folding them together, and twisting bottom tip of heart to hold case closed. Place cases in shallow baking pan and bake at 400° for 10 to 15 minutes. To serve, cut cases open with an X-shaped slit and fold back points. Serves 6.

Florida Red Snapper

Red snapper fillets 2 pounds
Onion ¼ cup grated
Orange juice 2 tablespoons
Lemon juice 2 tablespoons

Orange rind 2 teaspoons grated
Salt ½ teaspoon
Nutmeg ⅛ teaspoon
Pepper ⅛ teaspoon

Cut snapper into 6 portions and place in single layer, skin side down, in well-greased 8 by 12-inch baking dish. Combine next 5 ingredients; pour over fish. Cover and place in refrigerator to marinate for 30 minutes. Sprinkle fish with nutmeg and pepper. Bake at 350° for 25 to 30 minutes or until fish flakes easily. Serves 6.

Red Snapper with Vegetable Sauce

Red snapper fillets 2 pounds
Olive oil 2 tablespoons
Onion ½ cup chopped
Celery ¼ cup chopped
Green pepper ¼ cup chopped
Carrot ¼ cup chopped
Parsley 1 tablespoon chopped
Garlic clove 1, minced

Tomato sauce with tomato bits
  1 15-ounce can
Pale dry sherry ½ cup
Dillweed 1 teaspoon
Salt ½ teaspoon
Pepper ⅛ teaspoon
Lemon juice 1 tablespoon

Cut fillets into 6 portions. In saucepan, combine next 7 ingredients; cover and cook until tender. Stir in tomato sauce, sherry, and dillweed; bring to boil and simmer for 10 minutes. Ladle about ½ cup vegetable sauce into an 8 by 12 by 2-inch baking dish. Place fish portions on sauce and sprinkle with salt, pepper, and lemon juice. Pour remaining sauce over fish. Bake at 400° for 20 to 25 minutes or until fish flakes easily. Serves 6.

Broiled Red Snapper

Red snapper fillets or steaks
  2 pounds
Peanut oil ½ cup
Lemon juice ¼ cup
Salt 2 teaspoons

Worcestershire sauce ½ teaspoon
Pepper pinch
Liquid pepper sauce 2 to 3 drops
Paprika garnish
Lemon slices garnish

Cut fish into serving-size pieces and place in well-greased broiler pan. Combine next 6 ingredients and baste fish with this sauce. Broil about 3 inches from source of heat for 5 minutes on each side or until fish flakes easily and is nicely browned. Sprinkle with paprika and garnish with lemon slices. Serves 6.

Snappy Snapper

Red snapper fillets 2 pounds skinned
Frozen orange juice concentrate
  ½ cup, thawed
Salad oil ¼ cup

Soy sauce ¼ cup
Cider vinegar ¼ cup
Salt ½ teaspoon
Parsley chopped

Cut fillets into 6 portions and place in single layer, skinned side up, in well-greased shallow 10 by 15-inch baking pan. Combine next 5 ingredients; brush fish with this sauce. Broil about 4 inches from source of heat for 5 minutes; turn fish carefully and brush with sauce. Broil 5 to 7 minutes longer or until fish is lightly browned and flakes easily. Sprinkle with parsley. Serves 6.

Spicy Snapper

Red snapper or other fish fillets
  2 pounds skinned
Tomato juice ⅔ cup
Vinegar 3 tablespoons

Salad oil 2 tablespoons
Old-fashioned French dressing
  mix 1 ⅝-ounce envelope

Cut fillets into serving-size portions and arrange in single layer in shallow dish. Combine remaining ingredients; blend well. Pour sauce over fish and let stand for 30 minutes, turning once. Remove fish and arrange on well-greased broiler pan. Broil about 4 inches from source of heat for 4 to 5 minutes; turn carefully and brush with marinade. Broil 4 minutes longer or until fish flakes easily. Serves 6.

Red Snapper Supreme

Large red snapper fillets 4
Salad oil 3 tablespoons
Salt 1 teaspoon
Pepper ¼ teaspoon
Butter ¼ cup

Water ¼ cup
Button mushrooms 1 6-ounce
  can, drained
Sherry ¼ cup
Lemon wedges garnish

Fry fillets in oil over medium heat until well browned on each side; add seasonings while frying. Transfer to a clean skillet in which the butter has been melted; add water and mushrooms. Simmer for 5 minutes; add sherry and simmer 5 minutes longer. Serve mushroom sauce over fillets and garnish with lemon wedges. Serves 4.

Baked Salmon

Salmon   1 3- to 4-pound dressed
Salt   1½ teaspoons
Vegetable oil   4 tablespoons

Bacon slices   3 (optional)
Lemon wedges

Wash and dry fish; sprinkle inside and out with salt. Place in foil-lined baking pan, brush with oil, and lay strips of bacon over salmon. Measure fish at its thickest part, and allow 10 minutes baking time for each inch of thickness. Bake at 425° and do not overcook. Do not turn fish, and if it seems dry during baking, baste with oil. Garnish with lemon and serve immediately. Serves 6.
Variation: Fish may be stuffed with a dressing, skewered closed, and then baked.

Creamy Salmon Bake

Salmon steaks   2 pounds
Onion   2 tablespoons grated
Dillweed   1¼ teaspoons
Salt   1 teaspoon

Pepper   pinch
Butter or margarine   1 tablespoon
Half-and-half   ¾ cup

Place steaks in single layer in well-buttered 8 by 12 by 2-inch baking dish. Sprinkle with onion, dillweed, salt, and pepper; dot with butter and add cream. Bake at 350° for 25 minutes or until steaks flake easily. Serves 6.
Variation: Ten minutes before fish is done, top with crushed potato chips, buttered dry bread crumbs, or grated cheddar cheese; bake final 10 minutes.

Crispy Baked Salmon Fillets

Evaporated milk   1 13-ounce can
Salt   1 teaspoon
Lemon juice   of 1 lemon
Salmon fillets   2 pounds

Cornflakes   2 cups crushed
Butter or margarine   2 tablespoons, melted

Combine milk, salt, and lemon juice. Cut salmon into 6 pieces and dip into milk; roll in cornflakes. Place fish in buttered shallow baking pan and sprinkle with butter. Bake at 400° for 20 minutes or until fish is nicely browned and flakes easily. Serves 6.

Elegant Baked Stuffed Salmon

Salmon   1 3- to 4-pound dressed
Salt   1½ teaspoons
Bread Stuffing (see Index)
Onion   ½ cup finely chopped
Carrot   ½ cup finely chopped

Celery   ½ cup finely chopped
Dry white wine   1 cup
Butter   ¼ cup, melted
Lemon juice or white wine
   2 tablespoons

Wash and dry fish; sprinkle inside and out with salt. Stuff with Bread Stuffing and close opening with skewers laced with string. Line a baking pan with buttered foil; put onion, carrot, and celery on foil. Place fish on vegetables and pour wine over it. Measure fish at the thickest part, and allow 10 minutes baking time for each inch of thickness. Bake at 425° and baste periodically with a mixture of butter and lemon juice. Serves 6.
Variation: This recipe can be prepared more simply by omitting the stuffing and serving the baked fish on a bed of rice and mushrooms.

Salmon Paysanne

Salmon steaks   2 pounds
Salt   ½ teaspoon
White pepper   ¼ teaspoon
Sliced mushrooms   1 4-ounce
   can, drained

Green onions   ½ cup sliced
Catsup   ¼ cup
Butter or margarine   2 tablespoons,
   melted
Liquid smoke   ½ teaspoon

Arrange steaks in buttered 8 by 12 by 2-inch baking dish; sprinkle with salt and pepper. Combine remaining ingredients; spread over salmon. Bake at 350° for 25 minutes or until fish flakes easily. Serves 6.

Salmon Piquant

Salmon fillet   1 1½ to 2 pounds,
   skin on
Salt   to taste
Medium onion   1, sliced
Lemon   1, sliced

Pickling spice   1 teaspoon
Garlic clove   1, finely chopped
Mayonnaise or salad dressing   ½ cup
Cucumber   1, sliced

Sprinkle salmon with salt. Cover the bottom of well-buttered deep 1½-quart casserole with onion, lemon, pickling spice, and garlic. Place salmon, skin side up, over seasonings. Cover casserole tightly; bake at 350° for 1 hour. Chill salmon in covered casserole. Place fish on serving platter and remove skin carefully. Garnish with mayonniase and cucumber. Serves 6.

Salmon-Potato au Gratin

Salmon 1 2-pound piece, dressed
Salt 1 teaspoon
Pepper ⅛ teaspoon
Butter ⅓ cup
Flour ⅓ cup
Milk 3 cups

Salt 1 teaspoon
Pepper ⅛ teaspoon
Potatoes 4 cups boiled,
   cold and diced
Cheddar cheese ½ cup grated
Bacon slices 4, fried and crumbled

Place salmon in shallow baking pan; sprinkle with salt and pepper. In saucepan, melt butter over low heat; gradually stir in flour. Add milk, a little at a time so the mixture remains smooth. Heat until slightly thickened; season. Add potatoes to sauce and arrange mixture around and over fish; sprinkle with cheese and bacon. Bake at 325° for 45 minutes or until fish flakes easily. Serves 6.

Salmon with Shrimp Stuffing and Sherried Sauce

Large salmon fillets 2, with skin,
   from whole fish
Salt 1½ teaspoons
Pepper ½ teaspoon

Shrimp Stuffing
Butter 4 tablespoons, melted
Bacon slices 3 (optional)
Sherried Sauce

Sprinkle cut side of salmon with salt and pepper. Place 1 fillet, skin side down, in a buttered shallow baking pan; spread Shrimp Stuffing on top. Place the other fillet, skin side up, over stuffing. Brush with butter or lay bacon over fish. Bake at 375° for 45 to 60 minutes or until fish flakes easily. Serve with Sherried Sauce. Serves 8.

Shrimp Stuffing and Sherried Sauce

Sliced mushrooms 1 2½-ounce jar
Water ⅓ cup
Evaporated milk ⅔ cup
Eggs 3, slightly beaten
Butter 4 tablespoons
Flour 4 tablespoons
Salt ½ teaspoon

Pepper ⅛ teaspoon
Shrimp 1 4½-ounce can, drained,
   rinsed, and chopped
Chives 1 tablespoon chopped
Dry sherry ⅓ cup
Water ¼ cup

Drain liquid from mushrooms into small bowl; add water, milk, and eggs. In saucepan, melt butter over low heat; gradually stir in flour and seasonings. Carefully add egg mixture, stirring constantly, and cook below the simmering point until it thickens; remove from heat. Combine ½ of this cream sauce with mushrooms, shrimp, and chives. This is Shrimp Stuffing. Add sherry and water to other ½ of cream sauce and heat just to simmering point. This is Sherried Sauce.

Broiled Salmon

Salmon   1 or ½, split and boned
Salt and pepper   to taste
Catsup   1 14-ounce bottle
Worcestershire sauce   ½ 5-ounce bottle

Garlic butter   1 cup, melted
Parsley   garnish
Lemon wedges   garnish

Line broiler pan with foil and place salmon, skin side down, on foil; season fish. Combine catsup, Worcestershire sauce, and garlic butter; brush fish with this sauce. Broil about 4 inches from source of heat for 20 minutes or until fish flakes easily. Baste several times and do not turn fish. Flesh will peel away from the skin when served. Garnish with parsley and lemon. Serves 8.
Variation: A slightly different sauce can be had by combining ½ 14-ounce bottle of catsup with 1 cup of melted butter and the juice of 1 lemon.

Dilled Salmon Steaks

Salmon steaks   4
Salt   1 teaspoon
Pepper   ¼ teaspoon
Corn oil   2 tablespoons
Lemon   1, sliced

Corn oil   2 tablespoons
Dillweed   ¼ teaspoon
Parsley   garnish
Lemon wedges   garnish

Season salmon with salt and pepper. Brush shallow baking pan with oil. Place lemon slices in pan, top with salmon and brush with remaining oil. Broil about 4 inches from source of heat for 10 minutes or until fish flakes easily. Do not turn fish during cooking. Carefully place salmon on heated platter; sprinkle with dillweed. Garnish with parsley and lemon and serve at once. Serves 4.

Salmon Kabobs

Salmon fillets   2 pounds
Catsup   1 cup
Brown sugar   ¼ cup
Salt   2 teaspoons

Liquid pepper sauce   8 drops
Salad oil   6 tablespoons
Vinegar   ¼ cup

Cut salmon into 1-inch cubes. Combine last 6 ingredients; pour over salmon and marinate for 1 to 2 hours. Remove salmon from sauce; thread skewers through fish. Lay across a baking dish and bake at 375° for about 20 minutes. Baste once with sauce during baking. Serves 6.

Superb Broiled Salmon Steaks

Salmon steaks 2 pounds
Salt 1 teaspoon
Pepper ½ teaspoon
Monosodium glutamate ¼ teaspoon
Parsley 2 teaspoons finely chopped

Butter ¼ cup, melted
Tarragon ¼ teaspoon
Lemon juice or Madeira 2 tablespoons
Parsley or watercress garnish
Lemon slices garnish

Wipe steaks with paper towel. Combine seasonings and parsley; sprinkle both sides of steaks with mixture. Preheat oven to 500°. Line broiler pan with aluminum foil; heat and brush liberally with butter. Place steaks on pan so they do not touch each other; sprinkle with tarragon and lemon juice. Broil 6 inches from source of heat for about 10 minutes. Do not turn steaks. Baste with remaining butter during broiling. Lift salmon from pan to heated platter; garnish with parsley and lemon. Serves 4.

Old Salt's Cooked Salmon

This is a favorite method of preparing salmon on commercial fishing boats.

Water 4 quarts
Salt ¾ cup

Salmon 3 to 4 pounds dressed

Bring water to a rolling boil in a 6- to 8-quart kettle. Add salt. This large amount of salt is necessary to seal in the juices, and the fish usually absorbs just enough of it to be seasoned just right. Leave skin on salmon, and tie the fish in a piece of cheesecloth. Lower gently into boiling water; cover. Quickly bring water back to a full boil. Maintaining this temperature, cook about 45 minutes. The salmon will not break apart, but do not overcook it. It is done when the cut end turns pink at the backbone and it flakes easily. This fish will be moist and juicy but, if served hot, it must be served immediately. Trying to keep it warm will dry it out. It is also excellent served cold with dressings or in salads. Serves 6 to 8.

Baked Shad

Shad are difficult to eat whole because they have many small bones, and they are so difficult to fillet that it takes an expert to bone them. Here is a cooking method which softens the bones so they become edible.

Shad 1 3- to 5-pound dressed
Salt 1 teaspoon
Pepper pinch

Butter 2 tablespoons, melted or
Bacon slices 3
Milk or tomato sauce or condensed cream of mushroom soup ½ cup

Leave shad whole or cut into pieces; season inside and out. Place large piece of heavy-duty aluminum foil in shallow baking pan; put fish on this and brush with butter or top with bacon. Pour milk onto fish and wrap securely in foil, making double fold to seal package tightly. Bake at 275° for 5 hours. Serves 6 to 8.

Crusty Baked Shad

Shad 1 3- to 5-pound dressed, head attached
Salt ½ teaspoon
Medium onion 1, chopped

Celery stalks 3, chopped
Salt ½ teaspoon
Pepper ⅛ teaspoon

Rub a brown (it must be brown) paper bag, which is 4 inches longer than fish, inside and out with vegetable oil. Sprinkle fish with salt. Combine onion, celery, salt, and pepper and stuff fish cavity, including head, with the mixture; skewer opening and lace closed with string. Place fish in paper bag and close bag by double- or triple-folding the end and securing with safety pin. Place bag on cookie sheet and bake at 225° for 5 hours. The bones will be edible and the fish crusty and brown when it is done. Serves 6 to 8.

Planked Shad

Shad 1 3 to 5 pounds, split and boned
Salt 1 teaspoon
Pepper ¼ teaspoon

Butter 4 tablespoons, melted
Potatoes cooked and mashed
Lemon wedges garnish

Oil a wooden plank and heat in 225° oven for 30 minutes before using. Wipe fish dry and season; place skin side down on plank and brush with butter. Broil 4 inches from source of heat for about 10 minutes. Encircle fish with mashed potatoes and broil 5 minutes longer or until fish flakes easily; do not turn fish. Garnish with lemon wedges and serve from the plank. Serves 6 to 10.

Tasty Shad

Shad   1 3 to 4 pounds, split and boned
Salt
Lemon juice   of 1 lemon

Sweet or dry wine   ½ cup
Bacon slices   6

Place fish, skin side down, in baking dish; salt fish lightly. Combine lemon juice and wine and brush some of it into fish. Place 3 bacon slices lengthwise on each half of fish and slowly pour remaining wine mixture over fish; marinate for at least 1 hour. Broil, without turning, about 4 inches from source of heat for 15 minutes or until fish flakes easily. Serve hot. Serves 6.

Smelt Amandine

Smelt   2 pounds dressed
Salt   ½ teaspoon
Pepper   ⅛ teaspoon
Butter   ¼ cup

Blanched slivered almonds
   2 tablespoons
Lemon juice   2 tablespoons

Arrange smelt in shallow baking pan and season. In small, heavy pan, melt butter, add almonds, and brown slightly; stir in lemon juice and pour over smelt. Bake at 450° for 10 minutes or until fish flakes easily. Serves 4.

Smelt au Gratin

Smelt   2 pounds dressed
Cooking oil   3 tablespoons
Bread   6 slices, toasted and buttered
Eggs   2, slightly beaten
Salt   1 teaspoon

Prepared mustard   1 teaspoon
Paprika   ½ teaspoon
Milk   ½ cup
Cheddar cheese   1 cup grated

In large frying pan, fry smelt in oil over medium heat until fish flakes easily; remove fins and bones. Trim crusts from toast and arrange 3 slices in bottom of buttered shallow baking pan. Cover toast with smelt; cover smelt with remaining toast. Combine next 5 ingredients and pour over toast; sprinkle with cheese. Place pan in larger shallow pan of hot water; bake at 350° for 30 minutes or until brown and firm. Serves 6.

Smelt, Italian Style

Smelt   2 pounds dressed
Spaghetti sauce with mushrooms
  1 cup

Oregano   ½ teaspoon
Mozzarella cheese   ¼ cup grated

Place smelt in single layer in shallow baking pan. Combine sauce and oregano; spoon sauce over smelt. Sprinkle with cheese and bake at 400° for 12 to 15 minutes. Serves 4 to 6.

Smelt Kabobs

Smelt fillets   1 pound
French dressing   2 tablespoons
Salt   ¼ teaspoon
Pepper   pinch

Bacon slices   12
Tomatoes   4, cut into wedges
Butter   ¼ cup, melted

Marinate smelt in French dressing and seasonings for 30 minutes. Cook bacon over medium heat for about 2 minutes; drain on absorbent paper and cut each slice in half. Roll fillets (which have been cut in half lengthwise) and put them on skewers alternately with tomato wedges and folded bacon pieces. Place skewers over a shallow baking pan and brush with butter. Bake at 400° for 10 to 12 minutes. Serves 4.

Broiled Smelt

Smelt   2 pounds dressed
Butter   4 tablespoons, melted

Lemon juice   1 tablespoon

Place smelt in single layer in buttered shallow baking pan and brush with butter and lemon juice. Broil about 4 inches from source of heat for 5 minutes on each side or until fish is browned and flakes easily. Serve with tartar sauce. Serves 4 to 6.

Deep-Fried Smelt

Smelt   2 pounds dressed
Salt   1½ teaspoons
Pepper   pinch
Pancake mix   1 cup
Yellow cornmeal   ¼ cup

Salt   ½ teaspoon
Milk   1¼ cups
Flour   ½ cup
Oil   for deep frying

Sprinkle smelt, inside and out, with salt and pepper. Combine pancake mix, cornmeal, and ½ teaspoon salt; add milk and stir only until blended. Roll fish in flour and dip in batter; place in single layer in fry basket. Fry in deep fat at 350° for 3 minutes or until nicely browned. Drain on absorbent paper and keep warm until served. Serves 6.

Pan-Fried Smelt

Flour ½ cup
Cornmeal ½ cup
Salt 1 tablespoon
Pepper ½ teaspoon

Smelt 2 pounds dressed
Water shallow bowlful
Cooking oil, butter, or
  margarine ¼ cup

Combine flour, cornmeal and seasonings. Dip smelt in water; coat with flour mixture. In heavy frying pan, fry fish in oil over medium heat for about 5 minutes on each side or until nicely browned. Serves 4.

Baked Fillet of Sole

Dairy sour cream 1 cup
Salt 1 teaspoon
Pepper ½ teaspoon
Paprika pinch
Potatoes 4 cups cooked and diced
Mushrooms 1 8-ounce can,
  drained and chopped

Butter 2 tablespoons
White wine ⅔ cup
Sole fillets 2 pounds
Lemon slices garnish
Parsley garnish

Combine sour cream and seasonings; set aside. Spread potatoes and mushrooms in shallow 10 by 15-inch baking dish; dot with butter and add wine. Spread ½ of sour cream over top. Arrange sole over sour cream; spread remaining sour cream over sole. Bake at 375° for 45 minutes or until fish flakes easily. Garnish with lemon and bits of parsley. Serves 4 to 5.

Baked Sole Casserole

Butter ¼ cup
Flour ¼ cup
Salt ½ teaspoon
Pepper pinch
Mushroom liquid plus water
  1½ cups
Lemon juice 3 tablespoons

Egg yolks 2, beaten
Mushrooms 1 4-ounce can, drained
Onion 2 teaspoons finely chopped
Green beans and carrots
  2 cups, cooked
Sole fillets 1 pound
Cracker crumbs 1 cup, buttered

In saucepan, melt butter and blend in flour and seasonings; gradually add liquid and lemon juice. Cook over low heat, stirring constantly, until sauce is smooth and thick. Add a little of the hot sauce to egg yolks; stir yolks into the sauce in pan. Add mushrooms and onion and remove from heat. Place beans and carrots in buttered 1½-quart casserole and cover with sole. Pour sauce over fish and top with cracker crumbs. Bake at 350° for 20 minutes or until fish flakes easily. Serves 3 to 4.

Fillet of Sole in Foil

Green onion 1 teaspoon chopped
Soft bread crumbs 1½ cups
Egg 1, well beaten
Butter 1 tablespoon, melted
Sole fillets 8, about 2 pounds·

Condensed asparagus soup ½ cup
Large mushroom caps 8 or
  canned equivalent
Butter 1 tablespoon

Combine onion, crumbs, egg, and butter; mix well. Spread mixture on fillets; roll them up and fasten with toothpick. Place each fillet on a buttered square of aluminum foil large enough to enclose fish. Spoon soup over fillets and top each with a mushroom cap; dot with butter. Fold foil around each fillet. Place foil packages on hot baking sheet and bake at 400° for 25 to 30 minutes. To serve, place packages on individual plates and open slightly to disclose contents. Serves 8.

Sole Classé

Butter 2 tablespoons
Sole fillets 2 pounds
Salt ½ teaspoon
Pepper ⅛ teaspoon
Green onions 4, thinly sliced
Parsley 1 teaspoon minced

Tarragon 1 teaspoon minced
Chervil 1 teaspoon minced
Soft bread crumbs 1 cup
Dry vermouth ⅓ cup
Butter 3 tablespoons

Melt butter in bottom of shallow 10 by 15-inch baking pan. Sprinkle fillets with salt and pepper and dip in butter. Spread onions and herbs in baking pan and place fish, in single layer, on top. Cover with bread crumbs. Sprinkle vermouth over crumbs and dot top with butter. Bake, uncovered, at 375° for 30 minutes or until crumbs are browned and fish flakes easily. Serves 4 to 6.

Heavenly Sole

Sole fillets 2 pounds skinned
Lemon juice 2 tablespoons
Parmesan cheese ½ cup grated
Butter or margarine ¼ cup, softened

Mayonnaise or salad dressing
  3 tablespoons
Green onion 3 tablespoons chopped
Salt ¼ teaspoon
Liquid pepper sauce 2 drops

Place fillets in single layer on well-buttered 10 by 16-inch bake-and-serve platter. Brush fillets with lemon juice and let stand for 10 minutes. Combine remaining 6 ingredients; set aside. Broil fillets, without turning, about 4 inches from source of heat for 6 to 8 minutes or until fish flakes easily. Remove from heat and spread with cheese mixture. Broil 2 to 3 minutes longer or until lightly browned. Serves 6.

Sturgeon Rollups

Thin sturgeon fillets 2 pounds
Salt 1 teaspoon
Pepper pinch
**Condensed cream of chicken or
  cream of mushroom soup**
  1 10¾-ounce can

Water ½ cup
Butter 1 tablespoon
Paprika garnish
Lemon wedges garnish

Cut fillets into 1-inch strips lengthwise and season. Roll strips and secure with toothpicks. Arrange rolls in well-buttered shallow baking pan. Combine soup and water; pour over fish. Bake at 350° for 30 minutes or until fish flakes easily. Remove from oven and dot with butter; garnish with paprika and lemon wedges. Serves 4 to 6.
Variation: If you are in a hurry, fillets can be left whole and laid flat in the baking pan.

Ginger-Broiled Sturgeon

Sturgeon steaks 6 1-inch thick
Dry white wine ¾ cup
Salad oil 3 tablespoons
Soy sauce 2 tablespoons
Instant minced onions 1½ teaspoons

Salt 1½ teaspoons
Powdered ginger ½ teaspoon
Prepared horseradish ½ teaspoon
  (optional)
Lemon wedges garnish

Place steaks in well-greased broiler pan. Combine next 7 ingredients; pour over fish. Broil about 4 inches from source of heat for 5 to 7 minutes; turn carefully. Baste fish with sauce from pan and broil 5 minutes longer or until fish flakes easily. Garnish with lemon wedges. Serves 6.

Trout à la Tangerine

Trout fillets 2 pounds skinned
Frozen tangerine juice concentrate
  ½ cup, thawed
Salt 1 teaspoon
Pepper pinch

Cereal or toasted dry bread crumbs 1½ cups
Butter or margarine ¼ cup
Tangerine Sauce

Cut fillets into 6 portions. Combine tangerine juice and seasonings. Dip fish in juice and roll in crumbs; arrange in a single layer in shallow baking dish. Dot fish with butter. Bake at 350° for 15 to 20 minutes or until fish flakes easily. Serve with Tangerine Sauce. Serves 6.

Tangerine Sauce

White wine vinegar 2 tablespoons
Sugar 1½ tablespoons
Chicken broth ½ cup
Frozen tangerine juice concentrate
  ¼ cup, thawed

Water ¼ cup
Tangerine peel 1 tablespoon
  finely chopped
Dry white wine ¼ cup
Cornstarch 1 tablespoon

Combine all ingredients in saucepan. Heat, stirring constantly, until sauce is thickened. Makes about 1⅓ cups.

Sea Trout Meunière

Sea trout fillets 2 pounds, skinned
Egg 1, beaten
Milk 2 tablespoons
Flour 1 cup
Salt 1 teaspoon

Cayenne ½ teaspoon
Oil for deep frying
Meunière Sauce or Amandine Sauce
Parsley chopped

Cut fillets into 6 portions. Combine egg and milk. Mix together flour and seasonings. Dip fish into egg mixture and roll in flour mixture; allow fillets to dry a few minutes. Place in single layer in fry basket; fry in deep fat at 350° for 3 to 5 minutes or until fish is well-browned and flakes easily. Drain on absorbent paper and keep warm while remaining fish is fried. To serve, place each portion on a separate heated plate, top with Meunière or Amandine Sauce and sprinkle with parsley. Serves 6.

Meunière Sauce

Butter or margarine ½ cup

Lemon juice 1 tablespoon

In small, heavy saucepan, melt butter over low heat; continue cooking until it turns light brown. Add lemon juice. Makes ½ cup.

Amandine Sauce

Butter or margarine ½ cup
Blanched almonds 1 cup sliced

Lemon juice 1 tablespoon

In heavy frying pan, melt butter over low heat. Add almonds and heat and stir until butter and almonds turn light brown. Add lemon juice. Makes about 1 cup.

Ahi Baked Italian Style

Salt
Ahi (tuna) steak 1 pound
Olive oil 1 tablespoon
Tomatoes 1 cup drained and
   coarsely chopped
Garlic clove 1, chopped

Black pepper pinch
Oregano ¼ teaspoon
Thyme ¼ teaspoon
Rosemary pinch
Cayenne pinch (optional)
Olive oil 1 tablespoon

Salt fish lightly and let stand 20 to 25 minutes. Rub shallow baking pan with olive oil and place fish in pan. Combine next 7 ingredients and spread over fish; drizzle remaining olive oil over the top. Bake at 350° for 60 minutes. Serve hot or cold with rice. Serves 4.

Baked Clams

Salad oil ½ cup
Salt 1 teaspoon
Onion 1 tablespoon chopped

Shucked clams 1 pint
Cheddar cheese ½ cup grated
Dry bread crumbs 1 cup

Combine oil, salt, and onion. Place clams in mixture for 1 minute; remove and drain. Roll clams in cheese and then bread crumbs. Arrange in single layer in a well-buttered shallow baking pan. Bake at 450° for 12 minutes or until crumbs are golden. Serves 4.

Fried Clams

Eggs 2, slightly beaten
Milk 2 tablespoons
Salt 2 teaspoons
Pepper pinch

Shucked clams 1 quart, drained
Dry bread crumbs 3 cups
Oil for deep frying

Combine eggs, milk, and seasonings; dip clams in egg mixture and roll in crumbs. Arrange in single layer in fry basket. Fry in deep fat at 350° for 1 to 2 minutes or until brown. Drain on absorbent paper and keep warm until all clams are fried. Serve with tartar sauce. Serves 6.

Steamed Clams

Salt   1½ cups
Cold water   3 gallons
Clams   4 dozen, in shell and scrubbed

Boiling water   2 cups
Butter   ½ cup, melted

Combine ½ cup of salt and 1 gallon of water; let clams stand in this for 15 minutes. Drain. Repeat process 2 times with remaining cold water and salt. Place clams in large kettle, add boiling water, and cover. Steam over moderate heat for 8 to 10 minutes or until clams open. Strain liquor through cheesecloth to remove any sand. Serve hot clams with melted butter and clam liquor in cups. Serves 4 to 6.

1-2-3 Crab

Blue crab meat   1 pound
Butter or margarine   ½ cup, melted

Tarragon vinegar   1 tablespoon

Drain crab and remove any shell or cartilage; place in shallow 1-quart casserole. Combine butter and vinegar; pour over crab meat and mix lightly. Broil about 4 inches from source of heat for 12 to 15 minutes or until lightly browned. Serves 4.

Crawfish Newburg

Butter   2 tablespoons
Salt   ¼ teaspoon
Pepper   ¼ teaspoon
Onion powder   ¼ teaspoon
Mushrooms   1 cup coarsely chopped

Sherry or Madeira   ¼ cup
Egg yolks   3, slightly beaten
Whipping cream   1 cup
Crawfish meat   3 cups

In saucepan, melt butter and add seasonings and mushrooms; cook for 5 minutes. Add sherry and cook 3 minutes longer. Combine egg yolks and cream and beat well; add crawfish. Pour into mushroom mixture and stir gently. Continue stirring and cook, without boiling, for 2 minutes or until thickened. Serves 4 to 6.

Simple Crawfish Newburg

Butter ¼ cup
Flour ¼ cup
Salt ½ teaspoon
Pepper pinch
Milk 1½ cups

**Dry white wine or lemon
 juice** 2 tablespoons
Crawfish meat 2 cups*
Toast or patty shells 6 servings

Melt butter in top of double boiler and blend in flour, salt, and pepper; gradually add milk and cook, stirring constantly, until thickened. Add wine and crawfish and heat thoroughly. Serve immediately on toast. Serves 6.
*Lobster or crab meat may be substituted for crawfish.

Buttered Crawfish

Crawfish tails 3 cups shelled
Butter ¼ cup
Water 1 tablespoon
Salt ½ teaspoon

Pepper pinch
Dry mustard ¼ teaspoon
Lemon juice 1 teaspoon
Noodles or rice 4 servings

Steam crawfish in butter and water in tightly covered kettle for 5 minutes; shake pan occasionally. Sprinkle with salt, pepper, mustard, and lemon juice and serve over noodles. Serves 4.

Steamed Mussels

Live mussels 4 dozen, in shell
  and cleaned (see Introduction)
Salt 1½ teaspoons
Onion 1, sliced
Green pepper 1, sliced
Olive oil or salad oil ¼ cup

Dry white wine 1 cup
Bay leaf ½
Celery stalk 1
Liquid pepper sauce 2 to 3 drops
Butter 2 tablespoons

Place mussels in heavy, deep kettle; add next 7 ingredients and enough water to cover mussels. Cover kettle, place over high heat, and shake kettle for about 5 minutes; lower heat and continue to cook and shake for 5 minutes longer. Remove mussels from broth with slotted spoon; discard any that remain closed. Remove top shell of each, and arrange mussels in soup plates. Strain broth through several layers of cheesecloth to remove any sand. Add pepper sauce and butter to broth before pouring over mussels. Serves 4 to 6.

Stuffed Mussels

Mussels 2 pounds, 2 inches long, cleaned and steamed open
Fine dry bread crumbs 1½ cups
Parmesan cheese ½ cup grated
Garlic clove 1, minced

Parsley sprig 1, minced
Oregano ¼ teaspoon
Basil ¼ teaspoon
Olive oil or salad oil 2 tablespoons

Arrange a layer of mussels on the half-shell in a shallow baking pan. Mix remaining **7** ingredients and lightly spoon over the mussels — do not pack. If mixture seems dry, sprinkle with mussel broth. Bake at 375° for 8 to 10 minutes or until golden brown. Serve at once. Serves 4 to 6.

Festive Mussels

Mussels 36, 2 inches long, scrubbed
Dry wine ½ cup
Bay leaf 1
Thyme ½ teaspoon
Parsley ¼ teaspoon
Large onion 1, chopped
Butter 2 tablespoons

Flour 2 tablespoons
Lemon juice from 1 lemon
Salt and pepper to taste
Egg yolks 2, slightly beaten
Heavy cream 2 tablespoons
Parsley garnish

Place first 6 ingredients in a large kettle; cook, covered, over moderate heat for 7 to 10 minutes or until mussels open. Discard any unopened shells. Remove mussels from shells and place in covered dish to keep warm. In saucepan, melt butter and blend in flour; cook gently for about 2 minutes. Strain liquid from mussel kettle through several layers of cheesecloth; add to butter and flour gradually, stirring constantly. Add lemon juice and season; bring to a simmer. Combine egg yolks and cream; add a little hot mixture. Add egg mixture to hot mixture slowly; heat and stir gently only until hot and well blended. Pour over mussels, garnish with parsley, and serve at once. Serves 6.

Opulent Oysters

French fried onions 1 3-ounce can
Shucked oysters 1½ pints, drained
Half-and-half ¼ cup

Parmesan cheese 2 tablespoons grated
Butter or margarine 2 tablespoons

Spread ¾ of the onions in well-buttered round baking dish which is 8 inches in diameter and 2 inches deep. Cover with oysters; pour half-and-half over oysters. Combine remaining onions and cheese and sprinkle over top; dot with butter. Bake at 450° for 8 to 10 minutes or until oyster edges curl and top is lightly browned. Serves 4.

Oysters Casino

Bacon slices 8, diced
Onion ¼ cup chopped
Celery ¼ cup chopped
Green pepper ¼ cup chopped
Lemon juice 2 tablespoons

Salt 1 teaspoon
Worcestershire sauce 1 teaspoon
Liquid pepper sauce 4 drops
Pepper pinch
Shucked oysters 1 quart, drained

Partially fry bacon; add onion, celery, and green pepper and cook until tender. Add remaining ingredients; remove from heat. Arrange oysters in shallow baking dish and spread vegetable mixture over them. Bake at 400° for 10 to 12 minutes or until edges of oysters curl and topping is brown. Serve with toast points. Serves 6.

Pan-Roasted Oysters

Shucked oysters 1 pint, drained
Butter 2 tablespoons, melted
Salt ½ teaspoon

Pepper ⅛ teaspoon
Buttered toast

Arrange oysters in buttered shallow baking dish. Combine butter, salt, and pepper and pour over oysters. Bake at 400° for about 10 minutes or until edges begin to curl. Serve immediately on buttered toast. Serves 3 to 4.

Broiled Oysters on the Half Shell

Oysters 3 dozen in the shell*
Salt and pepper to taste

Butter or margarine 2 tablespoons, melted
Dry bread crumbs ½ cup

Shuck and drain oysters. Scrub deep half of shells thoroughly. Place an oyster on each shell and season. Combine butter and crumbs and sprinkle over oysters. Place shells on broiler pan. Broil about 3 inches from source of heat for 5 minutes or until edges curl and crumbs are brown. Serves 6.
*Clams are a good substitute.

Creamed Oysters and Eggs on Hot Biscuits

Margarine 1 tablespoon
Oysters 1 pint
Flour 1 tablespoon
Salt ½ teaspoon
Condensed cream of celery soup
   1 10¾-ounce can
Evaporated milk ½ cup

Eggs 2, hard-cooked and sliced
Mushroom stems and pieces
   1 2½-ounce can, drained
Pimiento 2 tablespoons diced (optional)
Parsley 2 teaspoons chopped
Large baking powder biscuits 4, hot

Melt margarine in saucepan; add oysters and cook slowly until edges curl. Remove oysters with slotted spoon to a hot covered dish to keep warm. Stir flour and salt into saucepan juices; add soup and milk and cook, stirring constantly, until sauce is smooth and hot. Add eggs, mushrooms, pimiento, parsley, and oysters; stir gently and heat thoroughly. Spoon over split biscuits. Serves 4.

Fried Oysters

Eggs 2, slightly beaten
Milk 2 tablespoons
Salt 1 teaspoon
Pepper ⅛ teaspoon
Shucked oysters 1 quart, drained

Dry bread or cracker crumbs
   or cornmeal 1 cup
Cooking oil ¼ cup
Lemon slices or tartar sauce

Combine eggs, milk, salt, and pepper; dip oysters in egg mixture and roll in crumbs. Fry oysters in oil over moderate heat until brown on both sides. Total cooking time will be about 5 minutes. Drain on absorbent paper and serve immediately with lemon. Serves 6.

Oysters Benedict Caper

White bread 6 slices
Canadian-style bacon 6 ounces, sliced
Shucked oysters 1½ pints

Caper Hollandaise Sauce hot
   (see Index)

Toast bread and place on warm serving platter or individual plates; keep warm. In 10-inch frying pan, fry bacon; drain on absorbent paper. Place bacon on toast. Pour oysters and their liquor into frying pan. Simmer for 3 to 5 minutes or until edges curl; remove oysters with slotted spoon and place on bacon. Pour Caper Hollandaise Sauce over oysters and serve immediately. Serves 6.

Baked Scallops

Scallops 1 pound, rinsed and dried
Dry bread crumbs 1 cup
Butter or margarine ¼ cup, melted

Worcestershire sauce 1 teaspoon
Lemon juice 1 tablespoon

Coat scallops with bread crumbs and arrange in shallow baking pan. Combine butter, Worcestershire sauce, and lemon juice; pour over scallops. Bake at 450° for 12 minutes. Serves 4.

Deviled Scallops

Scallops 1 pound, rinsed and dried
Garlic clove 1, chopped
Butter 2 tablespoons
Flour 2 tablespoons
Prepared horseradish 2 teaspoons
Dry mustard ½ teaspoon

Celery salt ½ teaspoon
Parsley 2 tablespoons chopped
Lemon juice 1 tablespoon
Pepper pinch
Dry crumbs ½ cup, buttered
Paprika garnish

If scallops are large, cut into halves crosswise. In saucepan, cook garlic in butter until golden; discard garlic. Add next 7 ingredients; add scallops and cook, stirring constantly, for 4 to 5 minutes. Arrange in 4 buttered shells or custard cups; top with crumbs and garnish with paprika. Bake at 350° for 20 minutes. Serves 4.

Scallops Baked in Shells

Scallops 1 pound, rinsed and dried
Salt and pepper to taste
Heavy cream 4 tablespoons

Fine dry bread crumbs 4 teaspoons
Butter or margarine 4 teaspoons, melted

Place 4 or 5 scallops in each of 4 buttered scallop shells or custard cups; season with salt and pepper. Add 1 tablespoon of cream to each shell; top each with 1 teaspoon of crumbs and 1 teaspoon of butter. Bake at 450° for 15 minutes. Serves 4.

Scallop Casserole

Scallops 1 pound, rinsed and dried
Condensed cream of mushroom soup 1 10¾-ounce can

Fine dry bread crumbs ¼ cup, buttered

If scallops are large, cut into halves crosswise. In buttered 1½-quart casserole, stir soup until smooth. Mix in scallops and top with crumbs. Bake at 450° for 20 minutes or until bubbling. Serves 4.

French-Fried Scallops

Scallops 2 pounds, rinsed
 and dried
Eggs 2, beaten
Milk 2 tablespoons

Salt 1 teaspoon
Pepper pinch
Dry bread crumbs 1 cup
Oil for deep frying

If scallops are large, cut into halves crosswise. Combine eggs, milk, salt, and pepper. Roll scallops in crumbs, dip in egg mixture, and roll again in crumbs. Place in single layer in fry basket and fry in deep fat at 375° for 2 to 5 minutes or until golden. Drain on absorbent paper and serve hot with catsup, tartar sauce, or lemon. Serves 6 to 8.

Skillet Scallops

Scallops 2 pounds, rinsed and dried
Butter or margarine ¼ cup
Frozen pea pods 1 6-ounce
 package, thawed and drained
Tomatoes 2, cut into eighths
Water ¼ cup
Cornstarch 2 tablespoons

Soy sauce 1 tablespoon
Salt ½ teaspoon
Pepper ⅛ teaspoon
Rice 3 cups cooked and hot,
 molded into a ring
Soy sauce

Cut large scallops into halves crosswise. Melt butter in a 10-inch frying pan; add scallops and cook over low heat for 3 to 4 minutes, stirring frequently. Add pea pods and tomatoes. Combine next 5 ingredients; add to scallop mixture and cook, stirring until thick. Serve in rice ring accompanied by soy sauce. Serves 6.

Baked Shrimp

Shrimp 5 to 6 cups, cooked
 and cleaned
Butter ½ cup
Onion 1 tablespoon minced
Parsley ¼ cup chopped

Paprika ¼ teaspoon
Cayenne pinch
Sherry ⅔ cup
Soft bread crumbs 2 cups

Place shrimp in shallow 7 by 11-inch baking pan. In saucepan, melt butter and add next 5 ingredients; simmer until onion is tender. Add bread crumbs to mixture and toss together; spoon over shrimp. Bake at 325° for 20 to 25 minutes or until crumbs brown. Serves 6.

Shellfish Kabobs

**Large shrimp or shucked clams
  or oysters** 1 pint
Bacon slices 6, cut in squares
Tomatoes 2, cut in wedges or
  Mild onions 2, cut in wedges or
  Green peppers 2, cut in cubes

Salt ½ teaspoon
Pepper pinch
Butter 3 tablespoons, melted

Arrange shellfish, bacon, and vegetables alternately on skewers. Combine seasonings and butter. Place skewers on buttered broiler pan and brush kabobs with butter. Broil 3 inches from source of heat for 5 minutes; turn. Brush with butter and broil 3 to 5 minutes longer. Serves 3.

Variations: Fish fillets may be used in place of shellfish. Cut fillets into 1 by 4-inch strips and sprinkle with salt and pepper. Roll strips before arranging on skewers. Use French dressing instead of butter for an easy basting sauce.

Cantonese Shrimp and Beans

Chicken stock base 1½ teaspoons
Boiling water 1 cup
Raw shrimp 1½ pounds
  peeled and deveined
Green onion ¼ cup thinly sliced
Garlic clove 1, crushed
Salad oil 1 tablespoon
Salt 1 teaspoon

Powdered ginger ½ teaspoon
Pepper pinch
Frozen cut green beans
  1 10-ounce package
Cornstarch 1 tablespoon
Cold water 1 tablespoon
Rice 6 servings

Dissolve stock base in boiling water. Sauté shrimp, green onion, and garlic in oil for 3 minutes, stirring frequently. If necessary, add a little chicken stock to prevent sticking. Stir in seasonings, green beans, and stock; cover and simmer 5 minutes longer or until beans are cooked but still slightly crisp. Combine cornstarch and water; add to shrimp mixture and cook, stirring constantly, until thick and clear. Serve over rice. Serves 6.

French-Fried Shrimp

Shrimp   2 pounds in shells
Flour   1 cup sifted
Salt   ½ teaspoon
Sugar   ½ teaspoon
Egg   1, slightly beaten

Salad oil   2 tablespoons
Ice water   1 cup
Oil   for deep frying
Lemon wedges or tartar sauce

Peel shell from shrimp, leaving last section of tail intact, and remove sand vein. To butterfly shrimp, cut ¾ of the way through the meat along the back and open and flatten. Combine flour, salt, and sugar. Combine egg, oil, and water; add to dry ingredients and beat well. Dip shrimp into batter and place in single layer in fry basket. Fry in deep fat at 375° for 3 to 5 minutes or until brown. Drain on absorbent paper and serve at once with lemon. Serves 4.

Savannah Stuffed Shrimp

Raw jumbo shrimp   2 pounds in shells
Salt   ¼ teaspoon
Butter or margarine   2 tablespoons
Onion   ¼ cup finely chopped
Green onions   2 tablespoons
  finely chopped
Celery   2 tablespoons finely chopped
Green pepper   2 tablespoons
  finely chopped
Parsley   1 tablespoon chopped

Garlic clove   1, minced
Crab meat   1 6½-ounce can, drained,
  flaked, and cartilage removed
Salt   ½ teaspoon
Cayenne   ¼ teaspoon
Eggs   2, beaten
Evaporated milk   1 5⅓-ounce can
Flour   1 cup
Soft white bread crumbs   3 cups
Oil   for deep frying

Peel shrimp, leaving last sections of tails intact. Devein, rinse, and dry on absorbent paper. To butterfly shrimp, cut along their outside curve about ¾ of the way through the meat, then carefully flatten them. Sprinkle with salt. In small saucepan, melt butter and add next 6 ingredients; cover and cook over low heat for 5 minutes or until tender. Remove from heat and stir in crab meat, salt, and cayenne. Pack stuffing mixture in a band down the center of each shrimp, dividing it equally among them. The shrimp should contract enough to hold the stuffing. Combine eggs and milk in shallow bowl. Place flour and bread crumbs in separate pie plates. One at a time, roll the shrimp in flour to coat evenly, dip into egg mixture, and then roll in crumbs. Arrange shrimp on baking sheet and refrigerate 1 hour to firm coating. Arrange 5 to 6 shrimp in single layer in fry basket. Fry in deep fat at 350° for 3 to 5 minutes or until golden brown. Drain on absorbent paper and keep warm in oven while remaining shrimp are being cooked. Serves 6.

Shrimp à la King

Sliced mushrooms 1 4-ounce can, drained
Green pepper 3 tablespoons chopped
Butter or oil 3 tablespoons
Flour 3 tablespoons
Salt ¼ teaspoon
Cayenne pinch

Milk 1½ cups
Pimiento 2 tablespoons chopped
Shrimp 3 4½-ounce cans, drained and rinsed
Patty shells, toast cups, or corn bread 6 servings

Sauté mushrooms and green pepper in butter until tender. Blend in flour and seasonings; add milk gradually and cook, stirring constantly, until thick. Add pimiento and shrimp and heat thoroughly. Serve in patty shells. Serves 6.

Shrimp Étouffé

Butter or margarine ¼ cup
Flour 3 tablespoons
Onion 1 cup chopped
Celery ½ cup chopped
Green pepper ¼ cup chopped
Green onion 2 tablespoons chopped
Parsley 2 tablespoons chopped
Garlic clove 1, minced

Water ½ cup
Lemon juice 1 tablespoon
Salt ¼ teaspoon
Cayenne ¼ teaspoon
Raw shrimp 3 pounds peeled and deveined
Rice 3 cups cooked

In 10-inch frying pan, melt butter and blend in flour; add next 6 ingredients. Cover and cook 5 minutes or until vegetables are tender. Gradually add water, stirring constantly. Stir in lemon juice, salt, and cayenne; push vegetables to one side of pan. Add shrimp to pan and spoon vegetables over them. Cover and simmer for 5 minutes or until shrimp are pink and tender. Serve over rice. Serves 6.

Shrimp Hurry-Curry

Butter or margarine 2 tablespoons
Raw shrimp 1½ pounds peeled and deveined
Condensed cream of shrimp soup 1 10¾-ounce can
Condensed cream of mushroom soup 1 10¾-ounce can

Dairy sour cream ¾ cup
Curry powder 1½ teaspoons
Parsley 2 tablespoons chopped
Rice, toast points, or patty shells 6 servings

Melt butter in 10-inch frying pan. Add shrimp and cook over low heat for 3 to 5 minutes, stirring frequently; add soups and stir until thoroughly blended. Stir in sour cream, curry powder, and parsley. When very hot, serve over rice. Serves 6.

Shrimp Victoria

Onion   ¼ cup finely chopped
Butter or margarine   ¼ cup
Raw shrimp   1 pound peeled and deveined
Sliced mushrooms   1 4-ounce can, drained

Flour   1 tablespoon
Salt   ¼ teaspoon
Cayenne   pinch
Dairy sour cream   1 cup
Rice   6 servings

Sauté onion in butter until limp. Add shrimp and mushrooms; cover and cook about 10 minutes or until shrimp are pink. Sprinkle with flour and seasonings; stir and cook until well blended. Mix in sour cream and heat gently to a simmer, but do not allow to boil. Serve over rice. Serves 6.

Sweet-and-Sour Shrimp

Onion   ½ cup diced
Celery   1 cup diced
Green pepper   1 cup diced
Salad oil   ¼ cup
Flour   2 tablespoons
Tomato juice   1½ cups
Brown sugar   ⅓ cup

Salt   ½ teaspoon
Lemon juice   ¼ cup
Lemon rind   1 tablespoon grated
Shrimp   1½ pounds cooked and cleaned
Pineapple slices   1 8¼-ounce can, drained
Rice   6 servings

Sauté onion, celery, and green pepper in oil until tender but not brown; blend in flour. Add next 5 ingredients; cook and stir for 5 minutes. Add shrimp and pineapple; heat thoroughly and serve with rice. Serves 6.

Bread Stuffing

Onion   ¼ cup chopped
Celery   1 cup chopped
Butter or margarine   ⅓ cup
Day-old bread   4 cups cubed
Salt   1 teaspoon

Pepper   pinch
Thyme, savory, or poultry seasoning   1 teaspoon
Milk, fish stock, or water   2 tablespoons (optional)

Cook onion and celery in butter until tender. Combine with bread cubes and seasonings. If stuffing seems dry, moisten with milk. Makes enough to stuff a 4-pound fish, or about 4 cups.

Crab Stuffing

Onion 1 tablespoon minced
Celery 1 tablespoon finely chopped
Parsley 2 teaspoons chopped
Butter or margarine 2 tablespoons

Cracker crumbs ½ cup
Crab meat ½ pound, flaked
Egg 1, slightly beaten
Salt and pepper to taste

In saucepan, sauté onion, celery, and parsley in butter until tender but not brown. Remove from heat and add remaining ingredients. Put spoonfuls on white-fleshed fish steaks before baking. Makes enough for 4 steaks.

Green Stuffing

Small onion 1, minced
Frozen chopped spinach
  1 10-ounce package
Butter or margarine 1 tablespoon

Salt to taste
Egg 1, well beaten
Day-old bread crumbs
  about ½ cup

Add onion to spinach and cook as directed on package until tender. Drain and add butter and salt; cool. Blend in egg and enough crumbs to hold mixture together. Makes enough to stuff a 2-pound fish, or about 1½ cups.

Mushroom Stuffing

Onion ¼ cup minced
Celery ¼ cup minced
Butter or margarine ¼ cup
Mushrooms ¼ to ½ pound, sliced or
  Mushrooms 1 4-ounce can,
  drained and sliced

Parsley 1 tablespoon minced
Coarse cracker crumbs 2 cups
Poultry seasoning ¼ teaspoon
Salt to taste

In large skillet, sauté onion and celery in butter until golden; add mushrooms and cook 3 minutes longer. Add parsley, cracker crumbs, and seasonings; mix lightly. Makes enough to stuff a 4- to 6-pound fish.

Oyster or Clam Stuffing

Shucked oysters or clams   ½ cup
  chopped
Fine cracker crumbs   2 cups
Butter   2 tablespoons, melted
Salt   to taste

Pickle   2 teaspoons chopped
Lemon juice   2 tablespoons
**Water or oyster or clam
  liquor**   ½ cup

Combine ingredients in order listed; if stuffing seems dry, add more water. Makes enough to stuff a 3- to 4-pound fish.

Plain Stuffing

Dry bread crumbs   1 cup
Hot water   ½ cup
Butter   ¼ cup, melted
Salt   ¼ teaspoon

Onion   ¼, minced
Sage   ¼ teaspoon
Pepper   ⅛ teaspoon

Combine all ingredients. Use to stuff a small fish. Makes about 1 cup.

Raisin Stuffing

Butter   3 tablespoons, melted
Soft bread crumbs   3 cups
Boiling water   2 cups
Seedless raisins   ½ cup
Walnuts or pecans   ½ cup chopped

Egg   1, beaten
Salt   1 teaspoon
Pepper   ⅛ teaspoon
Marjoram   ½ teaspoon

Pour butter over crumbs and mix lightly. Pour boiling water over raisins and allow to stand for 5 minutes; drain. Combine raisins and remaining ingredients; mix with crumbs. Makes enough to stuff a 3- to 4-pound fish.

Casseroles, Omelets, and Soufflés

Crunchy Fish Noodle Bake

Fish fillets 1 pound
Mandarin orange segments
  1 11-ounce can
Condensed cream of mushroom soup
  1 10¾-ounce can

Celery 1 cup sliced
Onion ½ cup chopped
Salted peanuts ½ cup
Salt ½ teaspoon
Chow mein noodles 1 3-ounce can

Cut fish into 1-inch pieces. Drain orange segments, reserving ¼ cup syrup; set aside ¼ of the orange segments for garnish. Combine fish, orange segments, reserved syrup, soup, celery, onion, peanuts, salt, and ½ of the noodles. Spread mixture in shallow 1½-quart casserole and cover. Bake at 350° for about 30 minutes. Uncover, sprinkle with remaining noodles, and bake 10 minutes longer or until it is bubbly and fish flakes easily. Garnish with orange segments. Serves 4.

Fish and Rice Bake

Fish fillets 1 pound
Condensed cheddar cheese soup
  1 11-ounce can
Rice 2 cups cooked, hot
Egg 1, beaten

Oil or melted margarine 2 tablespoons
Lemon juice 1 tablespoon
Onion salt ½ teaspoon
Paprika garnish

Cut fish into 1-inch pieces. Combine soup, rice, and egg; mix well. Spread in an even layer in shallow 1½-quart casserole; top with fish pieces and sprinkle with oil, lemon juice, and onion salt. Cover casserole and bake at 350° for 30 minutes; uncover and bake 5 minutes longer or until hot and bubbly and fish flakes easily. Sprinkle with paprika. Serves 4.

Fish and Vegetable Dinner

Fish fillets 1 pound
Onion 1 cup chopped
Margarine or vegetable oil
  3 tablespoons
Flour 2 tablespoons
Salt 1 teaspoon

Pepper pinch
Evaporated milk 1 13-ounce can
Potatoes 2 cups cooked and sliced
Frozen peas and carrots
  1 10-ounce package, thawed
Paprika garnish

Cut fish into 1-inch pieces. In saucepan, cook onion in margarine until tender but not brown. Stir in flour, salt, and pepper. Add milk; cook over low heat, stirring constantly, until thick. Add potatoes and peas and carrots; heat until bubbly. Fold in fish. Pour into shallow 1½-quart casserole and cover. Bake at 350° for about 30 minutes. Uncover and bake 5 to 10 minutes longer or until mixture is bubbly and fish flakes easily. Sprinkle with paprika. Serves 4.

Fish Casserole au Gratin

Fish 4 cups cooked and flaked
Butter ¼ cup
Flour ¼ cup
Dry mustard ½ teaspoon

Salt 1 teaspoon
Milk 2¼ cups
Cheese 1 cup grated
Cracker crumbs 1 cup, buttered

In saucepan, melt butter and add flour, mustard, and salt; gradually stir in milk and cook until thick. Add cheese and stir until melted. In buttered 1½-quart casserole, arrange alternate layers of fish and sauce; top with crumbs. Bake at 350° for 20 to 30 minutes or until golden brown. Serves 6.

Fish Casserole Deluxe

Fish 1 cup cooked and flaked
Rice 1 cup cooked
Butter 2 tablespoons
Onion ¼ cup chopped
Green pepper 2 tablespoons diced

Condensed cream of mushroom soup
 1 10¾-ounce can
Milk ⅔ cup
Potato chips 2 cups coarsely crushed
Blanched almonds ⅓ cup

Combine fish and rice. Melt butter and cook onion and green pepper in it until soft. In saucepan, combine soup and milk and stir over low heat until smooth; add onion mixture. Place ½ the potato chips in a buttered 1½-quart casserole. Cover with alternate layers of fish and rice mixture and sauce. Top with remaining potato chips. Sprinkle with almonds. Bake at 350° for 20 to 30 minutes. Serves 4.

Fish Loaf

Lemon juice 1 tablespoon
Fish 2 cups cooked and flaked
Butter ¼ cup
Flour ½ cup
Milk 1 cup
Celery ½ cup chopped

Dry bread crumbs ½ cup
Parsley 1 tablespoon chopped
Onion 1 teaspoon minced
 (optional)
Salt ¾ teaspoon
Tomato sauce (optional)

Add lemon juice to fish. Melt butter, stir in flour, then milk, and cook until mixture is smooth and very thick; allow to cool. Combine paste, fish, and next 5 ingredients; blend thoroughly. Mold into a loaf and place on greased brown paper on a rack in an open roasting pan. Bake at 350° for about 45 minutes. Serve with tomato sauce, if desired. Serves 6.

Fish Pie with Cheese Biscuit Topping

Fish fillets 1 pound
Frozen mixed vegetables
  1 10-ounce package, broken apart
Condensed cream of celery soup
  1 10¾-ounce can

Milk ½ cup
Onion salt ½ teaspoon
Prepared biscuit mix 1 cup
American cheese ½ cup shredded
Milk ½ cup

Cut fish into 1-inch pieces. Combine vegetables, soup, milk, and onion salt in a 10-inch frying pan with heatproof handle; mix well and heat slowly for 5 minutes. Add fish and heat until bubbly. Combine biscuit mix, cheese, and remaining milk in bowl; stir to make a smooth dough. Spoon into 8 even mounds on hot mixture. Bake at 400° for 18 minutes or until brown and thoroughly cooked. Serves 4.

Fish Portions Stroganoff Casserole

Margarine or other fat
  2 tablespoons, melted
Lemon juice 1 tablespoon
Frozen breaded fish portions
  1 12-ounce package
Medium noodles 6 ounces,
  cooked and drained
Peas and carrots 1 8½-ounce can,
  drained or frozen equivalent

Condensed cream of chicken soup
  1 10¾-ounce can
Dairy sour cream ½ cup
Milk ½ cup
Worcestershire sauce 1 teaspoon
Onion or garlic salt ½ teaspoon
Pepper pinch

Drizzle margarine and lemon juice over fish portions; broil 10 minutes less than directed on package label. Combine remaining ingredients, mix well, and pour into a shallow 1½-quart casserole. Bake at 350° for 15 minutes, then top with fish portions and continue to bake for 10 minutes or until noodle mixture is hot and bubbling. Serves 4.

Fish Sticks with Jalapeño Corn Bread

Flour ¾ cup
Yellow cornmeal ½ cup
Baking powder 2 teaspoons
Sugar 2 teaspoons
Salt 1 teaspoon
Milk ⅓ cup
Eggs 2, beaten

Margarine or bacon drippings
  3 tablespoons, melted
Cream-style corn 1 8¾-ounce can
Canned jalapeño pepper
  2 tablespoons finely chopped
American cheese 1 cup grated
Frozen fish sticks
  1 10-ounce package

Combine first 5 dry ingredients in a mixing bowl. In another bowl, combine next 5 ingredients; add to dry ingredients and stir until just moistened. Fold in ½ of the cheese and spread into buttered shallow 1½-quart casserole. Push fish sticks into batter in rows along the sides of casserole. Sprinkle remaining cheese evenly over top. Bake at 425° for 25 minutes or until corn bread is done. Cut into wedges or squares. Serves 4.

Scalloped Fish

Butter 3 tablespoons
Flour 2 tablespoons
Salt 1 teaspoon
Milk 2 cups

Bread crumbs 2 cups
Butter 1 tablespoon, melted
Fish 2 cups cooked and flaked

In pan, melt butter and add flour and salt; gradually stir in milk and cook until thick. Combine bread crumbs and butter. In buttered 1½-quart baking dish, place a layer of fish, a layer of bread crumbs, and ⅓ of the white sauce. Repeat and top with a layer of bread crumbs. Bake at 375° for 20 minutes or until bubbly and golden brown. Serves 4.
Variation: Add a layer of sliced hard-cooked eggs before baking.

Cheesy Fish and Sauerkraut Skillet

Fish fillets 1 pound
Onion ½ cup chopped
Margarine or vegetable oil
  2 tablespoons
Sauerkraut 3½ cups, well drained
Water ½ cup

Caraway seed ½ teaspoon
Garlic salt ½ teaspoon
Cream cheese 1 3-ounce
  package, cubed
American cheese 2 slices,
  cut in strips

Cut fillets into 1-inch pieces. In 10-inch frying pan, cook onions in margarine until tender but not brown. Add sauerkraut, water, caraway seed, and garlic salt; cover and simmer 30 minutes or until flavors are well blended. Stir cream cheese into sauerkraut; top with fish pieces. Cover and simmer 10 minutes or until fish flakes easily. Top fish with strips of cheese and allow cheese to melt before serving. Serves 4.

Creole Fish with Rice

Fish fillets 1 pound
Onion 1 cup sliced
Celery 1 cup sliced
Margarine or vegetable oil
  2 tablespoons
Flour 1 tablespoon
Tomatoes 1 16-ounce can

Green pepper ½ cup chopped
  (optional)
Garlic salt 1 teaspoon
Chili powder ½ teaspoon
Pepper pinch
Rice 4 servings

Cut fillets into 1-inch pieces. In saucepan, cook onion and celery in margarine until onion is tender but not brown; stir in flour. Add next 5 ingredients; cover and simmer 20 minutes. Add fish and simmer, uncovered, 10 minutes longer or until fish flakes easily. Serve over rice. Serves 4.

Fish Fritters

Fish 2 cups cooked and flaked
Egg yolks 3, well beaten
Flour ¼ cup
Salt ½ teaspoon
Pepper to taste

Onion juice 2 teaspoons
Parsley 1 tablespoon minced
Egg whites 3, stiffly beaten
Oil for deep frying

Combine first 7 ingredients; fold in egg whites. Drop batter by tablespoonfuls into deep fat and fry at 380° until golden brown. Drain on absorbent paper. Serves 4.

Mexican Fish with Beans and Rice

Fish fillets 1 pound
Onion 1 cup chopped
Margarine or vegetable oil
    2 tablespoons
Flour 1 tablespoon
Salt ½ teaspoon
Pepper pinch

Tomatoes 1 16-ounce can
Brown sugar 2 tablespoons
Vinegar 2 tablespoons
Prepared mustard 1 teaspoon
Kidney beans 1 15-ounce can,
    drained
Rice 1½ cups cooked

Cut fish into 1-inch pieces. In saucepan, cook onion in margarine until tender but not brown. Stir in flour, salt, and pepper; add tomatoes, brown sugar, vinegar, and mustard and simmer, uncovered, for about 10 minutes, stirring frequently. Add fish and simmer another 10 minutes or until fish flakes easily. Stir kidney beans into rice; heat slowly until hot. Serve fish mixture over beans and rice. Serves 4.

Baked Cod

Butter 2 tablespoons
Flour 2 tablespoons
Tomato juice 1¼ cups
Onion 1 tablespoon chopped

Green pepper
    1 tablespoon chopped
Cod or other fish 2 cups,
    cooked and flaked
Dry bread crumbs ½ cup, buttered

Melt butter in skillet and gradually blend in flour; add tomato juice slowly, stirring constantly as it thickens. Add onion and green pepper, remove from heat, and stir in the fish. Pour into buttered 1½-quart casserole; top with bread crumbs. Bake at 400° for 15 minutes or until crumbs are well browned. Serves 4.

Tomato-Fish Casserole

Whole tomatoes 1 16-ounce can
Onion 2 tablespoons finely minced
Salt ½ teaspoon
Pepper pinch

Sugar 1 tablespoon
Cod or flounder fillets 1 pound
Parsley chopped
Butter 1 tablespoon

Pour tomatoes in shallow baking dish and sprinkle with onion, salt, pepper, and sugar. Place fish fillets on top of tomatoes and sprinkle with a little parsley. Cover and bake at 350° for 20 to 25 mintues or until fish flakes easily. Top with butter before serving. Serves 4.

Codfish Balls

Dried salt codfish   1 pound
Eggs   2, well beaten
Potatoes   2 cups cooked and mashed
Onion   2 tablespoons grated
Pepper   pinch

Parsley   2 tablespoons chopped
   (optional)
Flour
Oil   for deep frying

Soak fish overnight; drain. Simmer in water until tender; drain and flake. Add next 5 ingredients to fish and mix well. Form into small balls and roll in flour. Fry in deep fat at 375° for 3 to 5 minutes or until golden brown. Serves 6.
Variation: Use this mixture for fish cakes, too. Form cakes instead of balls, and fry in heavy pan in ⅛ inch of oil over moderate heat, turning once, until both sides are crusty and brown.

Codfish, Maine Style

Cod   2 cups cooked and flaked
Egg whites   2, hard-cooked
   and chopped
Paprika   ¼ teaspoon
Celery salt   pinch

Salt   ¼ teaspoon
Bacon strips   3, diced
Rice   2 cups, cooked hot
Egg yolks   2, hard cooked and diced
Parsley   garnish

Combine first 5 ingredients; set aside. Heat skillet and brown bacon. Add fish mixture and turn frequently to prevent burning. Pile rice on serving dish, top with hot fish mixture, and garnish with egg yolks and parsley. Serves 4 to 6.

Flounder Fish Loaf

Flounder   2 cups cooked and flaked
Salt   ½ teaspoon
Egg yolks   2, beaten
Cream of chicken soup   1 cup

Egg whites   2, stiffly beaten
Buttered bread crumbs or crushed
   potato chips   ½ cup

Combine fish, salt, egg yolks, and soup; fold in egg whites. Pour into buttered shallow baking dish and top with buttered crumbs. Bake at 350° for 20 to 30 minutes or until firm. Serves 4.

Flounder Croquettes

Flounder 2 cups cooked and flaked
Onion juice 1 teaspoon
Salt ½ teaspoon
Pepper ¼ teaspoon
Parsley 1 tablespoon chopped

Medium white sauce 1 cup
Cracker crumbs 1 cup
Egg 1, slightly beaten
Oil for deep frying

Mix first 6 ingredients well and chill thoroughly. Mold into croquettes, roll in cracker crumbs, dip into egg, and roll in crumbs again. Fry in deep fat at 375° for about 3 minutes or until golden brown. Makes 6 medium-size croquettes; serves 3.

Baked Halibut Loaf

Chicken bouillon cube 1
Boiling water ¾ cup
Halibut 2 cups cooked and flaked
Soft bread crumbs 1½ cups
Celery ½ cup chopped
Parsley 1 tablespoon chopped
Light cream ½ cup
Onion 1 teaspoon grated

Salt 1 teaspoon
Pepper pinch
Lemon juice 2 teaspoons
Eggs 2, beaten
**White Sauce with cheese or
  shrimp** (see Index) or
  **Condensed cream of
  mushroom soup**

Dissolve bouillon cube in boiling water; combine with next 10 ingredients and place in a well-buttered 5 by 9-inch loaf pan. Bake at 350° for 1 hour or until loaf is firm in center. Serve with sauce. Serves 6.

Curried Halibut Casserole

Noodles 1 8-ounce package, cooked
Halibut 2 cups cooked and flaked
Curry powder 1 teaspoon
Butter or margarine 2 tablespoons,
  melted

Milk ½ cup
Condensed cream of mushroom soup
  1 10¾-ounce can
Asparagus 1 15-ounce can, drained
Cheese 1 cup grated

Place noodles in well-buttered 2½-quart casserole; cover with fish. Combine curry powder, butter, milk, and soup; pour over fish. Arrange asparagus over casserole and sprinkle with cheese. Bake at 350° for 25 minutes or until brown. Serves 6.

Glorified Halibut Pudding

Eggs   3, well beaten
Milk   4 cups, scalded
Halibut   1 cup cooked and flaked
Rice   2 cups cooked
Butter or margarine   ½ cup, melted

Sugar   1 tablespoon
Salt   2 teaspoons
Pepper   ¼ teaspoon
Nutmeg   ½ teaspoon

Butter a 9-inch casserole. Combine first 8 ingredients and stir until well blended. Pour into casserole and sprinkle nutmeg on top. Set casserole in pan of hot water and bake at 350° for 1 hour or until set. Serves 6.

Halibut Fondue

Bread   8 slices, cubed
Halibut   3 cups cooked and flaked
Mayonnaise   ½ cup
Small onion   1, chopped
Celery   1 cup diced
Green pepper   ½, diced

Condensed cream of mushroom soup
   1 10¾-ounce can
Eggs   4, slightly beaten
Milk   3 cups
Sharp cheese   1 cup grated

Place half of bread cubes in buttered 9 by 13-inch baking dish. Combine next 6 ingredients; place on bread in pan and top with remaining bread cubes. Combine eggs and milk and pour over mixture in baking dish; sprinkle with cheese and mix lightly. Cover and let stand overnight in refrigerator. Bake at 325° for 1 hour and 15 minutes. Serves 8 to 10.

Halibut in Potato Nests

Halibut   2 cups cooked and flaked
Cheddar cheese   ½ cup grated
Lemon juice   1 tablespoon
Salt   ½ teaspoon

Potatoes   2 cups cooked
   and seasoned
Tomato slices   4
Cheddar cheese   ¼ cup grated

Combine fish with ½ cup cheese, lemon juice, and salt. In individual casseroles make 4 nests of mashed potatoes. Fill each nest with fish mixture, top with tomato, and sprinkle with cheese. Bake at 350° for 20 minutes or until cheese has browned. Serves 4.

Halibut-Potato Casserole

Halibut   2 pounds cooked and flaked
Worcestershire sauce   1 teaspoon
Onion   2 teaspoons chopped
Butter   2 tablespoons
Flour   2 tablespoons
Pepper   pinch

Salt   ½ teaspoon
Milk   1½ cups
Potatoes   3 to 4 cups
   cooked and mashed
Cheese   ¼ cup grated

Place halibut in buttered 2-quart casserole; sprinkle Worcestershire sauce and onion over it. In saucepan, melt butter and blend in flour and seasonings; gradually add milk, stirring constantly until smooth and thick. Pour over fish. Top with mashed potatoes and sprinkle with cheese. Bake at 375° for 25 minutes. Serves 6.

Quick Halibut Casserole

Halibut   2 cups cooked and flaked
Rice   2 cups cooked
Onion   ½ cup chopped
Green pepper   ¼ cup diced
Butter   2 tablespoons

Condensed tomato soup
   1 10¾-ounce can
Milk   ½ cup
Potato chips   2 cups coarsely crushed

Combine fish and rice. Sauté onion and green pepper in butter until tender; add to fish and rice and mix lightly. Blend soup with milk. Place ½ the potato chips in the bottom of a buttered 2-quart casserole. Cover with alternate layers of fish and sauce. Top with remaining potato chips. Bake at 350° for 25 to 30 minutes. Serves 6.

Halibut and Cheese Soufflé

Milk   1 cup, scalded
Soft bread crumbs   1 cup
American cheese   ½ cup grated
Halibut   1 cup cooked and flaked
Lemon juice   1 tablespoon

Pimiento   2 tablespoons chopped
Salt   ½ teaspoon
Egg yolks   3, well beaten
Egg whites   3, stiffly beaten

Combine milk, bread crumbs, and cheese; add fish, lemon juice, pimiento, and salt, and then the egg yolks. Fold egg whites into the mixture. Spoon lightly into a buttered 1½-quart casserole set in a pan of hot water. Bake at 325° for 40 minutes or until soufflé is set and golden brown. Serves 4.

Halibut-Carrot Soufflé

Butter 3 tablespoons
Flour 3 tablespoons
Salt 1 teaspoon
Pepper pinch
Milk 1 cup
Halibut 1 cup cooked and flaked

Lemon juice 1 tablespoon
Carrot ¼ cup finely grated
Parsley 1 tablespoon chopped
Egg yolks 3, beaten
Egg whites 3, stiffly beaten
  but not dry

Melt butter in saucepan; stir in flour and seasonings. Gradually add milk and cook, stirring constantly, until it has thickened; remove from heat. Add halibut, lemon juice, carrot, and parsley, and then the egg yolks. Fold in egg whites. Pour mixture into an ungreased 1½-quart casserole set in a pan of boiling water. Bake at 350° for 45 minutes or until set. Serve immediately. Serves 4.

Golden Halibut Bits

Halibut fillets or steaks 2 pounds
Pancake mix 1 cup

Beer ¾ cup*
Oil for deep frying

Cut halibut into 1½-inch pieces. Combine pancake mix and beer; dip halibut into beer batter. Fry, a single layer at a time, in deep fat at 375° for 4 to 5 minutes or until golden brown. Drain on absorbent paper and serve immediately with French fried potatoes. Serves 4 to 6.
*1 cup of milk and 1 well-beaten egg may be used instead of beer.

Halibut Cakes

Halibut fillets 3 pounds
Medium onion 1
Egg 1
Flour 3 tablespoons
Nutmeg ½ teaspoon
Mace ¼ teaspoon

Pepper ½ teaspoon
Evaporated milk 1 13-ounce can
Salt 1½ teaspoons
Shortening for frying
Browned Butter Sauce

Put halibut and onion through fine blade of food chopper 3 times. Using an electric mixer, beat the egg into the fish; then beat in flour, nutmeg, mace, and pepper. Gradually add milk, beating thoroughly. Mixture must be light and fluffy; beating time will be about 15 minutes. Stir in salt. Dip a small serving spoon in cold water, then into halibut mixture to scoop out cakes. In a Dutch oven, over moderate heat, fry cakes in 2 inches of hot shortening, until browned. Drain on absorbent paper and place in 2-quart casserole. Pour Browned Butter Sauce over cakes. Bake, covered, at 350° for about 30 minutes. Serves 8 to 10.

Browned Butter Sauce

Butter ½ cup
Flour ½ cup
Water 4 cups

Small onion 1, grated
Salt 2 teaspoons
Pepper ½ teaspoon

In heavy pan, melt butter over low heat. Add flour and brown to a light mahogany; remove from heat. Gradually add water, onion, and seasonings. Return to heat and cook, stirring constantly, until smooth and thickened. Makes about 4 cups.

Smoked Halibut Oriental

Smoked halibut 1 pound, boned, skinned, and flaked
Bean sprouts 1 16-ounce can, drained
Eggs 6, beaten

Green onion ¼ cup finely chopped
Pepper to taste
Foo Yung Sauce
Sesame seeds garnish

Combine first 5 ingredients. Pour ⅓ cup fish mixture into a hot, lightly greased Teflon pan; fry over moderate heat for 2 to 3 minutes on each side, until browned. Repeat until all the batter is used, keeping patties warm while others are cooking. To serve, pour Foo Yung Sauce over patties and sprinkle with sesame seeds. Serves 6.

Foo Yung Sauce

Chicken bouillon cubes 2
Sugar ½ teaspoon
Boiling water 2 cups

Cornstarch 2 tablespoons
Soy sauce 2 tablespoons

Dissolve bouillon cubes and sugar in boiling water. Combine cornstarch and soy sauce; add to bouillon and cook over low heat, stirring constantly, until thick and clear. Makes about 1⅔ cups.

Rockfish French Puff

Rockfish   2 cups cooked and mashed*
Salt and pepper   to taste
Onion juice   1 tablespoon
Liquid pepper sauce   2 drops
Parsley   1 teaspoon minced
Bread   6 slices, buttered and
   cut in cubes

American cheese   1 cup grated
Eggs   2, slightly beaten
Milk   1 cup
Sherry   ⅓ cup (optional)
Worcestershire sauce   1 teaspoon

Mix together first 5 ingredients. Arrange bread cubes, cheese, and fish mixture in alternate layers in buttered shallow baking dish, ending with a layer of bread cubes. Mix remaining ingredients, adding other seasonings if you wish. Pour over mixture in baking dish. Bake at 325° for 1 hour. Serves 3 to 4.
*Other firm, white-fleshed fish may be used in this recipe.

Rockfish Loaves

Rockfish   2 cups cooked and flaked
Cheese   ⅔ cup grated*
Eggs   2, beaten*
Butter   2 tablespoons, melted

Salt   1 teaspoon
Lemon juice   2 tablespoons
Cracker crumbs or crushed
   cornflakes   ½ cup

Combine first 6 ingredients. Shape into 6 loaves and roll in crumbs. Bake at 350° for 25 to 30 minutes or until brown. Serve plain or with a sauce. Serves 6.
*The cheese and eggs should hold this mixture together to form loaves, but you may add sufficient crumbs to assist in forming loaves, if desired.

Seafood Swifty

Onion   2 cups chopped
Butter or oil   ¼ cup
Rockfish fillets   2 pounds
Salt   1½ teaspoons
Pepper   ¼ teaspoon
Tomatoes   2, sliced

Lemon   1, sliced
Large bay leaf   1
Water   ¼ cup
Sugar   1 teaspoon
Cider vinegar   1 teaspoon

In a 10-inch frying pan, cook onion in butter until tender. While onion is cooking, cut fillets crosswise into strips about ½-inch wide. Arrange fish over onion and season. Cover fish with tomato and lemon slices; add bay leaf. Combine water, sugar, and vinegar; pour over fish mixture. Cover and simmer 10 to 15 minutes or until fish flakes easily. Serve with French bread. Serves 6.

Scrambled Herring Roe and Eggs

Vinegar 1 tablespoon
Salt 1 teaspoon
Herring roe ½ pound
Boiling water 2 cups
Eggs 6

Milk 6 tablespoons
Salt ½ teaspoon
Pepper pinch
Butter or margarine 2 tablespoons
Paprika garnish

Add vinegar, salt, and roe to boiling water in saucepan; simmer 15 minutes. Drain, remove skin, and mash roe. Combine eggs, milk, seasonings, and roe. In skillet, scramble mixture in butter over low heat. When eggs are firm, garnish with paprika and serve hot. Serves 4 to 6.

Baked Salmon Croquettes

Onion ½ cup chopped
Butter or margarine 2 tablespoons
Flour 2 tablespoons
Milk ½ cup
Rice 2 cups cooked
Egg 1, beaten
Cheese ½ cup grated
Salt ½ teaspoon

Pepper pinch
Salmon 1 15½-ounce can,
   drained and flaked
Cereal crumbs 1 cup
Vegetable oil ¼ cup
Spiced apple rings 6
Parsley chopped

Cook onion in butter until tender; blend in flour. Add milk gradually and cook until thick, stirring constantly. Add next 6 ingredients; chill several hours. Shape into 6 cones and roll in crumbs. Place cones on well-buttered 10 by 15 by 1-inch baking pan and pour oil over them. Bake at 500° for 10 to 15 minutes or until light brown. Remove from oven and place apple rings on baking pan. Bake 4 to 5 minutes longer or until apples are heated. Arrange croquettes and apple rings on warm serving platter and sprinkle with parsley. Serves 6.

Salmon Ring with Dill Sauce and Peas

Salmon 2 pounds
Water 4 cups
Salt 1 tablespoon
Pepper ¼ teaspoon
Parsley sprigs 3 or
  Dried parsley 1 teaspoon
Medium onion 1, sliced
Bay leaf 1
Celery stalks 2, chopped
White wine ½ cup or
  Lemon slices 2

Butter 3 tablespoons
Flour 3 tablespoons
Milk 1½ cups
Salt 1 teaspoon
Pepper pinch
Onion salt ¼ teaspoon
Eggs 3, beaten until thick
Dill Sauce
Green peas 2 cups cooked
  and hot

Place salmon in wire basket or poacher. Combine next 8 ingredients in large kettle; boil for 5 minutes. Lower heat; place basket of fish in broth and gently poach for about 30 minutes. When salmon flakes easily, remove from kettle and cool. Save fish stock for later use. Remove skin and bones and flake fish. Melt butter in saucepan; gradually add flour, stirring constantly. Stir in milk, a little at a time, and add seasonings. Simmer gently, stirring the sauce until thickened; remove from heat. In large bowl, combine flaked salmon, eggs, and white sauce; blend thoroughly and pour into buttered 5-cup ring mold. Set mold in pan of hot water and bake at 325° for 45 minutes or until set. While this is baking, prepare Dill Sauce. When thoroughly baked, fill the center of the fish ring with peas and serve with Dill Sauce. Serves 6.

Dill Sauce

Butter 2 tablespoons
Flour 2 tablespoons
Strained fish stock ½ cup
Milk ¾ cup

Dillweed 3 teaspoons chopped or
  Dried dillweed 1 teaspoon
Lemon juice 1 teaspoon
Salt ½ teaspoon
Pepper pinch

In saucepan, melt butter and gradually add flour, stirring constantly. Stir in fish stock and milk, a little at a time; add remaining ingredients. Simmer gently, stirring sauce until thickened.

Salmon-and-Chips Bake

Frozen French fries ½ of
  16-ounce package
Condensed cream of celery soup
  1 10¾-ounce can
Salmon 2 cups cooked or
  Salmon 1 15½-ounce can, drained

Bacon slices 8, cut in half
  and partially cooked
Cheese ¼ cup grated
Paprika garnish
Parsley sprigs garnish

Arrange French fries in buttered shallow baking pan. Pour soup over potatoes and arrange salmon chunks on top. Cover with bacon strips and spread with cheese. Bake at 350° for 25 minutes or until potatoes are done. Garnish with paprika and parsley. Serves 4.

Salmon Pudding, Norwegian Style

Salmon 1½ pounds dressed
Salt 2 teaspoons
Nutmeg ¼ teaspoon

Butter or margarine ¼ cup, melted
Milk 2 cups
Egg whites 2

Remove skin and bones from salmon; grind enough to make 2 cups. Place fish, salt, and nutmeg in large bowl and beat for 10 minutes with an electric beater; continue beating and add butter slowly. Beat egg whites into milk. Add milk ½ cup at a time, beating after each addition. Beat for 15 minutes. Place in a well-buttered 1½-quart casserole; place casserole in a shallow pan of hot water. Bake at 350° for 1½ hours or until pudding is set. Serve hot. Serves 6.

Salmon Roll

Salmon 2 cups cooked and flaked or
  Salmon 1 15½-ounce can, drained
Mayonnaise ¼ cup
Lemon juice 1 tablespoon
Parsley 2 tablespoons chopped
White pepper ¼ teaspoon
Onion 1 tablespoon minced or
  Onion powder ¼ teaspoon
Biscuit mix 2 cups

Parsley flakes 1 tablespoon
Parmesan cheese 1 tablespoon grated
Butter ¼ cup
Evaporated milk ⅓ cup
Water · ⅓ cup
Condensed cream of celery soup
  1 10¾-ounce can
Peas 1 8½-ounce can, with liquid

Combine first 6 ingredients; set aside. Stir together biscuit mix, parsley flakes, and cheese; cut in butter until mixture becomes coarse crumbs; add milk and water. Stir only until ingredients cling together. Knead gently about 10 times and roll into 10 by 15-inch rectangle. Spread with salmon mixture; roll up like jelly roll. Slash top to mark 8 servings. Bake on cookie sheet at 425° for 15 to 20 minutes. Combine soup and peas and heat to boiling. Serve with salmon roll. Serves 6.

Salmon Casserole

Salmon 1 15½-ounce can,
  reserve liquid
Butter 2 tablespoons
Flour 3 tablespoons

Condensed cream of mushroom soup
  1 10¾-ounce can
Potato chips 2 cups crushed
Butter 2 tablespoons

Drain salmon; take off skin and flake. In saucepan, melt butter and blend in flour; add soup, stirring constantly. When hot, remove from heat; add salmon plus the liquid and 1⅔ cups potato chips. Pour mixture into a buttered 2-quart casserole and top with remaining potato chips. Dot with butter. Bake at 375° for 25 minutes or until mixture is bubbling. Serves 4.

Jiffy Salmon Casserole

Salmon 1 cup cooked and
  flaked or canned equivalent
**Condensed cream of mushroom or
  cream of chicken soup**
  1 10¾-ounce can

**Milk or liquid from canned
  salmon** ¼ cup
Peas 1½ cups cooked
Potato chips 1 cup crushed

Butter a 1-quart casserole. Combine salmon, soup, milk, and peas; pour into casserole and top with potato chips. Bake at 350° for 35 minutes. Serve with rice or noodles. Serves 4.

Quickie Salmon Casserole

Salmon 1 15½-ounce can
Condensed chicken noodle soup
    1 10¾-ounce can
Condensed cream of mushroom soup
    1 10¾-ounce can

Evaporated milk 1 5⅓-ounce can
Chow mein noodles 1 3-ounce can
Cracker crumbs ½ cup, buttered

Combine first 5 ingredients and pour into buttered 2-quart casserole. Sprinkle with crumbs and bake at 350° for 30 minutes or until casserole is bubbling. Serves 4.

Salmon Amandine Casserole

Salmon 1 cup cooked and flaked
    or canned equivalent
Rice 1 cup cooked
Onion ¼ cup minced
Green pepper 1 tablespoon chopped
Butter or margarine 2 tablespoons

Condensed cream of mushroom soup
    1 10¾-ounce can
Milk ⅔ cup
Potato chips 2 cups crushed
Blanched almonds ⅓ cup sliced

Mix salmon with rice. Cook onion and green pepper in butter over low heat until tender; gently fold into salmon mixture. Blend soup with milk. Place ½ of potato chips in buttered 1½-quart casserole; cover with alternate layers of salmon and soup mixtures. Top with remaining potato chips and sprinkle with almonds. Bake, uncovered, at 350° for 30 minutes or until bubbling. Serves 4 to 6.

Salmon Casserole Surprise

Butter 3 tablespoons
Flour 3 tablespoons
Liquid from salmon plus
    milk 2 cups
Potatoes 4 cups cooked and sliced

Salmon 1 15½-ounce can,
    drained and flaked
Mayonnaise or salad dressing ½ cup
Cheddar cheese ½ cup grated
Prepared mustard 1 teaspoon
Worcestershire sauce 1 teaspoon

In saucepan, melt butter and blend in flour; add liquid gradually and cook until thick and smooth; stirring constantly. Arrange potatoes, salmon, and sauce in alternate layers in well-buttered 2-quart casserole. Combine remaining ingredients; spread over top of casserole. Bake at 375° for 30 minutes or until mixture is bubbling. Serves 6.

Salmon Casserole with Corn Bread Topping

Salmon 1 15½-ounce can,
  liquid reserved
**Condensed cream of mushroom
  soup** 1 10¾-ounce can
Frozen cut green beans
  1 10-ounce package, thawed
Corn muffin mix ½ 18-ounce package

Green pepper ¼ cup finely
  chopped (optional)
Dry mustard ¼ teaspoon
Egg 1, well beaten
Milk ½ of amount called for
  on muffin package

Distribute flaked salmon evenly over bottom of shallow 1½-quart casserole. Combine salmon liquid, soup, and green beans in saucepan; heat and pour over salmon. Combine muffin mix, green pepper, and mustard in mixing bowl. Blend egg and milk; stir into muffin mix. Spoon muffin mix in 8 even mounds onto hot soup mixture and bake at 400° for 20 minutes or until topping is thoroughly cooked. Serves 4.

Salmon Loaf

Salmon 2 cups cooked and flaked or
  Salmon 1 15½-ounce can, drained
Salt ½ teaspoon
Pepper pinch
Salmon liquid or milk ¼ cup
Celery ⅓ cup finely chopped

Onion 1 teaspoon minced
Eggs 2, well beaten
Fine cracker crumbs ½ cup
Parsley garnish
Lemon wedges garnish

Combine first 8 ingredients in order given. Mix well and pack into buttered small loaf pan. Bake at 350° for 45 minutes or until nicely browned and firm. Unmold, garnish with parsley and lemon and serve. Serves 4 to 6.

Salmon and Cooked-Egg Loaf

Butter or margarine ¼ cup
Flour ¼ cup
Milk 2 cups
Salt ½ teaspoon
Onion salt ½ teaspoon
Pepper ⅛ teaspoon

Salmon 1 15½-ounce can, with liquid
Soft bread crumbs 1½ cups
Eggs 2, hard-cooked and
  coarsely chopped
Ripe olives ½ cup chopped

In saucepan, melt butter and gradually stir in flour; remove from heat and stir in ½ cup of milk. Return to heat and gradually add remaining milk, stirring constantly until sauce has thickened. Remove from heat and add seasonings and flaked salmon plus liquid; stir, and add bread crumbs, eggs, and olives. Pour into buttered 2-quart casserole and bake at 350° for 25 minutes or until loaf is firm. Serves 6.

Tasty Salmon Loaf

Salmon 1 15½-ounce can, with liquid
Soft bread crumbs 1 cup
Onion 1 tablespoon minced
Parsley 2 teaspoons minced
Celery salt ½ teaspoon

Salt ½ teaspoon
Pepper ⅛ teaspoon
Butter 2 tablespoons, melted
Eggs 2, well beaten

Combine all ingredients; blend well. Pour into well-buttered small loaf pan. Bake at 350° for 30 minutes or until firm. May be served with a sauce. Serves 6.

Choose-Your-Own Seafood Pie

Butter or margarine ⅓ cup
Flour ⅓ cup
Salt ½ teaspoon
Liquid from fish plus milk or diluted mushroom soup 2 cups
Onion 2 tablespoons chopped
Carrots, peas, celery 1 cup, cooked, singly or in combination

Salmon 1 15½-ounce can, drained and flaked or
  Black cod, halibut, rockfish, shrimp, or crab 2 to 3 cups cooked or
  Shucked clams 1 pint
Pastry enough for double-crust pie or
  Potatoes 2 to 3 cups cooked and mashed

Melt butter and blend in flour and salt; add liquid gradually and cook, stirring constantly, until thick. Add onion, cooked vegetables, and seafood; blend thoroughly and remove from heat. Line a well-buttered 1½-quart casserole with ½ of pastry; fill with seafood mixture and top with remaining pastry. Cut slits in pastry and bake pie at 425° until crust is flaky and brown. Serves 6.
Variation: Place filling directly into the buttered casserole and top with pastry for a single-crust pie or 1 cup of mashed potatoes. Bake as directed in recipe.

Salmon Pie

Salmon 2 cups cooked and flaked or
  Salmon 1 15½-ounce can, drained
Milk plus salmon liquid 1 cup
Soft bread crumbs ½ cup
Onion 1 teaspoon grated

Salt ¼ teaspoon
Parsley ½ tablespoon chopped
Lemon juice 1 teaspoon
Garlic salt ½ teaspoon (optional)
Eggs 2, slightly beaten

Combine all ingredients in order given; stir well. Pour into buttered 8-inch pie pan. Bake at 350° for 45 minutes or until pie is firm in center. Serves 6.

Deep-Dish Salmon Pie

Condensed green pea soup
2 11¼-ounce cans
Salmon 1 15½-ounce can,
liquid reserved
Milk ⅔ cup
Small potatoes 1 16-ounce can,
drained

Small onions 1 16-ounce can, drained
Parsley ½ teaspoon minced
Pepper ⅛ teaspoon
Celery salt ¼ teaspoon
Flaky baking powder biscuits
1 7½-ounce package

In saucepan, mix soup, liquid from salmon, and milk; heat and stir until smooth. Add salmon and next 5 ingredients; heat until mixture begins to simmer, stirring constantly. Pour into 2-quart casserole; top with biscuits. Bake at 400° for 15 minutes or until biscuits are browned. Serves 4.

Salmon Custard Pie

Pie pastry enough for 1 9-inch crust
Salmon 2 cups cooked and flaked or
 Salmon 1 15½-ounce can, drained
Onion ¼ cup chopped
Butter or margarine 2 tablespoons
Parsley 1 tablespoon chopped

Eggs 4, slightly beaten
Half-and-half 1½ cups* or
 Milk and evaporated milk
 ¾ cup each
Salt ½ teaspoon
Pepper pinch

Line 9-inch pie pan with pie crust and make a high, fluted edge. Spread salmon in unbaked crust. Sauté onion in butter until tender; do not brown. Sprinkle onion and parsley over salmon. Combine eggs, half-and-half, and seasonings; pour over salmon. Bake at 350° for 35 minutes or until pie is firm in center. Serves 6.
*Canned salmon liquid may be substituted for part of the half-and-half.

Salmon-Rice Pie

Salmon 1 15½-ounce can,
drained and flaked
Salmon liquid ¼ cup
Rice 1 cup cooked
Lemon juice 1 tablespoon

Medium onion 1, grated
Celery stalks 2, chopped
Pastry mix 2 cups
Butter or margarine 2 tablespoons

Combine first 6 ingredients. Prepare pastry mix as directed on package; line shallow 1-quart casserole with half of pastry. Place fish mixture in casserole and dot with butter. Cover casserole with remaining pastry and score the top so steam can escape. Bake at 400° for 45 minutes or until crust is golden brown. Serves 6.
Variation: To make this Russian style, pour sour cream over the finished pie.

Salmon-Potato Pie

Potatoes 4 cups cooked and mashed
Butter ¼ cup, melted
Onion ½ cup finely chopped
Salt ¼ teaspoon
Pepper pinch

Poultry seasoning ¼ teaspoon
Salmon 2 cups cooked and flaked or
  Salmon 1 15½-ounce can,
  drained and flaked
Butter 1 tablespoon, melted

Combine first 6 ingredients; spread ½ of mixture in buttered 2-quart casserole. Cover with salmon. Cover salmon with remaining potato mixture and brush with melted butter. Bake at 400° for 25 minutes or until top is golden. Serves 4.

Variation: For a festive occasion, top the pie with pastry before baking. Flute the edges firmly around the casserole and cut a 3-inch X in the center of the pastry to allow the steam to escape. Fold the corners of the X back so the potatoes will brown where they are exposed. Bake until crust is nicely browned.

Salmon Turnovers

Biscuit mix 3 cups
Sliced mushrooms 2 2½-ounce jars,
  drained
Butter ¼ cup

Salmon 1 15½-ounce can,
  drained and flaked
Parsley 1 tablespoon chopped
Lemon juice 2 tablespoons

Prepare biscuit mix according to package directions. On lightly floured board, roll out dough to ¼-inch-thick rectangle; cut dough into 4-inch squares. Sauté mushrooms gently in butter for about 4 minutes; do not brown. Combine mushrooms and salmon and place about ¼ cup of this mixture on each square of dough; sprinkle each with parsley and lemon juice. Bring dough up around salmon and pinch edges together, leaving a little opening in center so steam can escape. Place on buttered baking sheet and bake at 350° for 20 minutes or until golden brown. Serve these hot with a warm sauce (see Index). Serves 4.

Salmon Soufflé

Butter 2 tablespoons
Flour 2 tablespoons
Salt ½ teaspoon
Milk 1 cup*
Mayonnaise ½ cup

Egg yolks 3, beaten until light
Salmon 1 cup cooked and flaked
  or canned equivalent
Egg whites 3, beaten stiff
  but not dry

Melt butter in saucepan; blend in flour and salt. Add milk gradually and cook until thickened, stirring constantly; remove from heat. Blend in mayonnaise; cool slightly. Fold in egg yolks, then salmon, and egg whites last. Combine gently, but thoroughly. Pour into unbuttered 1½-quart casserole; set in pan of hot water. Bake at 350° for 45 minutes or until soufflé is puffed and set. Do serve immediately; it will sag if kept waiting. Serves 4 or 5.
*Canned salmon liquid may be substituted for part of the milk.

Elaine's Salmon Soufflé

Butter or margarine 3 tablespoons
Flour 3 tablespoons
Evaporated milk 1 cup
Water ½ cup
Salt ¼ teaspoon

Egg yolks 4, slightly beaten
Salmon 2 cups cooked and flaked or
  Salmon 1 15½-ounce can, drained
Egg whites 4, stiffly beaten

Melt butter in saucepan over low heat and blend in flour. Gradually add milk and water, stirring constantly until thickened; add salt. Remove from heat and stir in egg yolks; return to heat and cook gently for 1 minute. Remove from heat and stir in salmon. Pour cooked mixture into egg whites and fold whites into it. Pour into buttered 2-quart casserole; set in pan of hot water. Bake at 350° for 45 minutes or until soufflé is set. Serve immediately. Serves 6.

Salmon Croquettes

Condensed cream of chicken soup
  1 10¾-ounce can
Salmon 2 cups cooked and flaked or
  Salmon 1 15½-ounce can,
  drained and flaked
Lemon juice 2 tablespoons
Onion 2 tablespoons finely chopped

Pepper pinch
Coarse cracker crumbs 1 cup
Milk ¼ cup
Egg 1, beaten
Fine cracker crumbs 1 cup
Oil for deep frying

Fold 1 cup of soup into salmon along with lemon juice, onion, pepper, and coarse crumbs; shape into 6 or 8 cones. Combine milk and egg. Roll each cone in fine crumbs, then the milk mixture, and again in crumbs. Fry in deep fat at 375° for 3 to 5 minutes or until golden brown; drain on absorbent paper. Heat remaining soup and serve as a sauce with croquettes. Serves 4.

Salmon Pancakes

Pancake mix 1 cup
Milk 1 cup
Egg 1, beaten
Salad oil 1 tablespoon

Salmon 1 7¾-ounce can,
  drained and flaked
White sauce (see Index) **or**
  dairy sour cream 1 cup*

Combine pancake mix, milk, egg, and salad oil; mix until smooth. Add ½ of salmon. Heat griddle, grease lightly, and fry spoonfuls of batter until each cake is brown on both sides. Heat white sauce and add remaining salmon; serve over hot pancakes. Serves 2 to 3.
*Any favorite sauce may be used, or sour cream mixed with remaining salmon.

Salmon Patties

Salmon 1 15½-ounce can with liquid
Soft bread crumbs 1 cup or
  Cracker crumbs 1 cup finely crushed
Egg 1, beaten

Salt ½ teaspoon
Pepper pinch
Onion 1 teaspoon minced
Butter or bacon fat 2 tablespoons

Combine first 6 ingredients and mix thoroughly. Pan fry in butter until nicely browned on each side and serve at once. Serves 4.
Variation: Serve these patties on hamburger buns garnished with tomato and bacon and you have salmonburgers.

Quick Salmon and Corn Dinner

Salmon 1 15½-ounce can, liquid
  drained and reserved
Elbow macaroni 3 cups cooked
  and well-drained
Cream-style corn 1 17-ounce can

Onion ½ cup chopped
Peas 1 8½-ounce can, drained
American cheese 2 slices
  cut in half diagonally

Flake salmon and set aside. In 10-inch frying pan, mix together macaroni, corn, onion, and salmon liquid; cover and simmer about 5 minutes. Fold in peas and salmon and heat thoroughly. Arrange cheese on top and allow to soften. Serves 4.

Salmon à la King

Butter or margarine 3 tablespoons
Flour ¼ cup
Salt ½ teaspoon
Pepper pinch
Nutmeg pinch
Salmon liquid plus milk 2 cups

Salmon 1 15½-ounce can, drained
  and flaked
Eggs 2, hard-cooked and chopped
Rice 3 cups cooked and hot or
  Bread 6 slices, toasted

In saucepan, melt butter and blend in flour and seasonings; add liquid gradually and cook until thick and smooth, stirring constantly. Add salmon and eggs and heat thoroughly. Serve over rice. Serves 6.

Salmon Jambalaya

Salmon 1 15½-ounce can, liquid
  reserved
Celery 1 cup sliced
Onion ½ cup chopped
**Margarine or bacon drippings or
  cooking oil** 2 tablespooons
Water 1½ cups
Tomatoes 1 16-ounce can

Rice ¾ cup
Chicken bouillon cube 1
Garlic salt 1 teaspoon
Salt ½ teaspoon
Pepper pinch
Bay leaf 1
Parsley ¼ cup chopped (optional)

Flake salmon and set aside. In saucepan, cook celery and onion in margarine until tender but not brown. Stir in salmon liquid and next 8 ingredients; cover and simmer 20 to 25 minutes or until rice is done. Remove bay leaf, fold in salmon and parsley, and heat thoroughly. Serves 4.
Variation: Substitute a 15-ounce can of mackerel for salmon. Drain mackerel, discard liquid, and increase the amount of water in the recipe to 2 cups.

Salmon Newburg

Butter or margarine 4 tablespoons
Flour 4 tablespoons
Milk 2 cups
Salmon 1½ cups cooked and
  coarsely flaked or canned equivalent
Egg yolks 2, slightly beaten

Salt ½ teaspoon
Pepper ⅛ teaspoon
Sherry ¼ cup
Liquid pepper sauce 2 drops
Rice, noodles, or toast 4 servings

In saucepan, melt butter and blend in flour; do not brown. Add milk gradually and cook over medium heat, stirring constantly, until slightly thickened and smooth; add fish. Remove from heat and slowly add egg yolks; return to heat and cook just below simmering for 2 or 3 minutes. Add seasonings. Just before serving, add sherry and pepper sauce. Serve over rice. Serves 4.

Individual Maine Sardine Pizzas

Butter or margarine 2 to 4 tablespoons
Hamburger buns 6
Maine sardines 3 3¾-ounce cans,
  drained and broken into large pieces
Catsup ¾ cup

Onion 1 tablespoon chopped
Oregano ¾ teaspoon
Garlic powder pinch
Cheese ½ cup grated

Spread butter on bun halves; place buns, butter side up, on 12 by 15-inch cookie sheet. Distribute sardines evenly over buns. Combine catsup, onion, oregano, and garlic powder; pour about 1 tablespoon of this mixture over each bun half. Sprinkle with cheese and bake at 450° for 8 minutes or until cheese melts and buns toast. Serve hot. Serves 6.

Saucy Sardine Rollups

Refrigerated crescent rolls
  1 8-ounce can

Maine sardines 2 4-ounce cans,
  drained
Mustard Sauce

Unroll crescent dough and separate into 8 triangles. Place a sardine on the wide end of each triangle and roll up; place rolls on unbuttered 10 by 15-inch baking sheet. Bake at 375° for 12 to 15 minutes or until rolls are golden brown. Serve with hot Mustard Sauce. Serves 6.

Mustard Sauce

Dairy sour cream ½ cup
Prepared mustard 1½ tablespoons
Butter or margarine 2 teaspoons

Parsley flakes ½ teaspoon
Salt ⅛ teaspoon

Combine all ingredients in saucepan. Heat, stirring occasionally, but do not boil. Makes about ⅔ cup.

Scalloped Shad Roe

Shad roe 2 pairs
Condensed cream of mushroom soup
  2 10¾-ounce cans
Milk ½ cup
Parsley 2 tablespoons chopped

Parmesan cheese ¼ cup grated
Salt 1 teaspoon
Pepper ⅛ teaspoon
Cracker crumbs ¼ cup, buttered

Wipe the shad roe dry and cut into cubes. In saucepan, combine and heat soup and milk; add roe, parsley, cheese, and seasonings, and mix gently so as not to break up the roe. Pour into shallow 1-quart casserole; sprinkle with crumbs. Bake at 425° for 10 to 15 minutes. Serves 4.

Sole and Egg Casserole

Butter 2 tablespoons
Flour 2 tablespoons
Salt ½ teaspoon
Pepper pinch
Milk 1 cup

Cornflakes 1 cup finely crushed
Sole 2 cups cooked and flaked
Egg 1, hard-cooked and chopped
Pimiento 1 tablespoon chopped
Butter 1 tablespoon

In saucepan, melt butter and blend in flour and seasonings; gradually add milk and cook, stirring constantly, until thick. Sprinkle ½ of cornflakes on bottom of buttered 1½-quart casserole. Arrange fish, egg, pimiento, and sauce in layers over cornflakes; top with remaining cornflakes. Dot with butter. Bake at 350° for 25 to 30 minutes or until bubbling. Serves 4.

Sole and Salmon Casserole

Salmon 1 15½-ounce can,
  liquid drained and reserved
**Sole or other white-fleshed fish
  fillets** 2 pounds
Day-old bread 4 cups cubed
Celery 2 cups sliced
Onion ½ cup finely chopped
Parsley ¼ cup chopped

Egg 1, beaten
Mayonnaise or salad dressing 1 cup
Lemon juice 2 tablespoons
Dry mustard 1 tablespoon
Worcestershire sauce 1 tablespoon
Parsley garnish
Lemon wedges garnish

Break up salmon and mix with sole, cut into 2-inch pieces, bread cubes, celery, onion, and parsley. In separate bowl, combine next 5 ingredients with salmon liquid. Fold the 2 mixtures together and pour into well-buttered 3-quart casserole. Bake at 350° for 45 to 60 minutes. Before serving, garnish with parsley and lemon. Serves 12 for lunch, 8 for dinner.

Sturgeon Casserole

Sturgeon fillets 1½ pounds
Minute rice 1 cup
Frozen peas 1 cup
Condensed cream of mushroom soup
  1 10¾-ounce can
Milk ¼ cup

Salt 1 teaspoon
Pepper ¼ teaspoon
Worcestershire sauce 1 tablespoon
Onion 1 teaspoon finely chopped
Paprika garnish

Cut fillets into 2-inch squares and arrange in shallow baking dish; set aside. Combine next 8 ingredients; cover fish with this mixture. Sprinkle lightly with paprika and bake at 350° for 30 minutes or until fish flakes easily. Serves 4.

Sturgeon and Chinese-Noodle Casserole

Sturgeon fillets 1 pound
Salt and pepper to taste
Chow mein noodles 1 5-ounce can
Green onions ½ cup chopped
Celery 1 cup chopped

Condensed cream of mushroom soup
  1 10¾-ounce can
Water ½ soup can
Cashews ½ cup

Cut fish into small chunks; season very lightly. Line bottom of buttered 1½-quart casserole with ⅔ of noodles; arrange fish on noodles. Combine next 5 ingredients and pour over fish; top with remaining noodles. Bake at 325° for 45 minutes. Serves 4.

Tomato-Tuna Casserole

Rice 1 cup cooked
Peas 1 cup cooked
Tuna 1 6½-ounce can,
  drained and flaked
Onion ¼ cup chopped
Butter 2 tablespoons
Flour 2 tablespoons

Milk 1 cup
Worcestershire sauce ½ teaspoon
Salt ½ teaspoon
Pepper pinch
Medium tomatoes 2, thinly sliced
Cheddar cheese ½ cup grated

Spread rice in bottom of buttered 1½-quart casserole; add peas and tuna in layers. Sauté onion in butter until tender; sprinkle with flour and gradually add milk. Stir constantly until thick. Add Worcestershire sauce, salt, and pepper; pour sauce over rice, tuna, and peas. Arrange tomatoes on top and sprinkle with cheese. Bake at 350° for 25 to 30 minutes. Serves 4.

Tuna and Corn Casserole

Onion ½ cup chopped
Green pepper ¼ cup chopped
Butter ¼ cup
Tuna 2 6½-ounce cans,
  drained and flaked
Macaroni 8 ounces, cooked

Cream-style corn 1 17-ounce can
Milk ¾ cup
Salt ¾ teaspoon
Pepper pinch
Paprika garnish

Cook onion and green pepper in butter until tender. Combine all ingredients except paprika; pour into well-buttered 2-quart casserole. Sprinkle with paprika. Bake at 350° for 50 minutes. Serves 6.

Tuna and Noodles, Italian Style

Tuna in oil   1 9¼-ounce can
Celery   1 cup sliced
Onion   ½ cup chopped
Tomatoes   1 16-ounce can
Tomato paste   1 6-ounce can
Water   ½ cup
Sugar   1 teaspoon

Garlic salt   1 teaspoon
Oregano   1 teaspoon
Sweet basil   ½ teaspoon
Medium noodles   4 ounces,
  cooked and drained
Parmesan cheese   ¼ cup grated

Pour tuna oil into saucepan and cook celery and onion in it until tender but not brown. Add next 7 ingredients and simmer, covered, for 30 minutes or until flavors are blended; remove from heat. Flake tuna and fold into sauce. Spread ½ of noodles over bottom of shallow 1½-quart casserole; top with ½ of tuna mixture and ½ of cheese. Repeat layers, using remaining ingredients. Bake at 350° for 30 minutes or until bubbling. Serves 4.

Tuna au Gratin

Condensed cream of mushroom soup
  1 10¾-ounce can
Milk   ¼ cup
Flour   2 tablespoons
Onion flakes   2 tablespoons
Frozen peas   1 10-ounce package,
  thawed and drained

Tuna   2 6½-ounce cans, drained
Pimiento   1 4-ounce can,
  drained and chopped
**9-inch pastry shell and
  scraps of pastry**   baked
American cheese   1 cup grated

Combine soup, milk, flour, and onion in saucepan; cook, stirring constantly, until thickened. Add peas, tuna, and pimiento; bring to boil and pour into pastry shell. Sprinkle with cheese. Crumble pastry scraps and sprinkle over cheese. Bake at 425° for 12 minutes or until mixture is thoroughly hot and cheese has melted. Serves 5 to 6.

Tuna Dinner Pie with Cheese Sauce

Onion   ½ cup chopped
Margarine or cooking oil
  2 tablespoons
Flour   2 tablespoons
Salt   ½ teaspoon
Pepper   pinch
Evaporated milk   1½ cups

Eggs   2, beaten slightly
9-inch pastry shell   unbaked
Tuna   2 6½-ounce cans,
  drained and flaked
Tomato slices   garnish (optional)
Cheese Sauce

In saucepan, cook onion in margarine until tender but not brown; blend in flour and seasonings. Gradually add milk and cook, stirring constantly, until thickened. Pour mixture very slowly over eggs, beating constantly; set aside. Bake pastry at 375° for 5 minutes; remove from oven and spread tuna on bottom. Pour egg mixture over tuna and return pie to oven. Bake for 25 minutes or until filling is set. Let stand 10 minutes before cutting into wedges. Garnish with tomato slices and serve with Cheese Sauce. Serves 4 to 6.

Cheese Sauce

Condensed cheddar cheese soup
  1 11-ounce can

Evaporated milk   ½ cup

In saucepan, combine soup and milk; heat, stirring until hot and smooth. Makes about 1¾ cups.

Vegetable-Tuna Casserole

Potatoes   1½ cups diced
Carrots   1½ cups diced
Onion   ½ cup chopped
Peas   1½ cups, cooked
Butter   ¼ cup
Flour   ¼ cup

Salt   1 teaspoon
Pepper   pinch
Milk   2 cups
Tuna   2 6½-ounce cans,
  drained and flaked
Soft bread crumbs   1 cup, buttered

Cook potatoes, carrots, and onion together in lightly salted water until tender; remove from heat and add peas. In saucepan, melt butter and blend in flour and seasonings; gradually add milk and stir constantly until thickened. Drain vegetables. Arrange alternate layers of tuna and vegetables in buttered 1½-quart casserole. Top with white sauce and sprinkle with bread crumbs. Bake at 350° for 25 to 30 minutes. Serves 6.

Texas Tuna

Tuna in oil 1 9¼-ounce can
Onion ¾ cup chopped
Celery ½ cup chopped (optional)
Catsup ¾ cup
Water ¾ cup
Sugar 1 tablespoon
Vinegar 1 tablespoon

Worcestershire sauce 1 tablespoon (optional)
Prepared mustard 1 teaspoon
Salt ¼ teaspoon
Pepper pinch
Rice, pasta, corn bread, or hamburger buns 4 servings

Drain oil from tuna into saucepan; cook onion and celery in it until tender but not brown. Add next 8 ingredients and simmer, uncovered, 10 minutes or until flavors are blended. Fold in tuna. When it is hot, serve over rice. Serves 4.

Tuna Newburg Rolls

Butter 3 tablespoons
Flour 4 tablespoons
Milk 1½ cups
Worcestershire sauce ½ teaspoon
Liquid pepper sauce 2 drops
Sherry 3 tablespoons (optional)
Lemon juice ½ teaspoon

Mushrooms 1 4-ounce can, drained (optional)
Tuna 1 6½-ounce can, drained and flaked*
Hard-crust rolls 4
Cheddar cheese 2 tablespoons grated
Paprika

In saucepan, melt butter and blend in flour; add milk gradually and cook, stirring constantly, until thick and smooth. Blend in next 6 ingredients; remove from heat. Cut off top of each roll and scoop out some of the inside bread. Pile fish mixture into each roll and sprinkle with cheese and paprika. Heat quickly under broiler and serve as soon as cheese is bubbling. Serves 4.

*Crab and salmon are tasty substitutes for tuna.

Tuna-Spaghetti Dinner

Onion   ½ cup chopped
Celery   2 tablespoons chopped
Cooking oil   ¼ cup
Garlic powder   pinch
Parsley   1 teaspoon minced
Salt   ½ teaspoon
Pepper   ¼ teaspoon
Paprika   ¼ teaspoon

Tomato sauce   ½ cup
Tuna   2 6½-ounce cans,
   drained and flaked
Sherry   ½ cup (optional)
Salt   3 tablespoons
Spaghetti   1 pound
Boiling water   4 quarts
Butter   2 tablespoons

In skillet, brown onion and celery in oil mixed with next 5 ingredients. Add tomato sauce and tuna, then sherry; simmer gently for 5 minutes. Add salt and spaghetti to boiling water; when spaghetti is tender but not soft, drain it well. Serve sauce over spaghetti and top with butter. Serves 4.

Tuna Taipei

Green onion   ½ cup chopped
Salad oil   ¼ cup
Rice   4 cups cooked
   without salt, cold
Soy sauce   3 tablespoons

Eggs   2, beaten
Water chestnuts   1 5-ounce can,
   drained and chopped
Tuna   2 6½-ounce cans,
   drained and flaked

In 10-inch frying pan, cook onion in oil over medium heat until tender. Add rice and soy sauce and stir over low heat until rice is hot; push rice to one side. Pour in eggs and cook, stirring frequently. Add water chestnuts and tuna; mix well and heat. Serves 6.

Clambursts

Shucked large clams   12
Butter   ¼ cup
Green onions   ½ cup chopped
Mushrooms   ½ pound, sliced
Ham   1 cup chopped

Flour   3 tablespoons
Monosodium glutamate   1 teaspoon
Cleaned clam shells   24 or
   Baking shells   18
Egg whites   6, stiffly beaten

Clean and chop clams. Melt butter in skillet over medium heat; add onions and mushrooms, sautéing until limp. Stir in clams, ham, flour, and monosodium glutamate; cook until thick, stirring constantly. Butter shells and fill with clam mixture; cover with egg whites and arrange on cookie sheet. Bake at 400° for 10 minutes or until lightly browned. Serves 6.

Clam-Corn Casserole

Clams 1 10-ounce can
Clam liquor plus milk 1 cup
Eggs 3, slightly beaten
Onion 1 tablespoon chopped
Pimiento 2 tablespoons chopped
Cream-style corn 1 cup

Salt ½ teaspoon
Cayenne a few grains
Butter or margarine 1 tablespoon, melted
Cracker crumbs ½ cup

Drain clams and reserve liquor. Rinse clams under cold water. Combine all ingredients and pour into buttered 1½-quart casserole. Bake at 350° for 1 hour or until firm. Serves 4 to 5.

Razor Clam Crumb Pie

Soft bread crumbs 2 cups
Onion 1 tablespoon grated
Celery salt ¼ teaspoon
Salt ½ teaspoon
Sage pinch
Pepper pinch
Butter or margarine ¼ cup, melted
Minced razor clams 1 7-ounce can
Butter or margarine 6 tablespoons

Flour 6 tablespoons
Clam liquor plus water 1 cup
Milk 1 cup
Salt ½ teaspoon
Pepper pinch
Celery salt ¼ teaspoon
Butter 2 tablespoons, melted
Dry bread crumbs ¼ cup

Combine first 7 ingredients; mix well. Press into an 8- or 9-inch pie pan and bake at 375° for 25 minutes or until brown. Drain clams and reserve liquor. In saucepan, melt butter and blend in flour; add liquor plus water and milk gradually and cook, stirring constantly, until thick and smooth. Add clams and seasonings; pour into baked crust. Combine butter and crumbs; sprinkle over top. Bake at 425° for 12 minutes or until brown. Serves 6.

Scalloped Clams

Shucked clams 1 pint
Cracker crumbs 2 cups
Salt ½ teaspoon
Pepper pinch

Butter or margarine ½ cup, softened
Worcestershire sauce ¼ teaspoon
Clam liquor plus milk 1 cup

Saving liquor, drain and chop clams. Combine crumbs, seasonings, and butter; spread ⅓ of mixture in bottom of buttered 1½-quart casserole. Add a layer of ½ of clams, a layer of another ⅓ of crumbs, and a layer of remaining clams. Add Worcestershire sauce to clam liquor and milk and pour into casserole; top with remaining crumbs. Bake at 350° for 30 minutes or until browned. Serves 4.

Clam-Corn Griddle Cakes

Flour 1½ cups sifted
Baking powder 2 teaspoons
Salt 1 teaspoon
Yellow cornmeal 1 cup
Clams 2 cups minced and drained

Clam liquor plus milk 1½ cups
Eggs 2, slightly beaten
Butter or other fat ⅓ cup, melted
Cran-Applesauce
Butter or margarine

Sift together flour, baking powder, and salt; stir in cornmeal. Combine clams, liquor plus milk, eggs, and butter; add to dry ingredients and stir only until blended. Drop batter in ¼-cup portions onto hot, well-greased griddle; fry 1 to 2 minutes. Turn carefully and fry other side for 1 to 2 minutes. Serve hot with Cran-Applesauce and butter. Serves 6.

Cran-Applesauce

Jellied cranberry sauce
 1 16-ounce can

Applesauce ½ cup
Cinnamon ¼ teaspoon

Combine all ingredients; blend thoroughly and chill. Makes 2½ cups.

Clam Fritters

Milk 1 cup
Clam liquor ½ cup
Eggs 2, slightly beaten
Flour 2 cups
Salt ½ teaspoon

Baking powder 2 teaspooons
Pepper pinch
Shucked clams 24, drained and
 chopped

Combine milk, clam liquor, and eggs. Sift together flour, salt, baking powder, and pepper; add liquid ingredients and mix well. Add clams. Drop batter by spoonfuls onto well-greased griddle and fry over moderate heat until golden brown on each side. Serves 6 to 8.

Clam Patties

Clams 1¼ cups minced and drained
Mashed potatoes 2 cups
Butter or margarine 2 tablespoons, melted
Salt ½ teaspoon

Pepper ¼ teaspoon
Lemon juice 1 tablespoon
Eggs 2, slightly beaten
Cooking oil 3 tablespoons

Combine first 7 ingredients and mix well; shape into 12 patties of equal size. In skillet, fry patties in hot oil over moderate heat until all are golden brown on both sides. Serves 6.

Razor Clam Croquettes

Razor clams 2 cups ground with liquor
Eggs 2, slightly beaten
Cracker crumbs 2 cups
Salt or garlic salt 1 teaspoon

Pepper pinch
Dry onion soup mix 2 tablespoons
Lemon juice 2 tablespoons
Flour 4 tablespoons sifted
Oil for deep frying

Combine first 8 ingredients and blend thoroughly; shape into 8 cones. Arrange in single layer in fry basket and fry in deep fat at 375° for 2 to 4 minutes or until golden. Drain on absorbent paper. Serves 4.

Clamghetti

Butter 2 tablespoons
Flour 4 tablespoons
Milk 1 cup
American cheese ¼ pound, cubed
Condensed cream of mushroom soup 1 10¾-ounce can

Sliced mushrooms 1 4-ounce can, drained
Chopped or minced clams 2 8-ounce cans, drained
Spaghetti 4 servings

In large saucepan, melt butter over medium heat; blend in flour. Add milk gradually and cook, stirring constantly, until mixture has thickened slightly. Add cheese and stir until melted; reduce heat and add soup, mushrooms, and clams. Simmer 10 minutes and serve over spaghetti. Serves 4.

Clam Fettucini

Margarine 2 tablespoons
Onion ½ cup chopped
Flour 3 tablespoons
Sugar 1 teaspoon
Oregano 1 teaspoon
Salt ½ teaspoon
Pepper pinch
Whole tomatoes 1 16-ounce can,
  undrained

Tomato sauce 1 8-ounce can
Minced clams 1 8-ounce can,
  undrained*
Ripe olives ¼ cup sliced
Noodles 4 cups cooked and hot
Margarine 2 tablespoons, softened
Parmesan cheese ¼ cup grated

In saucepan, melt margarine; add onion and cook until tender but not brown. Combine next 5 ingredients; stir into onion mixture. Add tomatoes, tomato sauce, clams, and olives and cook, stirring constantly, until mixture thickens; simmer briefly. Combine noodles, margarine, and cheese; toss until noodles are evenly coated with cheese. Turn into deep serving dish and pour sauce over top. Serves 4.
*You may substitute 2 6½-ounce cans of minced clams for the 8-ounce can, but 1 can should be drained to keep proportions correct.

Artichoke Crab

Dungeness crab meat 1 pound
Artichoke hearts 1 14-ounce can,
  drained and halved
Sliced mushrooms 1 4-ounce
  can, drained
Butter or margarine 2 tablespoons
Flour 2½ tablespoons

Salt ½ teaspoon
Cayenne pinch
Half-and-half 1 cup
Sherry 2 tablespoons
Cereal crumbs 2 tablespoons
Parmesan cheese 1 tablespoon grated
Paprika garnish

Drain crab and remove any shell or cartilage. Place artichokes in well-buttered shallow 1½-quart casserole; cover with mushrooms and crab meat. In saucepan, melt butter and blend in flour and seasonings; add half-and-half gradually and cook, stirring constantly, until thick. Stir in sherry and pour over crab. Combine crumbs and cheese and sprinkle over sauce. Garnish with paprika and bake at 450° for 12 to 15 minutes or until bubbling. Serves 4.

Crab Baked in Shells

Butter or margarine 4 tablespoons
Flour 4 tablespoons
Mushroom liquid plus water 1 cup
Milk 1 cup
Sherry 1 tablespoon
Soy sauce 1 teaspoon
Worcestershire sauce 1 teaspoon

Liquid pepper sauce 2 to 3 drops
Mushrooms 1 4-ounce can, liquid
  drained and reserved
Crab meat 2 cups flaked
Eggs 2, hard-cooked and chopped
Crab shells 6, well scrubbed
Dry bread crumbs ¼ cup, buttered

In large saucepan, melt butter and blend in flour; add mushroom liquid plus water and milk gradually and cook, stirring constantly, until thick and smooth. Add next 7 ingredients and pour mixture into shells; top with crumbs. Bake at 350° for 10 minutes or until golden brown. Serves 6.

Crab Casserole

Crab meat 1 pound
**Condensed cream of celery, chicken,
  or mushroom soup** 1 10¾-ounce
  can
Whole-kernel corn 1 17-ounce
  can, drained

Peas 1 17-ounce can, drained
Mushrooms 1 4-ounce can, with liquid
Pimientos 1 2-ounce can
Pepper to taste
Dry bread crumbs buttered

Combine first 7 ingredients. Pour into buttered casserole; cover with crumbs. Bake at 350° for 40 minutes. Serves 6.

Crab and Potato Chip Casserole

Condensed tomato soup
  1 10¾-ounce can
Water ¼ cup
Mayonnaise ½ cup

Potato chips 2 cups crushed
Crab meat 2 6½-ounce
  cans, flaked
Cheddar cheese ½ cup grated

Combine soup, water, and mayonnaise. Place alternate layers of potato chips, crab meat, and soup mixture in buttered 1½-quart casserole. Sprinkle cheese over top and bake at 350° for 20 to 30 minutes. Serves 5 to 6.

Crab Divan

Crab meat 1½ pounds or
  Crab meat 3 6½-ounce cans, drained
Frozen broccoli spears
  2 10-ounce packages
Butter or margarine 1 tablespoon
Flour 2 tablespoons

Salt 1 teaspoon
Pepper ¼ teaspoon
Milk ½ cup
American cheese ¼ cup grated
Tomatoes 1 16-ounce can, well drained
Cornflakes 2 tablespoons crushed

Remove any shell or cartilage from crab and cut meat into 1-inch pieces. Cook broccoli half as long as directed on package; drain thoroughly. Arrange broccoli in greased 8 by 8 by 2-inch baking dish; spread crab meat over broccoli. In saucepan, melt butter and blend in flour and seasonings; add milk gradually and cook, stirring constantly, until thick and smooth. Add cheese and stir until melted. Add tomatoes to sauce and pour over crab; sprinkle with cornflakes. Bake at 400° for 20 minutes or until lightly browned. Serves 6.

Crab Lasagne

Lasagne noodles 8 ounces
Salt 2 tablespoons
Boiling water 6 quarts
Condensed shrimp soup
  2 10¾-ounce cans
Crab meat 2 cups
Egg 1, beaten
Fresh basil 2 tablespoons minced

Medium onion 1, chopped
Salt 1 teaspoon
Pepper ½ teaspoon
Small-curd cottage cheese 2 cups
Cream cheese 1 8-ounce
  package, softened
Tomatoes 2, thinly sliced
Sharp cheddar cheese 1 cup grated

Add noodles and salt to water and cook for 15 minutes. Drain and cover with cold water; set aside. Put soup in saucepan; add crab and heat. Combine next 7 ingredients and blend well. Drain noodles. In buttered 9 by 13 by 2-inch baking dish, make a layer of ½ of noodles and a layer of ½ of cheese mixture. Add all soup and crab as one layer. Cover with remaining noodles and then remaining cheese mixture. Top with sliced tomatoes and bake at 350° for 30 minutes. Cover with grated cheese and bake until browned. Serves 10.

Crab-Pineapple Imperial

Crab meat 1 pound
Mayonnaise or salad dressing ¼ cup
Pimiento 1 teaspoon chopped
Salt ½ teaspoon
Worcestershire sauce ½ teaspoon
Liquid pepper sauce 3 drops
Pineapple slices 6
Fine cornflake crumbs 1 cup

Combine first 6 ingredients; mix well. Dip both sides of pineapple slices in ⅔ cup of the crumbs; place in a shallow baking dish. Place ⅓ cup of crab mixture on top of each pineapple slice. Sprinkle remaining crumbs over top of crab mixture. Bake at 350° for 15 to 20 minutes. Serves 6.

Gypsy Fisherman Stew (Gypsea Casserole)

Shortening ¼ cup
Medium onion 1, diced
Small green pepper 1, chopped
Celery ½ cup diced
Mushrooms 1 cup sliced
Tomatoes 1 16-ounce can
Tomato sauce 1 8-ounce can
Salt 1 teaspoon
Garlic powder ¼ teaspoon
Pepper ½ teaspoon
Crab meat 1 cup flaked
Small shrimp 1 cup cooked, peeled, and deveined
Flour 3 cups
Eggs 3, beaten
Water about ½ cup
Salt 1½ teaspoons
Water 2 quarts
Paprika garnish

In Dutch oven, melt shortening; add onion, green pepper, and celery and sauté until tender. Add next 6 ingredients and bring to a boil; simmer slowly for 20 minutes. Add crab and shrimp; cover and simmer gently for 10 minutes. To make dumplings, mix together flour, eggs, and enough water to form a medium-thick batter. In large kettle, bring to boil salt and water. Drop dumpling batter by teaspoonfuls into boiling water; cover and cook for 5 minutes. Drain dumplings, rinse with cold water, and drain again. Arrange on stew mixture and sprinkle with paprika. Bake at 325° for 20 minutes. Serve immediately. Serves 6 to 8.

Quick Seafood Casserole

Crab meat or combination of seafood 2 cups
Potato chips 1 4½-ounce package, crushed
Condensed cream of mushroom soup 2 10¾-ounce cans
Milk ½ cup
Butter 1 tablespoon

Keeping crab in large pieces, remove any shell or cartilage. Arrange alternate layers of crab meat and potato chips in well-buttered 2-quart casserole. Blend soup and milk and pour over top; dot with butter. Bake at 400° for 15 minutes or until thoroughly heated and browned. Serves 4.

Seashore Casserole

Potato chips   1 4½-ounce
 package, slightly broken
Pimiento   1 2-ounce jar,
 drained and chopped
Mushrooms   2 8-ounce cans, drained

Condensed cream of mushroom soup
 2 10¾-ounce cans
Crab, tuna, salmon, or shrimp
 1 6½-ounce can, drained
Evaporated milk   1 13-ounce can

Place potato chips in buttered casserole. Lightly mix together remaining ingredients. Pour over potato chips and bake at 350° for 20 minutes or until thoroughly heated. Serves 6 for lunch, 4 for dinner.

Crab Chops

Blue crab meat   1 pound
Butter or margarine   ¼ cup
Flour   ¼ cup
Salt   ½ teaspoon
Cayenne   ¼ teaspoon
Milk   1 cup
Parsley   ¼ cup chopped
Green onion   ½ cup chopped

Flour   ½ cup
Eggs   2, slightly beaten
Soft bread crumbs   2 cups
Butter or margarine   ¼ cup
Cooking oil   ¼ cup
Lemon wedges   garnish
Tartar sauce

Drain crab and remove any shell or cartilage. In small saucepan, melt butter and blend in flour and seasonings. Gradually stir in milk and cook, stirring constantly, until thickened. Mix in crab meat, parsley, and green onion. Cover and refrigerate for 2 hours. Divide crab mixture into 6 equal portions; pat and shape each portion into a "chop" about 5 inches long and ½ inch thick. Coat each chop on both sides with flour. Dip into egg and coat evenly with crumbs. Refrigerate at least 30 minutes to firm coating. In heavy 12-inch frying pan, heat butter and oil until hot but not smoking; fry chops over moderate heat about 5 minutes on each side or until delicately browned. Serve with lemon and tartar sauce. Serves 6.

King Crab Crunch

King crab meat 1 pound
Crushed pineapple 1 8¼-ounce can
Cornstarch 2 tablespoons
Butter or margarine 3 tablespoons
Celery ½ cup thinly sliced

Chicken broth 2 cups
Blanched slivered almonds
  ½ cup, toasted
Lemon juice 1 tablespoon
Chow mein noodles 1 5-ounce can

Remove any crab shell or cartilage. Drain pineapple and dissolve cornstarch in its juice; set aside. In 10-inch frying pan, melt butter; add celery, pineapple, and crab meat and cook over low heat for 5 minutes, stirring frequently. Stir cornstarch and pineapple juice into crab mixture; add chicken broth gradually and cook, stirring constantly, until thick. Add almonds and lemon juice and serve over noodles. Serves 6.

Crab Chow Mein

Butter or margarine 2 tablespoons
Celery 1½ cups chopped
Medium green pepper 1, chopped
Medium onions 2, chopped
Bean sprouts 1 16-ounce can, drained

Crab meat 2 cups in large pieces
Condensed cream of mushroom soup
  1 10¾-ounce can
Chow mein noodles 2 5-ounce cans

In frying pan, melt butter and cook celery, green pepper, and onion until tender; add sprouts and crab meat and heat. Pour soup over top and simmer 10 minutes. Serve over noodles. Serves 6.

Rich Crab Newburg

Half-and-half or evaporated
  milk 1 cup
Butter or margarine 3 tablespoons
Crab meat 2 cups flaked
Salt ¾ teaspoon
Paprika ½ teaspoon

Nutmeg ⅛ teaspoon
Egg yolks 2, slightly beaten
Worcestershire sauce 1 teaspoon
Sherry 1 tablespoon
Bread 6 slices, toasted and buttered

Heat half-and-half with butter in top of double boiler. Add crab and seasonings. Combine egg yolks, Worcestershire sauce, and sherry; mix a little of the hot liquid into the yolk mixture. Pour egg mixture into hot crab mixture; cook over simmering water for 1 to 2 minutes or until sauce thickens slightly. Serve immediately over toast. Serves 6.

Oyster Pie

Large potatoes 6
Milk ¾ cup, hot
Butter 3 tablespoons
Egg yolks 3, well beaten
Salt 1½ teaspoons
Pepper ⅛ teaspoon
Nutmeg ⅛ teaspoon (optional)
Egg whites 3, stiffly beaten
Fine dry bread crumbs ¼ cup

Shucked oysters 1 pint with liquor
Butter 2 tablespoons
Onion 2 tablespoons chopped
Flour 3 tablespoons
Oyster liquor plus milk 1½ cups
Cream 1 cup
Salt and pepper to taste
Parsley 1 tablespoon finely chopped

Boil potatoes until tender; drain and mash. Add milk, butter, and egg yolks, beating constantly; add seasonings. Fold in egg whites. Butter a 2-quart casserole and coat with crumbs. Spread bottom and sides with ½ of potato mixture. Remove any bits of shell from oysters and simmer them in their liquor over low heat for 3 minutes or until edges ruffle. If oysters are large, cut into halves. Drain, saving liquor. In saucepan, melt butter; add onion and sauté until tender but not brown. Stir in flour. Gradually add liquor plus milk and then add cream and season to taste. Cook and stir over low heat until sauce thickens slightly. Add oysters and spoon mixture into potato-lined casserole. Carefully spread remaining potato mixture over the top. Bake at 400° for 30 minutes. Garnish with parsley. Serves 6.

Oyster Pie Rappahannock

Oysters 1 pint
Bacon slices 6
Mushrooms 2 cups sliced
Onion ½ cup chopped
Green onions ½ cup chopped
Flour ¼ cup

Salt ½ teaspoon
Cayenne ¼ teaspoon
Parsley ¼ cup chopped
Lemon juice 2 tablespoons
Margarine 1 tablespoon, softened
Biscuit Topping

Drain oysters and dry between absorbent paper. In 10-inch frying pan, fry bacon until crisp. Remove bacon from pan, drain, and crumble. Reserve 3 tablespoons of bacon fat in pan; add mushrooms, onion, and green onion. Cover pan and simmer 5 minutes or until tender. Blend in flour, salt, and cayenne. Stir in oysters, bacon, parsley, and lemon juice. Rub margarine in 9-inch pie plate. Turn oyster mixture into pie plate; cover with Biscuit Topping. Score to make a design on top. Bake at 400° for 20 to 25 minutes or until lightly browned. Cut into wedges. Serves 6.

Biscuit Topping

Flour 1½ cups
Baking powder 2¼ teaspoons
Salt ¼ teaspoon

Butter or margarine 3 tablespoons
Milk ½ cup

Sift dry ingredients together. Cut in butter until mixture is like coarse crumbs. Add milk all at once; mix quickly to a soft dough—no more than 20 strokes. Turn onto lightly floured surface; knead gently 5 or 6 times. Shape into a ball and roll into a 9-inch circle.

Scalloped Oysters

Cracker crumbs 2 cups
Shucked oysters 1 quart,
  drained, liquor reserved
Oyster liquor plus rich
  milk 2 cups

Onion ¼ cup finely chopped
Salt 1 teaspoon
Monosodium glutamate ½ teaspoon
Pepper ⅛ teaspoon
Butter or margarine ½ cup

Line buttered 1½-quart casserole with ½ of crumbs. Arrange ½ of oysters on crumbs. Combine next 5 ingredients; pour ½ of this over oysters. Dot with ½ of butter. Make another layer of remaining oysters and add remaining liquid. Melt remaining butter, stir in remaining crumbs, and sprinkle over oysters. Bake at 350° for 20 to 25 minutes. Serves 6 to 8.

Seafood au Gratin

Bread 6 slices, toasted and buttered
Eggs 2, slightly beaten
Salt 1 teaspoon
Prepared mustard 1 teaspoon
Paprika ½ teaspoon

Milk ½ cup
Oysters, crab meat, or
  cooked fish 2 cups
Cheddar cheese 1 cup grated

Trim crusts from toast and cut into quarters. Combine next 5 ingredients. Arrange ½ of toast in bottom of buttered casserole; cover with seafood. Make another layer with remaining toast; cover with egg mixture and sprinkle with cheese. Place casserole in pan of hot water; bake at 350° for 30 minutes or until brown. Serves 3 to 4.

Oyster Soufflé

Shucked oysters 1 pint
Butter or margarine ¼ cup
Flour ¼ cup
Oyster liquor ½ cup
Milk ⅓ cup
Salt ½ teaspoon
Pepper pinch

Cayenne pinch
Liquid pepper sauce 2 or 3 drops
Egg yolks 3, well beaten
Egg whites 3, stiffly beaten
  but not dry
Cracker crumbs ¼ cup

Cook oysters in their liquor until edges begin to ruffle; drain well, save liquor, and dice oysters. In saucepan, melt butter and blend in flour; gradually add oyster liquor and milk; cook, stirring constantly, until thickened. Add seasonings and allow to cool slightly. Stir in egg yolks and oysters; fold in egg whites. Sprinkle crumbs in bottom of buttered 1½-quart casserole; pour in soufflé mixture. Bake at 350° for 40 minutes or until puffed and set. Serve at once. Serves 5 to 6.

Oyster Omelette

Bacon slices 2, chopped or
  Bacon drippings 2 tablespoons
Shucked oysters 2 cups chopped
Oyster liquor ½ cup
Green onions ¼ cup chopped

Eggs 6, well beaten
Whole-kernel corn 1 7-ounce
  can, drained
Seafood seasoning to taste
Tomato wedges or paprika garnish

Fry bacon in heavy 8-inch skillet until crisp. Add oysters and liquor; cook gently over moderate heat until edges curl and liquor is nearly gone. Toss in green onion and pour eggs and corn over mixture. Sprinkle with seafood seasoning. Cover pan and continue to cook gently for 15 minutes or until eggs are firm. Garnish with tomatoes or paprika. Serves 4.

Oyster-Egg Fry

Shucked Pacific oysters 1 pint
Boiling water 1 cup
Soy sauce 2 teaspoons
Powdered ginger ¼ teaspoon
Salad oil 1½ teaspoons
Eggs 6, slightly beaten

Milk ¼ cup
Salt ½ teaspoon
Pepper pinch
Green onion 1 tablespoon
  finely diced
Salad oil 1½ teaspoons

In saucepan, gently simmer oysters in water for 4 minutes; drain well and cut into bite-size pieces. Place in bowl and add soy sauce and ginger. Place Teflon pan over moderate heat; pour in oil and then oyster mixture. Stir and fry for about 1½ minutes. Return oysters to bowl and clean pan. Combine eggs, milk, salt, pepper, and green onion. Return pan to moderate heat; pour in remaining oil and the egg mixture. Cook and stir until eggs are almost set; add oysters, mix gently, and continue cooking until eggs are firm. Serves 4 to 6.

Baked Pacific Scallops

Scallops 1 pound, rinsed and dried
Salt 1 teaspoon
Butter or margarine 2 tablespoons
Celery 1½ cups diced
Mushrooms 1 cup chopped or
  Sliced mushrooms 1 4-ounce
  can, drained

Green pepper 1 cup diced
Butter or margarine 4 tablespoons
Flour 4 tablespoons
Salt 1 teaspoon
Milk 2 cups
Soft bread crumbs 1 cup, buttered
Cheddar cheese ¼ cup finely grated

Separate scallops and sprinkle with salt. In a frying pan, melt 2 tablespoons butter and add celery, mushrooms, and green pepper; cook until tender. In saucepan, melt remaining butter over low heat and blend in flour and salt; gradually add milk and stir until thickened. Combine scallops, vegetables, and sauce and pour into buttered 1½-quart casserole. Top with crumbs and cheese. Bake at 350° for 20 to 30 minutes. Serves 6.

Peachy Scallops

Scallops 1 pound, rinsed and dried
Butter or margarine 2 tablespoons
Lemon juice 2 tablespoons
Salt ¼ teaspoon
Pepper pinch

Canned peach halves 12, drained
Cinnamon ¼ teaspoon
Cloves ¼ teaspoon
Mace ¼ teaspoon
Bacon slices 3, cut into fourths

Cut scallops into ½-inch pieces. Melt butter in skillet; add scallops, lemon juice, salt and pepper; stir-fry for 2 minutes. Remove from heat. Arrange peach halves, cut side up, in shallow baking dish; sprinkle with spices. Divide scallops and pan juices among peaches; top with bacon pieces. Bake at 375° for about 15 minutes, or until sizzling. Serves 6.

Carolina Shrimp Pilaf

Bacon slices 8
Onion 2 cups chopped
Long-grain rice 1½ cups
Chicken broth 3 cups
Tomatoes 1 28-ounce can,
  cut up and undrained
Worcestershire sauce 2 teaspoons

Salt 1 teaspoon
Ground mace 1 teaspoon
Cayenne ¼ teaspoon
Raw shrimp 2 pounds
  peeled and deveined
Parsley 2 tablespoons chopped

In heavy 3- or 4-quart Dutch oven, cook bacon until crisp; drain on absorbent paper. Crumble and set aside. Reserve 3 tablespoons of bacon fat and cook onion in it, pan covered, until tender. Stir in rice. Add next 6 ingredients and bring to a boil. Cover and bake at 350° for 15 minutes. Stir in shrimp and bacon; cover and return to oven for 10 minutes or until shrimp turn pink. Remove from oven, fluff with a fork, and sprinkle with parsley. Serves 6.

Shrimp and Rice Casserole

Condensed cream of mushroom soup
  1 10¾-ounce can
Onion 1 tablespoon chopped
Green pepper 2 tablespoons chopped
Butter 2 tablespoons, melted
Lemon juice 1 tablespoon
Dry mustard ½ teaspoon

Worcestershire sauce ½ teaspoon
Pepper pinch
Cheese ½ cup cubed
Rice 2 cups cooked
Shrimp ½ pound, cooked and cleaned,
  a few reserved for garnish
Slivered almonds ¼ cup

Combine first 11 ingredients and spread in 2-quart casserole. Garnish with a few shrimp and the almonds. Bake at 375° for 30 minutes. Serves 4 to 6.

Shrimp Fondue

Shrimp 3 4½-ounce cans,
    drained and rinsed
Day-old white bread
    8 slices, crusts removed
Butter 3 tablespoons, softened
Green pepper ¼ cup chopped
Cheese 1 cup grated

Eggs 3
Dry mustard ¼ teaspoon
Salt ½ teaspoon
Pepper pinch
Milk 2 cups
Paprika

Cut large shrimp into halves. Spread bread with butter and cut into ½-inch cubes; place ½ of cubes in well-buttered 8 by 12-inch baking dish. Cover with shrimp, green pepper, and ½ of cheese. Top with remaining bread cubes and cheese. Combine eggs, mustard, salt, and pepper; beat with egg beater. Mix in milk. Pour over bread cubes and sprinkle with paprika. Bake at 350° for 45 minutes or until firm in the center. Remove from oven and let stand for 5 minutes before serving. Serves 6.

Shrimp Pizza

Onion ⅓ cup chopped
Garlic cloves 3, finely chopped
Butter or oil ½ cup
Italian-style tomato paste
    3 6-ounce cans
Parsley ⅓ cup chopped

Oregano 1½ teaspoons
Pizza crusts 3 9-inch, unbaked
Shrimp 3 4½-ounce cans,
    drained and rinsed
Mozzarella cheese ¾ pound,
    thinly sliced

Sauté onion and garlic in butter until tender. Add tomato paste and simmer for 5 minutes; remove from heat and add parsley and oregano. Place pizza crusts on well-greased baking sheets. Cover each crust with ⅓ of sauce, ⅓ of shrimp, and ⅓ of cheese. Bake at 425° for 20 minutes or until crust is brown and cheese melts. Serves 6.

Shrimp-Stuffed Baked Potatoes

Medium baking potatoes 6
Butter or margarine   1 tablespoon
Salt 1½ teaspoons
Pepper pinch
Onion 1½ tablespoons grated

Parsley ½ cup chopped or
  Celery ½ cup finely chopped
Milk ¾ to 1 cup
Shrimp 3 4½-ounce cans,
  drained and rinsed
Cheese ¾ cup grated

Bake potatoes at 425° for 35 to 60 minutes or until soft. Cut a slice off top of each potato and carefully scoop out insides. Mash potatoes with next 6 ingredients and blend well; fold in shrimp. Stuff potato shells with mixture and sprinkle with cheese. Bake at 400° for 15 minutes or until potatoes are hot and cheese is melted. Serves 6.

Note: To avoid last-minute hurry, prepare potatoes early in the day and refrigerate. About 25 minutes before serving time, return them to 400° oven to get hot.

Shrimp Thermidor

Mushroom stems and pieces
  1 4-ounce can, drained
Butter or oil ¼ cup
Flour ¼ cup
Cayenne pinch
Dry mustard ½ teaspoon
Milk 2 cups

Shrimp 3 4½-ounce cans,
  drained and rinsed
Parsley 2 tablespoons chopped
Salt to taste
Parmesan cheese 2 tablespoons grated
Paprika garnish

Sauté mushrooms in butter for 2 minutes; blend in flour, cayenne, and mustard. Add milk gradually and cook, stirring constantly, until thick. Add shrimp and parsley and, if necessary, salt. Arrange in 6 well-buttered shells or custard cups and sprinkle with cheese and paprika. Bake at 400° for 10 to 15 minutes or until lightly browned. Serves 6.

Creole Jambalaya

Butter or margarine 2 tablespoons
Onion ¾ cup chopped
Celery ½ cup chopped
Green pepper ¼ cup chopped
Parsley 1 tablespoon chopped
Garlic clove 1, minced
Cooked ham 2 cups cubed
Tomatoes 1 28-ounce can,
  cut up and undrained

Condensed beef broth 1 10½-ounce
  can
Water 1 soup can
Long-grain rice 1 cup
Sugar 1 teaspoon
Thyme leaves ½ teaspoon crushed
Chili powder ½ teaspoon
Pepper ¼ teaspoon
Raw shrimp 1½ pounds
  peeled and deveined

Melt butter in Dutch oven; add next 5 ingredients. Cover and cook until tender. Add ham and next 8 ingredients; cover and simmer 25 minutes or until rice is tender. Add shrimp; simmer, uncovered, for 5 to 10 minutes or until shrimp are pink and most of liquid has evaporated. Serves 6 to 8.

Shrimp Jambalaya

Green pepper 1 cup chopped
Onion ½ cup chopped
Garlic cloves 2, finely chopped
Butter or oil ¼ cup
Tomatoes 1 16-ounce can
Water 1½ cups
Rice 1 cup

Thyme leaves ½ teaspoon crushed
Salt ¼ teaspoon
Bay leaf 1
Pepper pinch
Parsley ¼ cup chopped
Shrimp 3 4½-ounce cans,
  drained and rinsed

Sauté green pepper, onion, and garlic in butter until tender; add next 7 ingredients. Cover and simmer for 25 minutes or until rice is tender; stir occasionally. Add parsley and shrimp. When hot, remove bay leaf and serve. Serves 6.

Shrimp Fried Rice

Rice 4 cups cooked, cold
Eggs 2, well beaten
Baby shrimp 1 cup
  cooked and cleaned
Peanut or other oil

Medium onion 1, thinly sliced
Soy sauce 4 tablespoons
Cooking sherry 2 tablespoons
Garlic powder ¼ teaspoon
Freshly ground pepper ⅛ teaspoon

Add a little water to rice to separate grains. Combine eggs and shrimp in bowl. In skillet or wok, heat oil and sauté onion until tender. Add shrimp mixture and cook over moderate heat, stirring constantly. Add rice; cook and stir for 2 minutes. Add remaining ingredients; fry and stir 2 minutes longer. Serves 4.

Spaghetti Shrimp Marinara

Margarine or oil 3 tablespoons
Flour 3 tablespoons
Lemon juice 2 teaspoons (optional)
Salt 1 teaspoon
Dillweed ¼ teaspoon (optional)
Evaporated milk 1 cup
Water 1 cup

Small shrimp ½ pound cooked
  and cleaned or
  Small shrimp 2 4½-ounce cans,
  drained and rinsed
Eggs 2, hard-cooked and quartered
Peas ¾ cup cooked
Ripe olives ¼ cup sliced (optional)
Spaghetti 1 8-ounce package, cooked

In saucepan, melt margarine and stir in flour, lemon juice, salt, and dillweed; gradually add milk and water and cook, stirring constantly, until smooth and thick. Fold in shrimp, eggs, peas, and olives. Heat 3 to 4 minutes and serve over spaghetti. Serves 4.

Quick Shrimp Scramble

Tiny shrimp 1 4½-ounce can, drained
Eggs 6
Salt and pepper to taste

Butter 1 tablespoon
Toast 4 slices, buttered

Combine shrimp, eggs, and salt and pepper and cook in butter as an omelette or scrambled eggs. Serve with toast as a quick supper. Serves 2.

Outdoor Cooking and Groups of 25

Beach Barbecue for a Crowd

Dig a trench in the sand which is 1 foot deep, 3 feet long, and wide enough to accommodate the fish. In the trench, build a fire with plenty of wood and let it burn down to coals, which will take about 2 hours. Alder, maple, or applewood make excellent fires.

Make a rack for the fish using 2 layers of chicken wire fastened to 2 metal pipes. One edge of the top layer of wire should remain unfastened until you place the fish on the bottom layer.

Rub salt into both halves of a salmon or other large fish and lay them, skin side down, on one piece of greased chicken wire. Then fasten the top layer over the fish to hold it securely in place. Using the ends of the pipe as handles, 2 people can place the rack of fish over the bed of coals. If the heat is too intense, raise fish farther from the fire by resting ends of pipe on pieces of rock.

Cook fish, skin side toward the coals, about 30 to 45 minutes; basting occasionally with lemon, butter, and herbs or with some other mild barbecue sauce. Turn rack (using potholders if pipes are hot), and cook skin side up for 20 minutes longer or until fish flakes easily.

If you do not have the makings of a rack, you can get a similar effect by building a fire directly on the sand, nailing the fish, skin side down, to a green or water-soaked plank of maple, alder, post oak, spruce, or other non-resinous wood, and leaning the plank against a railing or other support near the fire. The exact distance from the fire will vary with the heat of the coals and the thickness of the fish.

Baked Fish-In-A-Hole

Fish 1 4-pound dressed, head and tail intact (if desired)	**Salt** 1 teaspoon or **Bacon or salt pork** 4 slices **Small onion** 1, sliced (optional)

If the fish is lean, slash the skin on both sides 3 times; salt the inside or lay bacon and onion slices inside the cavity. Dig a trench 10 inches deep, 10 inches wide, and long enough to hold the fish. Build a fire in the trench with plenty of wood and let burn down to about a 2-inch depth of coals. Remove all flaming wood and about half of the hot coals. Make a smooth bed with the remaining coals and cover with a 1-inch thickness of green grass. Place fish on grass and cover with another 1-inch layer of grass. Place remaining live coals over the grass and cover the coals with warm earth from the edges of the hole. Cook fish 1 hour; carefully remove from hole. The flesh will separate easily from skin and bones. Serves 6.

Steaks Baked-in-the-Coals

Fish steaks or fillets 2 pounds or
  Trout 6, cleaned and dressed
Salt and pepper to taste
Butter ¼ cup, melted

Onion slices 6
Lemon slices 6
Green pepper 1, chopped (optional)
Bacon strips 6 (optional)

Cut fish into serving size portions, season, and brush with melted butter. Place fish on 12-inch lengths of heavy-duty aluminum foil. Divide onion, lemon, and green pepper among portions; cover with bacon. Make an airtight package by lifting side edges of foil over the fish and double-folding them together, then double-fold ends, being careful not to tear or puncture the foil. Place on a bed of hot coals, turning frequently for even cooking, and bake about 12 to 15 minutes. Remove packages from coals, cut big crisscross in the top of each package, and fold the foil back; serve in foil package. Serves 6.

Note: Increase baking time to 1 hour for 3 to 4 pound fish.

Barbecued Fillets or Steaks

Onion ¼ cup chopped
Green pepper 2 tablespoons chopped
Garlic clove 1, finely chopped
Butter or cooking oil 2 tablespoons
Tomato sauce 1 8-ounce can
Lemon juice 2 tablespoons

Worcestershire sauce 1 tablespoon
Sugar 1 tablespoon
Salt 2 teaspoons
Pepper ¼ teaspoon
Fish fillets or steaks 2 pounds

In saucepan, sauté onion, green pepper, and garlic in butter until tender. Add next 6 ingredients and simmer for 5 minutes, stirring occasionally; cool. Cut fish into 6 portions and arrange in single layer in shallow dish. Pour sauce over fish and let stand for 15 minutes; turn and let stand 15 minutes longer. Remove fish and reserve sauce for basting. Place fish in well-oiled hinged wire grills. Cook about 4 inches from moderately hot coals for 5 to 8 minutes; baste with sauce. Turn and cook 5 to 8 minutes longer or until fish flakes easily. Serves 6.

Charcoal-Broiled Pan-Dressed Fish

Fish 1 3-pound pan-dressed
Butter or other fat ¼ cup, melted
Lemon juice ¼ cup

Salt 1½ teaspoons
Paprika ¾ teaspoon
Pepper pinch

Wipe fish dry and place in well-oiled hinged wire grills. Combine remaining 5 ingredients; brush fish with mixture. Cook about 4 inches from moderately hot coals for 5 to 8 minutes. Baste with sauce and turn. Cook 5 to 8 minutes longer or until fish flakes easily. Serves 6.

Charcoal Broiled Fish Portions or Sticks

Frozen fried fish portions
  12 2½-3 ounce pieces or
Frozen fried fish sticks
  24 ¾-1¼ ounce pieces

Tartar Sauce   (see Index)

Place fish in single layer on well-greased, hinged grills; cook about 4 inches from moderately hot coals for 4 to 5 minutes per side, or until fish is heated through and flakes easily. Serve with a tartar sauce. Serves 6.

Fish Dinner-In-One

Fish fillets, steaks, or dressed trout
  2 pounds
Bacon slices   6, chopped
Tomatoes   1 pound, sliced
Onion   2 tablespoons chopped

Potatoes   1½ cups sliced
Green beans   1½ cups sliced
Salt   3 teaspoons
Pepper   pinch

Cut 6 pieces of heavy-duty aluminum foil in 12-inch lengths. Cut fish into serving-size portions. In center of each piece of foil, arrange equal servings of fish, bacon, tomato, onion, potato, and green beans. Sprinkle with salt and pepper. Wrap foil around food and seal all seams with double-folds. Place on a bed of hot coals and cook 20 minutes, turning frequently to cook evenly. Serve hot directly from packages. Serves 6.

Flounder Birds, Camp Style

Flounder fillets   2 pounds
Salt and pepper   to taste

Sweet Pickle Stuffing
Bacon slices   6

Cut fish into 6 pieces; season both sides. Place a spoonful of stuffing on each piece of fish; roll fish around stuffing. Wrap each roll with a slice of bacon and fasten with a toothpick. Wrap heavy-duty aluminum foil around each roll and seal all seams with double-folds. Place directly on a bed of hot coals and cook for 20 minutes, turning frequently to cook evenly. Serve hot directly from packages. Serves 6.

Sweet Pickle Stuffing

Soft bread crumbs 2 cups
Sweet pickle relish ¼ cup
Lemon juice 1 tablespoon
Onion 1 tablespoon minced
Salt ½ teaspoon

Pepper ¼ teaspoon
Parsley 1 teaspoon chopped
Shortening or bacon drippings
  3 tablespoons, melted

Combine all ingredients, mixing lightly. Makes enough to stuff a 5-pound fish.

Barbecued Halibut

Halibut steaks 4 1-inch thick
Barbecue sauce for basting

Lemon wedges garnish
Parsley garnish

Pile charcoal briquets pyramid style under grill about 45 minutes before cooking time and light; spread briquets out when lightly coated with ashes. Brush steaks lightly with sauce and place on well-greased rack approximately 3 inches from coals. Cook about 5 minutes on each side or until halibut flakes easily, basting frequently with sauce. Garnish with lemon wedges and parsley. Serves 4.

Texas-Grilled Spanish Mackerel

Lemon juice ½ cup
Olive oil ¼ cup
Salt 1 teaspoon
Oregano leaves 1 teaspoon crushed
Garlic salt ¾ teaspoon

Pepper ½ teaspoon
Monosodium glutamate ½ teaspoon
Spanish mackerel or other fish
  3 pounds dressed

Combine first 7 ingredients for basting sauce. Make 4 or 5 shallow slits on each side of each fish and brush, inside and out, with sauce. Place fish on well-oiled hinged wire grills. Cook about 4 inches from moderately hot coals for 5 to 8 minutes; baste with sauce. Turn and cook 5 to 8 minutes longer or until fish flakes easily. Serves 6.

Salmon Baked on a Spit

Salmon 1 6 to 8 pounds, cleaned and dressed
Salt and pepper to taste

Lemon wedges garnish
Hollandaise Sauce or favorite sauce (see Index)

Season inside of salmon and insert 30-inch spit along backbone. Balance fish so it will turn easily, adjusting the forks and tightening the screws. Fold a piece of chicken wire around the fish with metal skewers to prevent flesh from falling off bones while cooking. Place spit about 8 inches from slow coals and start turning. Cook for 1 to 1½ hours or until fish flakes easily. Serve with lemon and a sauce. Serves 12-16.

Salmon Baked in the Sand

Salmon cleaned and dressed
Salt

Potatoes (optional)

About 5 hours before eating time build large bonfire on a sandy beach. Rub inside cavity of salmon generously with salt, wrap in clean wet muslin and 4 or 5 layers of wet newspaper or wet seaweed, then sew snugly into wet burlap. Wrap potatoes in several layers of wet newspaper. Push hot coals and stones aside enough to dig pit about 10 inches deep; put salmon and potatoes in hole and cover with 3 inches of hot sand and stones. Allow 1 hour cooking time for serving-size pieces of salmon; 3 hours for 30 pounds.

Barbecued Salmon

Salmon fillets 2, 3 to 4 pounds each, with skin
Barbecue sauce ½ cup

Lemon juice from 1 lemon
Worcestershire sauce 1 tablespoon
Butter ½ cup, melted

Place fish, flesh side down, on a hot oiled grill 2 to 3 inches above hot coals; cook for 10 to 15 minutes. While fish cooks, combine remaining ingredients. Turn fish and baste frequently with sauce. Cook 10 to 15 minutes longer or until fish flakes easily. Serves 10 to 12.

Barbecued Salmon with Sesame

Salmon steaks 2 pounds, 1-inch thick
Vegetable oil 2 tablespoons
Sesame seeds 2 tablespoons
Tomato-cheese sauce 1 8-ounce can
Brown sugar 1½ tablespoons packed
Lemon juice from 1 lemon

Oregano ½ teaspoon
Worcestershire sauce 1 scant teaspoon
Dry mustard ¼ teaspoon
Parsley 1 tablespoon finely chopped

Brush fish with oil and sprinkle with sesame seeds. In a saucepan, combine next 6 ingredients and simmer gently for about 10 minutes. Place steaks on a hot grill, 2 to 3 inches from glowing coals. Baste frequently with sauce. Cook about 8 minutes and turn. Cook about 7 minutes longer or until fish flakes easily. Add parsley to any remaining sauce and serve with the fish. Serves 4.

Grilled Gourmet-Salmon Steak

Salmon steaks 2 pounds
Dry vermouth 1 cup
Butter or other fat ⅔ cup, melted
Lemon juice ¼ cup
Onion 2 tablespoons finely chopped
Salt 2 teaspoons

Marjoram ¼ teaspoon
Thyme ¼ teaspoon
Pepper ¼ teaspoon
Garlic clove 1, crushed
Sage pinch

Arrange steaks in single layer in shallow pan. Combine remaining 10 ingredients and pour over fish. Marinate for about 4 hours, turning steaks occasionally. Remove steaks and reserve sauce. Place steaks in an oiled hinged wire grill. Cook about 4 inches from hot coals for about 8 minutes; basting occasionally. Turn and cook other side, basting occasionally, until fish flakes easily. Serves 6.

Outdoor Shad Bake

Shad 1
Salt to taste

Bermuda onions 3, chopped

Scale shad by forcing water spray from a hose nozzle against the scales. Dress the fish and remove head and tail. Slit from the inside along the backbone through to the skin (do not cut the skin) so the fish will open flat. Season with salt and spread onions over fish; fold halves together and secure opening with small skewers and thread. Dig a hole 6 inches deep and wide and long enough to hold fish; line hole with leaves. Wrap fish in several thicknesses of heavy-duty aluminum foil and place it in the hole. Cover fish with leaves and fill the hole with dirt. Build a hot fire on the dirt above the fish and keep it burning all day — at least 6 to 8 hours. When shad is removed, the bones will be soft enough to eat and the fish will be very moist and tasty.

Smelt Beach Fry

Freshly caught smelt
  2 or more pounds

Fry mix 1½ cups
Cooking oil ¼ cup or more

Do not dress smelt; dip in clean salt water to wash. Drain and coat with fry mix. In a large, heavy skillet, fry smelt in hot oil over beach fire until brown on each side. Eat with your fingers, stripping the flesh from the bones, leaving the skeleton and body cavity. Serve with garlic bread. Serves 2 to 4.

Barbecued Clams or Oysters

Oysters or clams
Butter melted

Salt and pepper in shakers
Cocktail Sauce (see Index)

Scrub oyster or clam shells with a brush under running water; place around the edge of a hot, open fire. In about 15 minutes, the shells will pop open. Break off the top shells and serve meat on the bottom shells with butter, salt and pepper, and Cocktail Sauce.

Family Clambake

Clams 2½ gallons, scrubbed
Small white potatoes 2 dozen

Corn 12 ears, in husks
Butter melted, to dip clams in

Dig a hole approximately 4 feet square and 1 foot deep; line with rocks. Build a fire with plenty of wood and allow it to burn to coals. Remove any smoking pieces and cover the rocks and embers with at least 4 inches of fresh, wet seaweed. (Avoid old or dead seaweed; it imparts a bad flavor to the food.) Immediately spread clams, potatoes, and corn over seaweed and cover with cheesecloth (optional) and another 4 inches of wet seaweed. Cover the whole pile with old canvas or with hot sand from around the fire if you are on the beach. Cook 40 minutes, or until potatoes are tender. Serve clams with melted butter for dipping.

Grilled Oysters

Oysters 36, in the shell

Butter or margarine ½ cup, melted

Scrub oyster shells. Place oysters on a grill about 4 inches from hot coals. Roast for 10 to 15 minutes or until shells begin to open. Remove top shells and serve in bottom shells with melted butter. Serves 6.

Chesapeake Bay Crab-Clambake

Live hard-shell blue crabs 50
Soft-shell clams 25 dozen,
  well washed
Onions 50, 2 ounces each, peeled
Potatoes 50, 2 ounces each, scrubbed

Corn 25 ears, husked and halved
Lemons 6, cut into wedges
Butter or margarine 8 cups,
  melted

Cut 50 pieces of cheesecloth and heavy-duty aluminum foil, each 18 by 24 inches. For each serving, place 2 pieces of cheesecloth on top of 2 pieces of foil. Place 2 crabs, 12 clams, 2 onions, 2 potatoes, and 2 pieces of corn on each wrapper. Tie opposite corners of cheesecloth together. Pour 1 cup of water over each package. Bring foil up over food and close edges with tight double folds. Place packages on grills about 4 inches from hot coals. Cover with hoods or aluminum foil. Cook 45 to 60 minutes or until onions and potatoes are tender. Serve with lemon wedges and butter. Serves 25.

Fish-Salad Bunwiches

Halibut, cod, pollock, or other
  firm fish fillets or steaks 4 pounds,
  poached, chilled, and flaked
Celery 2½ cups finely chopped
Mayonnaise or salad dressing
  2⅔ cups
Sweet pickle relish ½ cup well drained

Onion ¼ cup finely chopped
Lemon juice ¼ cup
Salt 1 teaspoon
Hamburger or sesame buns 25,
  split and toasted
Lettuce leaves 25

Combine fish and celery. Combine next 5 ingredients; mix gently into fish and celery. Cover bottom half of each bun with a lettuce leaf and top with a scant ⅓ cup of salad mixture. Cover with bun tops. Serves 25.

Deep-Sea Treat

Frozen breaded fish portions
  25 2-ounce portions
Cooking oil   ½ cup
Paprika   to taste
American cheese   1½ pounds, grated
Catsup   ⅔ cup

Prepared mustard   ¼ cup
Horseradish   ¼ cup grated
Hamburger buns   25, split
Butter or margarine   ½ cup,
  softened

Place unthawed fish portions in single layer on well-greased shallow baking pans. Drizzle oil over fish; sprinkle with paprika. Bake at 500° for 10 to 15 minutes or until fish is browned and flakes easily. Combine cheese, catsup, mustard, and horseradish. Spread buns with softened butter. Place a fish portion on bottom half of each bun. Spread cheese mixture evenly over fish; cover with bun top. Bake at 350° for 8 minutes or until cheese melts. Serve hot. Serves 25.

Fish-In-Foil

**Cod, pollock, haddock, whitefish, or
  other fish fillets**   8 pounds
Butter or margarine   1½ cups
Flour   1½ cups
Salt   4½ teaspoons
Hot milk   1½ quarts
Lemon juice   ¾ cup
Paprika   1½ teaspoons

Salt   4½ teaspoons
Pepper   ½ teaspoon
**Celery-Green Pepper-Onion Topping
  or Onion-Carrot Topping or
  Shrimp-Mushroom Topping**
Tomato slices   25
Parsley   ½ cup chopped

Cut fillets into 25 serving-size portions. In large heavy saucepan, melt butter and stir in flour and salt; gradually add milk and cook, stirring constantly, until thick. Stir in lemon juice and paprika; set aside. Place a piece of fish on the oiled center of each piece of heavy-duty aluminum foil; sprinkle with salt and pepper. Arrange your choice of topping over fish; top with tomato slices. Spoon white sauce over tomato slices. Double-fold side edges of foil over center; double-fold ends. Place sealed packages in shallow baking pans. Bake at 425° for 40 minutes. To serve, place each package on a plate, cut crosses in the centers of packages, and turn back edges of crosses. Sprinkle with parsley and eat directly from foil. Serves 25.

Celery-Green Pepper-Onion Topping

Celery   1½ quarts chopped
Green pepper   1½ quarts chopped

Onion   1½ pints chopped

Toss ingredients together before using.

Onion-Carrot Topping

Medium onions 6, sliced

Medium carrots 24, peeled and cut into thin strips

Arrange equal amounts of onion and carrot on each piece of fish.

Shrimp-Mushroom Topping

Small mushrooms 1½ pounds, sliced
Butter or margarine ½ cup

Alaska or Maine shrimp 1½ pounds cooked and cleaned

In a large frying pan, sauté mushrooms in butter until golden brown. Combine with shrimp before using.

Beer-Batter-Fried Fish

Ocean perch, yellow perch, croaker, sea bass, sole, or other small fish fillets 8 pounds
Salt 2 teaspoons
Lemon juice 1½ tablespoons
Flour 4 cups

Paprika ¼ cup
Salt 4 teaspoons
Beer 3 12-ounce cans
Water ½ cup
Cooking oil
Tartar Sauce (see Index)

Cut fillets into serving-size pieces; sprinkle with salt and lemon juice. Combine flour, paprika, and salt; gradually add beer and water, beating until batter is thin and smooth. Dip fish in batter; drain slightly. Arrange in single layer in a fry basket; fry in deep fat at 350° for 3 minutes or until fish is brown and flakes easily. Drain on absorbent paper and keep warm until all fish is cooked. Serve with Tartar Sauce. Serves 25.

East Oven-Fried Fillets

Ocean perch, cod, pollock, flounder, sole, or other fish fillets 8 pounds
Salt 1 tablespoon

Milk 2 cups
Dry bread crumbs 1 quart, toasted
Cooking oil 1 cup

Cut fillets into serving-size portions. Add salt to milk; dip fillets in milk and roll in crumbs. Place fish, skin side down, in single layer in well-greased shallow baking pans; drizzle oil over top. Bake, without turning, at 500° for 10 to 15 minutes or until fish is browned and flakes easily. Serves 25.

Salmon, Seattle Style

Salmon 4 2-pound center cuts
Salt ¾ cup
Sugar ¾ cup

Peppercorns ¼ cup crushed
Fresh dillweed 2 bunches
Mustard-Dill Sauce

Fillet salmon, leaving skin intact. Mix together salt, sugar, and peppercorns; rub 3 table-spoons of mixture into flesh side of all 8 fillets. Place a fillet skin side down in each of 4 8 by 8 by 2-inch glass, enamel, or stainless steel containers; place ½ bunch of dillweed on each fillet. Place remaining 4 fillets, skin side up, over dillweed. Cover fish with double thick-nesses of heavy-duty aluminum foil. Place a plate on top of each piece of foil and a weight on top of each plate. Refrigerate for 48 hours; turn fish every 12 hours, separating halves slightly to baste flesh with liquid accumulated in dishes. When ready to serve, scrape seasonings from fish. Place fillets, skin side down, on cutting board; cut salmon away from skin diagonally in thin slices. Serve cold with Mustard-Dill Sauce. Serves 25.

Mustard-Dill Sauce

Dijon-style mustard 1 cup
Sugar ¾ cup
Vinegar ½ cup

Dry mustard 1 tablespoon
Salad oil 1⅓ cups
Fresh dillweed ¾ cup chopped

Beat together mustard, sugar, vinegar, and dry mustard; add oil very slowly, beating constantly, until a thick emulsion is formed. Fold in dill; cover and chill. Makes about 3 cups.

Maine Fisherman's Coleslaw

Cabbage 1 gallon shredded
Green pepper 2 cups chopped
Onion 1 cup chopped
Sweet pickle relish ¼ cup
Mayonnaise or salad dressing 2 cups

Salt 1 tablespoon
Maine sardines 10 3¾-ounce
  cans, drained
Paprika

Combine first 6 ingredients; mix well. Break sardines into ½-inch pieces and mix lightly into salad; chill. Serve in ⅔-cup portions sprinkled with paprika. Serves 25.

Rainbow Trout with Orange-Rice Stuffing

Rainbow trout   25 8-ounce pan-dressed
Salt   3 tablespoons
Orange-Rice Stuffing

Butter or margarine   ½ cup, melted
Orange juice   ½ cup
Paprika   garnish

Wipe trout dry; sprinkle, inside and out, with salt. Fill trout with scant ½-cup portions of stuffing; arrange in well-greased shallow baking pans. Combine butter and orange juice; brush fish with mixture and sprinkle with paprika. Bake at 350° for 35 to 45 minutes or until fish flakes easily, basting occasionally with pan drippings.

Orange-Rice Stuffing

Celery   1 quart chopped
Onion   1 cup chopped
Cooking oil   1 cup
Water   3 cups
Orange juice   1 cup
Lemon juice   ½ cup

Orange rind   ¼ cup grated
Salt   1 tablespoon
Rice   1 14-ounce box
   precooked (4½ cups)
Slivered almonds   2 cups, toasted
Parsley   ½ cup chopped

In a large saucepan, sauté celery and onion in oil until tender but not brown. Add next 5 ingredients; bring to a boil. Stir in rice; cover and remove from heat. Let stand for 5 minutes or until liquid is absorbed. Stir in almonds and parsley. Makes about 2 quarts.

Tuna and Kidney-Bean Salad

Tuna   4 6½-ounce cans, drained*
Kidney beans   2 15-ounce cans, drained
Sweet pickle   2 cups chopped
Celery   2 cups chopped
Onion   1 cup chopped

Eggs   6, hard-cooked and chopped
Mayonnaise or salad dressing   2 cups
Sweet pickle juice   ⅓ cup
Prepared mustard   3 tablespoons
Salad greens

Break tuna into large pieces; combine with next 8 ingredients by tossing lightly. Refrigerate for 1 hour to blend flavors. Serve in ½-cup portions on salad greens. Serves 25.
*Use 2 15½-ounce cans of drained salmon instead of tuna if you wish.

Tuna Barbecue

Catsup 3 cups
Celery 2 cups chopped
Onion 1 cup chopped
Worcestershire sauce ½ cup
Vinegar ½ cup
Brown sugar ½ cup packed

Dry mustard 4 teaspoons
Tuna oil or salad oil ¼ cup
Tuna-in-oil 9 6½-ounce
  cans, drained
Hamburger buns 25, split and toasted
Butter or margarine ½ cup, softened

In large saucepan, combine first 8 ingredients and bring to a boil; reduce heat and simmer, covered, for 30 minutes, stirring occasionally. Break tuna into large pieces and add to saucepan ingredients; continue cooking, uncovered, for 10 to 20 minutes, stirring carefully to keep tuna in chunks. Spread buns with butter. Serve ½-cup portions of barbecue between bun halves. Serves 25.

Manhattan Chowder

Shucked clams 3 quarts, liquor
  reserved, or
  **Sea bass, snapper, rockfish,
  sea trout or other fish fillets**
  2½ pounds, skinned
Salt pork or bacon ¼ pound, diced
Onion 2 cups chopped
Celery 2 cups chopped
Potatoes 2 quarts diced

Tomatoes 2 28-ounce cans or
  Tomato juice 2 quarts
Hot water 1 quart
Salt 1 tablespoon
Pepper ½ teaspoon
Butter or margarine ¼ cup
  (for clam chowder)
Parsley ¼ cup chopped

Cut fillets into ½-inch pieces. In large, heavy saucepan, fry salt pork until crisp. Add onion and celery and cook until tender. Add potatoes, tomatoes, and water. Cover and simmer for 20 minutes or until potatoes are tender. Add chopped clams and liquor (or fish pieces), salt, and pepper and simmer 5 to 10 minutes longer or until seafood is cooked. For clam chowder, add butter and heat until it melts. Serve in 1-cup portions garnished with parsley. Serves 25.

New England Chowder

Shucked clams 3 quarts or
   Haddock, cod, pollock, or other
   fish fillets 2½ pounds
Salt pork or bacon 4 ounces, diced
Onion 2 cups chopped
Celery 2 cups chopped
Potatoes 2 quarts diced

Boiling water 1 quart
Bay leaves 2
Salt 1½ tablespoons
Pepper ½ teaspoon
Hot milk 2½ quarts
Butter or margarine 4 tablespoons
Parsley chopped

Drain clams and chop, saving liquor; or cut fish into ½-inch pieces. Fry salt pork until crisp. Add onions and celery and cook 2 minutes. Add potatoes, water, and seasonings. Cover and simmer about 20 minutes, or until potatoes are tender. Add clams and liquor (or fish pieces) and simmer 5 to 10 minutes. Add milk and butter, heat to simmering and remove bay leaves. Serve garnished with parsley. Serves 25.

Crab Newburg

King crab meat 3 pounds,
   cut in 1-inch pieces
Butter or margarine 1⅛ cups
Flour 1⅛ cups
Salt 1½ teaspoons

Paprika 1 tablespoon
Cayenne ¼ teaspoon
Hot milk 1½ quarts
Sherry ½ cup
Large biscuits 25, hot

Remove any shell or cartilage from crab meat. Place crab meat in top of double boiler and heat. In large saucepan, melt butter and blend in flour and seasonings. Gradually stir in milk and cook, stirring constantly, until thickened. Add crab meat and sherry. Serve in ½-cup portions over split biscuits. Serves 25.

Shrimp-Macaroni Casserole

Shrimp 1½ pounds, cooked,
   peeled, and deveined
Butter or margarine 3 tablespoons
Flour ½ cup
Salt 1 tablespoon
Dry mustard 2 teaspoons

Hot milk 1 quart
Cheese 1½ quarts grated
Macaroni 1 pound, cooked,
   rinsed, and drained
Tomatoes 1 pound, cut into 25 slices
Cheese 1 cup grated

If shrimp are large, cut into ½-inch pieces. In large saucepan, melt butter and blend in flour, salt, and mustard. Gradually add milk and cook, stirring constantly, for 5 to 10 minutes or until thickened. Remove from heat and blend in cheese. Stir in macaroni and shrimp. Pour into well-buttered baking pans. Arrange tomatoes over top and sprinkle with 1 cup cheese. Bake at 350° for 40 minutes or until cheese is melted. Serves 25.

Shrimp Creole

Onion   2 cups chopped
Green pepper   2 cups chopped
Garlic clove   ½, minced
Cooking oil or margarine   ½ cup
Flour   ⅔ cup
Salt   1½ tablespoons

Pepper   1 teaspoon
Stewed tomatoes   2½ quarts
Medium shrimp   5 pounds peeled and
   deveined
Rice   1½ pounds, cooked and hot

Sauté onion, green pepper, and garlic in oil until tender but not brown. Blend in flour, salt, and pepper; gradually add tomatoes and cook, stirring constantly, until thickened. Add shrimp and simmer for 3 to 5 minutes or until shrimp are pink and tender. Serve ¾-cup portions of creole over ½-cup portions of rice. Serves 25.

Spaghetti with Seafood Sauce

Onion   3 cups sliced
Margarine or cooking oil   ½ cup
Tomatoes   2 16-ounce cans, cut
   into small pieces, juice included
Tomato sauce   2 8-ounce cans
Mushroom stems and pieces
   2 4-ounce cans, drained
Garlic salt   4½ teaspoons
Oregano   1 tablespoon

Small shrimp   3 pounds cooked,
   peeled, and deveined or
Shrimp   12 4½-ounce cans,
   rinsed and drained or
Minced clams   6 8-ounce cans,
   drained
Spaghetti   2 pounds, cooked
Parmesan cheese   1½ cups grated
   (optional)

In large saucepan, sauté onion in margarine until tender but not brown. Add next 5 ingredients; simmer, uncovered, for 20 to 30 minutes or until slightly thickened. Add shrimp and heat thoroughly. Serve sauce over spaghetti; sprinkle with cheese if desired. Serves 25.

Index

www.ingramcontent.com/pod-product-compliance
Lightning Source LLC
Chambersburg PA
CBHW080459110426
42742CB00017B/2945